D0901454

Self-Hypnosis
FOR
DUMMIES®

Clinch-Powell Regional Library
130 N. Main St. Suite 2
Clinton, TN 37716-3691

Self-Hypnosis FOR DUMMIES®

by Mike Bryant and Peter Mabbutt

WILEY

DISCARD

A John Wiley and Sons, Ltd, Publication

Clinch-Powell Regional Library
130 N. Main St. Suite 2
Clinton, TN 37716-3691

Self-Hypnosis For Dummies®

Published by
John Wiley & Sons, Ltd
The Atrium
Southern Gate
Chichester
West Sussex
PO19 8SQ
England

E-mail (for orders and customer service enquires): cs-books@wiley.co.uk

Visit our Home Page on www.wiley.com

Copyright © 2010 John Wiley & Sons, Ltd, Chichester, West Sussex, England

Published by John Wiley & Sons, Ltd, Chichester, West Sussex

All Rights Reserved. No part of this publication may be reproduced, stored in a retrieval system or transmitted in any form or by any means, electronic, mechanical, photocopying, recording, scanning or otherwise, except under the terms of the Copyright, Designs and Patents Act 1988 or under the terms of a licence issued by the Copyright Licensing Agency Ltd, Saffron House, 6-10 Kirby Street, London EC1N 8TS, UK, without the permission in writing of the Publisher. Requests to the Publisher for permission should be addressed to the Permissions Department, John Wiley & Sons, Ltd, The Atrium, Southern Gate, Chichester, West Sussex, PO19 8SQ, England, or emailed to permreq@wiley.co.uk, or faxed to (44) 1243 770620.

Trademarks: Wiley, the Wiley Publishing logo, For Dummies, the Dummies Man logo, A Reference for the Rest of Us!, The Dummies Way, Dummies Daily, The Fun and Easy Way, Dummies.com and related trade dress are trademarks or registered trademarks of John Wiley & Sons, Inc. and/or its affiliates in the United States and other countries, and may not be used without written permission. All other trademarks are the property of their respective owners. Wiley Publishing, Inc., is not associated with any product or vendor mentioned in this book.

LIMIT OF LIABILITY/DISCLAIMER OF WARRANTY: THE CONTENTS OF THIS WORK ARE INTENDED TO FURTHER GENERAL SCIENTIFIC RESEARCH, UNDERSTANDING, AND DISCUSSION ONLY AND ARE NOT INTENDED AND SHOULD NOT BE RELIED UPON AS RECOMMENDING OR PROMOTING A SPECIFIC METHOD, DIAGNOSIS, OR TREATMENT BY PHYSICIANS FOR ANY PARTICULAR PATIENT. THE PUBLISHE, THE AUTHOR, AND ANYONE ELSE INVOLVED IN PREPARING THIS WORK MAKE NO REPRESENTATIONS OR WARRANTIES WITH RESPECT TO THE ACCURACY OR COMPLETENESS OF THE CONTENTS OF THIS WORK AND SPECIFICALLY DISCLAIM ALL WARRANTIES, INCLUDING WITHOUT LIMITATION ANY IMPLIED WARRANTIES OF FITNESS FOR A PARTICULAR PURPOSE. IN VIEW OF ONGOING RESEARCH, EQUIPMENT MODIFICATIONS, CHANGES IN GOVERNMENTAL REGULATIONS, AND THE CONSTANT FLOW OF INFORMATION RELATING TO THE USE OF MEDICINES, EQUIPMENT, AND DEVICES, THE READER IS URGED TO REVIEW AND EVALUATE THE INFORMATION PROVIDED IN THE PACKAGE INSERT OR INSTRUCTIONS FOR EACH MEDICINE, EQUIPMENT, OR DEVICE FOR, AMONG OTHER THINGS, ANY CHANGES IN THE INSTRUCTIONS OR INDICATION OF USAGE AND FOR ADDED WARNINGS AND PRECAUTIONS. READERS SHOULD CONSULT WITH A SPECIALIST WHERE APPROPRIATE. THE FACT THAT AN ORGANIZATION OR WEBSITE IS REFERRED TO IN THIS WORK AS A CITATION AND/OR A POTENTIAL SOURCE OF FURTHER INFORMATION DOES NOT MEAN THAT THE AUTHOR OR THE PUBLISHER ENDORSES THE INFORMATION THE ORGANIZATION OR WEBSITE MAY PROVIDE OR RECOMMENDATIONS IT MAY MAKE. FURTHER, READERS SHOULD BE AWARE THAT INTERNET WEBSITES LISTED IN THIS WORK MAY HAVE CHANGED OR DISAPPEARED BETWEEN WHEN THIS WORK WAS WRITTEN AND WHEN IT IS READ. NO WARRANTY MAY BE CREATED OR EXTENDED BY ANY PROMOTIONAL STATEMENTS FOR THIS WORK. NEITHER THE PUBLISHER NOR THE AUTHOR SHALL BE LIABLE FOR ANY DAMAGES ARISING HEREFROM.

For general information on our other products and services, please contact our Customer Care Department within the U.S. at 877-762-2974, outside the U.S. at 317-572-3993, or fax 317-572-4002.

For technical support, please visit www.wiley.com/techsupport.

Wiley also publishes its books in a variety of electronic formats. Some content that appears in print may not be available in electronic books.

British Library Cataloguing in Publication Data: A catalogue record for this book is available from the British Library

ISBN: 978-0-470-66073-7

Printed and bound in Great Britain by Bell & Bain Ltd., Glasgow.

10 9 8 7 6 5 4 3

WILEY

About the Authors

Mike Bryant is a Hoosier from Indianapolis who has lived in England since 1984. Mike is also qualified psychiatric social worker, counsellor, and hypnotherapist.

Having worked in both America and the United Kingdom as a counsellor and mental health professional, Mike was a consultant for the Sainsbury Centre for Mental Health, advising NHS Trusts across the UK, and now works as a Mental Health Act Commissioner for the national Care Quality Commission.

Mike has also worked as a clinical supervisor to both counselling and hypnotherapy training organisations and is currently a part-time staff counsellor at Goldsmiths, University of London.

Mike currently lives in London with his wife and family and has a private practice as a counsellor and hypnotherapist. You can find more information about Mike's clinical practice at `www.mikebryant-hypnotherapy.co.uk`.

Peter Mabbutt is CEO and Director of Studies at the London College of Clinical Hypnosis (LCCH). He lectures extensively throughout the UK and the Asia Pacific region to students of hypnotherapy, the medical profession and the general public. Peter also makes regular appearances on radio promoting and discussing hypnotherapy.

Peter is responsible for the development of the LCCH's core courses that lead to the award of a Masters degree. With his colleagues he has introduced many new techniques and subjects to the curriculum, ensuring that it continues to meet the needs of the modern-day hypnotherapist.

Peter has a background in psychopharmacology and co-authored a range of papers on tranquilisers, anxiety, and learning and memory. He was involved in the development and management of several innovative international research projects designed to further understanding of the neurological and psychological basis of hypnotherapy. Peter has specialist interests in the mind-body connection, pain management, lifestyle improvement, performance enhancement, the treatment of trauma, and cardiovascular hypnotherapy.

Dedication

From Mike Bryant: I would like to dedicate this book to my girls: my wife Toni, and my brilliant, beautiful daughters Jodie and Jessie.

From Peter Mabbutt: I would like to dedicate this book to my partner Steven Winston. A big thank you for the past 10 years. Here's to our future together.

Mum and dad, watching from above, thanks for all the happy memories.

Authors' Acknowledgments

From Mike Bryant: I would like to thank my clients and supervisees who have provided a two-way learning process for me. I owe them a great deal in my development as a clinician, trainer, and author.

Many thanks to Nicole at Wiley for pitching this book and helping it to fly. Much appreciation also to Mario, Ogun and Nelson for their encouragement.

Peter, many thanks for bringing your expertise and humour to this project. It was great fun working with you.

From Peter Mabbutt: ¡Hola! to my sister Nadine and all the clan in sunny España. Thanks to my 'other' family of Sandra, Gerald, Andrea Winston and Veronica Fernandez for continuing to put up with me. To my own family, Linda, Barrie, Barry, Gillian, Anna, Sally and Sam a big hallo again.

Elijah and Dalya Winston, you are now at that age when you will be doing your utmost to ensure that your parents and I require prolonged therapy. Do your worst, kids – we can take it!

Sara Winston Fernandez, a true personality in the making. So young and yet so bossy and with the innate ability to make us all smile and laugh. Thank you.

Here's to the newbies: Sheila Menon, Principal of LCCH Asia Pacific, many thanks for the opportunities and doors opened and for becoming such a good and close friend - oh, and for our gin and tonic post-lecturing debriefs in various hotel bars across Malaysia and Singapore! Allan Dodgeon, media mogul and radio raconteur, thanks for bringing hysterical laughter into the serious business of work and for the incredible friendship that grew from a Tweet.

I would like to say a big thank you for all the support and encouragement given to me by my colleagues past, present and future at the LCCH right across the globe.

A big thanks to Nicole, Simon and all at Wiley who made this possible, you really made a challenging process such a breeze.

And Mike, it's always a pleasure working with you. We have another one under our belt. When do we start the next?

Publisher's Acknowledgments

We're proud of this book; please send us your comments through our Dummies online registration form located at www.dummies.com/register/.

Some of the people who helped bring this book to market include the following:

Commissioning, Editorial, and Media Development

Project Editor: Simon Bell

Commissioning Editor: Nicole Hermitage

Assistant Editor: Ben Kemble

Content Editor: Jo Theedom

Copy Editor: Sally Osborn

Technical Editor: Mark Haynes

Publisher: David Palmer

Production Manager: Daniel Mersey

Cover Photos: © Stephane106 / Alamy

Cartoons: Rich Tennant (www.the5thwave.com)

Composition Services

Project Coordinator: Lynsey Stanford

Layout and Graphics: Carrie A. Cesavice, Timothy C. Detrick, Joyce Haughey

Proofreader: Lindsay Littrell

Indexer: Claudia Bourbeau

Publishing and Editorial for Consumer Dummies

Diane Graves Steele, Vice President and Publisher, Consumer Dummies

Joyce Pepple, Acquisitions Director, Consumer Dummies

Kristin A. Cocks, Product Development Director, Consumer Dummies

Michael Spring, Vice President and Publisher, Travel

Kelly Regan, Editorial Director, Travel

Publishing for Technology Dummies

Andy Cummings, Vice President and Publisher, Dummies Technology/General User

Composition Services

Gerry Fahey, Vice President of Production Services

Debbie Stailey, Director of Composition Services

Contents at a Glance

Table of Contents

Introduction

*H*ypnosis brings to many people's minds images of mysticism and thought control, enclosed in a veneer of magic, wielded by sinister Svengali types who have dark ambitions as they take control of their poor victim! Thankfully this is a wild and fanciful notion that has absolutely nothing to do with reality. As you get to know and understand hypnosis and self-hypnosis, you find that the technique has a focus that's firmly based on helping you regain control of an area of your life where you perceive you've lost control – a far cry from the fiction of Svengali.

People come to self-hypnosis for a variety of reasons. You may be reading this book because you want to take control of stress and discover how to relax. Maybe you're seeing a hypnotherapist and you're asked to practise self-hypnosis as a homework assignment. Maybe you simply want to make a change to some aspect of your life and you've heard how powerful and effective self-hypnosis can be. Or maybe you're a student of hypnotherapy who wants to find out more about the ins and outs of self-hypnosis. Whatever your reason, this really is the book for you. Read on to find out why.

About This Book

Self-Hypnosis For Dummies helps you understand the realities of self-hypnosis. As you read this book you can discover how self-hypnosis maximises your own innate ability to change, and how you can use self-hypnosis to help overcome a wide variety of anxiety, emotional and behavioural issues, while at the same time promoting a healthy lifestyle, well-being and an inner sense of positivity.

Despite some of the seemingly miraculous outcomes some people achieve using self-hypnosis, in this book we focus on reality as we show you how self-hypnosis can help you achieve what you want to achieve while making you aware of its limitations. Of course, we give advice on how to overcome these limitations by getting further professional help.

This book gives you both a technical and a practical grasp of self-hypnosis, focusing primarily on practical aspects. After all, self-hypnosis is a very practical subject. You can find exercises, hints and tips that allow you use self-hypnosis as a means of taking control, bringing in changes that enable you to lead a more satisfying life.

Conventions Used in This Book

To help you navigate through this book, we've set up a few conventions:

- ✔ *Italics* give emphasis and highlight new words or define terms.
- ✔ **Boldfaced** text indicates the key concept in a list.
- ✔ Monofont denotes Web and e-mail addresses.

We (the authors, Mike and Peter) use the pronoun 'we' to signify both of us or 'one of us' followed by '(Mike)' or '(Peter)', depending on who the author writing that particular paragraph is.

Also, when speaking generally we use the female pronoun 'she' in odd-numbered chapters and the male 'he' in even-numbered chapters, just to be fair to both genders.

Foolish Assumptions

When authors write books they tend to do so while holding on to several assumptions about their prospective readership. We, the authors of this fair tome, are no different and we've made the following assumptions about you and your reasons for parting with your hard-earned cash in order to read what we have to say. At least one of the following applies to you:

- ✔ You're interested in hypnosis and want to find out more about a very fascinating subject, yet you don't want to plough through something more technical.
- ✔ You want to practise self-hypnosis because you want to make some kind of change to your life.
- ✔ Your hypnotherapist has suggested that you use self-hypnosis to aid your treatment programme.
- ✔ You already practise self-hypnosis and want to make sure that you do so properly.
- ✔ You're a trained therapist or are training in hypnotherapy and want some new tips to give to your patients.

Why You Need This Book

Self-hypnosis is a wonderful way of helping yourself to take control of your own life, making those tweaks and modifications that you've always wanted to make but were perhaps unsure of the best way of doing.

As practising hypnotherapists we understand the challenges some people face when carrying out self-hypnosis. This book, like all *For Dummies* books, is written in a people-friendly way that helps you to do the following:

- Understand the reality of self-hypnosis.
- Overcome any challenges you may have had when practising self-hypnosis previously.
- Work through simple and effective exercises as you bring about self-insight and change.

Remember, you're a goal-directed being. That means that your behaviours, anxieties, problems and successes, and the way you handle your emotions, are heavily influenced by the way you think. As you read this book you see how to focus your mind in a positive way, getting a good and realistic handle on your thinking as you bring about change to your life.

How This Book Is Organised

As this is a *For Dummies* book, you don't have to read the whole book from cover to cover in order to get the most out of it.

We've split this book into five parts, each broken down into its respective chapters. Each chapter's a story in its own right that you can read alone or in conjunction with others. We reference information you can find in other chapters, maybe directing your attention towards specific parts of those chapter in order to make the most out of what you're reading.

Part I: Identifying Your Needs and Preparing the Way

This section provides the foundation on which self-hypnosis is based. We break down any barriers of misunderstanding by defining what self-hypnosis is. We then look at how your mind and body work together as a team in order to create problems and, most importantly, how to overcome them. We explore the goal-directed nature of your mind and how you can best put your mind to use in order to help you achieve what you want to achieve, while at the same time discussing ways of overcoming any resistance to change.

Part II: Training Your Mind with Self-Hypnosis

Here we open up the self-hypnosis toolkit and take an in-depth look at the techniques you can use. We explore ways for you to take yourself into the trance state, and lovingly linger over the language that hypnotherapy uses so that you get the most out of each practice session. We help you to become conscious of your unconscious as you discover how to harness its power for your own benefit.

Part III: Improving Your Outlook with Self-Hypnosis

If you're searching for that feel-good factor, this is the section for you. Whether you're looking to calm yourself or your anger, ease your pain and sleep well, or confidently step out into the world brimming with self-esteem, here you can find strategies to help you accomplish a more fulfilling life.

Part IV: Overcoming Problems with Self-Hypnosis

If your health is important to you then you want to read through this section, as we cover eating and drinking issues as well as smoking here. We show you how to recognise the emotional and behavioural factors that push you towards making unhealthy lifestyle choices and how to gain power over those factors.

Let's be realistic, self-hypnosis alone doesn't magic away the unhealthy. Rather, self-hypnosis builds on your inner willpower and becomes a positive driving force, helping you create motivational strategies that eradicate the unhealthy as you stride purposefully into a healthy new lifestyle and a healthy new you!

Part V: The Part of Tens

This is the supplemental resource section of the book. Do you want to put your creativity to good use? If so, we expand on what you can find out in Chapter 5 as you discover 10 creative ways to enter trance. If you're not sure how to tell whether you're in trance, peruse the 10 reasons that show you are. To do self-hypnosis or not to do self-hypnosis – if that is the question then we give you 10 reasons why you should be seeking help from a professional source first.

Icons Used in This Book

As you read this book you find many icons that are designed to highlight certain information or give you pointers to ponder on.

This icon indicates an anecdote that we feel usefully illustrates something that we're saying in the text.

We highlight technical terms and language that you may find unfamiliar and explain them under this icon.

This icon draws your attention to an important point that we want you to bear in mind as you continue reading and practising.

Here you can find something of technical interest that relates to the paragraph you're reading.

This icon indicates that we're emphasising information that you may find useful later on.

This icon does what it says on the tin – it highlights something that you really do need to pay attention to.

Where to Go from Here

Julie Andrews may say 'start at the very beginning, it's a very good place to start' and in general we agree with her, except for the fact that this is a *For Dummies* book. That means that you can start anywhere, at any chapter and still get the most out of your reading. So, turn to the table of contents and jump to the chapter that most appeals to you or to the one that directly addresses the issue you want to work on.

As you read this book, remember that if your mind has had the power to create a problem, it certainly has the power to resolve that problem. We wish you luck as you discover how to take control of your life!

Part I
Identifying Your Needs and Preparing the Way

In this part . . .

The first Part of this book gives you the basics for understanding and practising self-hypnosis. In it, we define what self-hypnosis is, and briefly look at what it isn't. We then examine how you can get started on overcoming your problems by getting your mind and body working together.

We also take a look at how to help you achieve what you want to achieve, whilst at the same time discussing how you can overcome your own resistance to change and avoid relapses.

Chapter 1

What Is Self-Hypnosis?

*W*hether you realise you are or not, you're doing self-hypnosis continually, every hour of the day. In this book we guide this natural tendency to help you get what you want using the raw skills you already possess. In this book we will help you to understand how hypnosis works and how you can hypnotise yourself using different techniques – old and new.

We also help you to develop powerful self-hypnosis skills across a range of topics, including:

✔ How to clarify your goals.

✔ How to train your mind for a range of different self-hypnosis approaches.

✔ How to improve your outlook.

✔ How to achieve more with *less effort*.

✔ How to apply self-hypnosis to specific problems.

You may be *pleasantly surprised*, as hypnotherapists frequently like to say, at your new-found abilities after applying the ideas and practical suggestions in this book.

Understanding Self-Hypnosis

As you read this book, you're in a slight trance state. You're hearing the words on the page in your mind; they're stimulating you to think in a certain way. In a literal sense, you're simply looking at dried ink on paper. Yet the letters are forming words that give you a certain meaning that they don't to someone who can't read or comprehend what you're able to understand easily.

Unconscious self-hypnosis

We show you a new and exciting approach to self-hypnosis that we've developed based on our clinical practice – *unconscious self-hypnosis*.

Unconscious self-hypnosis works without you having to think about what's happening, unlike traditional self-hypnosis methods that can involve very self-conscious approaches. This is a significant departure, as you don't have to close your eyes and sit in a quiet room or to do artificial countdowns or deepeners.

Unconscious self-hypnosis is fast and you can do it in many real-world situations, including:

✓ With your eyes open

✓ In the workplace,

✓ In noisy, public places

✓ While you're talking or listening to others

Traditional methods of self-hypnosis often require some form of isolation from your daily routine, which isn't always possible for people living a busy life. Some methods require you to take an hour of undisturbed time. For most people, finding a regular hour of undisturbed time's probably difficult – but that's not a requirement of unconscious self-hypnosis.

Unconscious self-hypnosis works rapidly and in very light trance states that can be indistinguishable from daydream states. We're all natural born experts at daydreaming – we bet you've wondered a few times what you may do if you won the lottery.

Once you've mastered unconscious self-hypnosis, you have a skill for life that works like a thermostat, continually adjusting itself when you need to access the resources of your inner mind.

Self-hypnosis is like that: simply by focusing, you can go into a relaxed state of mind, sometimes called 'trance'. In this trance state you can allow your mind to create new meanings and discoveries in your life that can help you *spontaneously create new behaviours* and *form helpful beliefs*.

Creating a trance state's the first part of doing self-hypnosis. The second part's giving yourself a hypnotic suggestion for change. This is called the *hypnotic suggestion*. The italicised words in the previous paragraph – *spontaneously create new behaviours* and *form helpful beliefs* – are direct examples of two hypnotic suggestions. Already your unconscious mind understands that effective self-hypnosis changes your unhelpful behaviours and beliefs. When these changes occur, you're doing effective self-hypnosis.

In this book we take you through a range of topics that help you develop skills of self-hypnosis.

The ins and outs of self-hypnosis

The first time one of us (Mike) was hypnotised, it was by someone informally many years ago. I was speaking to a well-known hypnotherapist and enquired what being hypnotised felt like. This person was keen to stay within his professional boundaries, but I was persistent. The hypnotherapist simply asked me two or three questions and I was in an altered state. The questions he asked me that sent me into a light trance state were:

- ✔ Do you know what a *trance state* is?
- ✔ What do you think it *feels* like to *go into a trance*?
- ✔ How may you *use hypnosis* if you were to *go into a trance*?

This happened during the middle of a conversation in a noisy room full of people who were unaware what was happening. Without realising the power of these three sentences, I noticed a shift in my state of mind – I was only slightly more relaxed, but in a dramatically different state.

The hypnotherapist then explained how the unconscious can perceive questions as hypnotic commands. Look again at the italicised words in his three questions and this may begin to make sense to you.

Some people don't like the phrase 'trance state'. Specifically, disagreement occurs over the existence of the concept of a hypnotic trance state. Some people argue that trance, as first proposed by Scottish surgeon and hypnotherapy pioneer James Braid (1795–1860), doesn't exist. Instead, they propose a *non-state theory of hypnosis* and believe that a hypnotised person is simply role playing because this is what others expect and that no altered state of consciousness exists. We disagree with this view, but include the debate for your information.

Finding out how to induce hypnosis

No limits exist to the methods that enable you to go into trance. But one thing's clear: you can forget about any impressions of trance inductions that you may have seen on television or in the movies. Media representations of hypnotherapy tend towards the sensational and are invariably a misrepresentation.

Trance is an everyday state of mind. Trance can be as simple as daydreaming or as complicated as you want.

When you go to sleep each night, do you think about your technique for falling asleep? Perhaps if you're an insomniac, but otherwise, probably not.

You can induce trance from just about any state. The most common approach is to relax to go into trance, as you do to sleep naturally at night. But athletes go into trance by the opposite method: tensing their bodies and creating a very tough, super-focused mindset. Few rules exist except that the method you choose should be appropriate for your hypnosis goals.

As you find out more about unconscious self-hypnosis, you become increasingly nonchalant about technique in your self-hypnosis practice – and you begin simply to enjoy the process.

Delving into your unconscious mind

Think of your unconscious mind as the unknown part of you that school never showed you how to use. This is the part of your mind that isn't concerned with logic, words or the 'real world'.

> *I think that cognitive scientists would support the view that our visual system does not directly represent what is out there in the world and that our brain constructs a lot of the imagery that we believe we are seeing.*
>
> Galen Rowell

We're convinced that by practising self-hypnosis you begin to construct a new imagery and perspective about the potential you can achieve. This will help you to free your self from your previous limitations.

Scoping out the uses of self-hypnosis

Hypnosis works on any areas connected to your mind and central nervous system – that's an immense territory of potential applications. Areas that hypnosis can potentially help with include the following:

- ✔ Anxiety
- ✔ Breaking habits
- ✔ Confidence
- ✔ Infertility
- ✔ Memory enhancement
- ✔ Pain management
- ✔ Performance issues
- ✔ Phobias
- ✔ Stopping smoking

If you need to work on deep emotional problems, however, generally speaking we recommend you begin with a counsellor or a hypnotherapist. Then through self-hypnosis you can sustain and reinforce the insights you gain.

Seeing How Self-Hypnosis Works

Hypnotherapy helps you reprogram your behaviour and give messages to the body to support these changes. Trance induction relaxes your body and pushes away the totalitarian grip of your conscious mind. You usually induce trance by slowing your breathing and relaxing your muscles with each out breath, so that your body becomes increasingly relaxed. This also slows down your pulse rate.

Relaxation has a knock-on effect on your central nervous system and endocrine system, which is why self-hypnosis can help with things like skin disorders, pain reduction and even fertility – some women who've been unable to conceive have fallen pregnant after using hypnotherapy.

As your body slows your pulse and metabolism, eventually your conscious mind slows down. In fact, your conscious mind – a creature of habit – so habitually associates these slowed body functions with the sleep process that it relaxes its grip and allows your unconscious to take over. This is akin to the factory day-shift worker clocking out to allow the night-shift worker to clock in.

Using suggestibility

As your conscious mind takes a background place – or even goes completely on vacation – your unconscious is primed and ready to receive hypnotic suggestions.

The suggestions you use in self-hypnosis can come in two flavours:

✔ Suggestions to further deepen initial trance states (optional)
✔ Suggestions for therapeutic change

If you feel ready to deepen the trance, you have at your disposal an array of options that can help you to go deeper. As you progress through this book, not only will you learn different ways to use self-hypnosis, but you will also become confident enough to improvise and even record your own self-hypnosis CDs.

If you're ready to do the therapy part of your self-hypnotherapy, then you simply think your pre-planned, concisely worded hypnotic suggestion to yourself. (For more on how to construct self-hypnosis suggestions see Chapter 6 'Working with Words: Becoming Your Own Recording Star'.)

These two categories of suggestions that you can use in self-hypnosis form the backbone of your future hypnosis sessions. Within this structure exists a great deal of room for creativity.

Working with dissociation

Dissociation means to separate or to stop associating with. One of the first things you let go of in hypnosis are your own critical thoughts that are restricting you and keeping you stuck with a particular problem. A hypnotherapist does this by helping you to see a different perspective that empowers you. In this way the problem doesn't control you, you control the problem. This is termed *reframing*. For example, reframing 'pain' as 'discomfort' is a common hypnotherapy technique for managing chronic migraines and is also used with hypnosis in childbirth situations.

Dissociation, most importantly, focuses on intentionally separating the *conscious mind* (which deals with concrete, logical thinking) from the *unconscious mind* (which deals with abstractions, feelings, intuition).

Your conscious mind keeps you firmly grounded, but is also the seat of your critical and limiting thinking. Your conscious mind's your 'rule keeper': it thinks 'You have this problem, so you behave in the following manner.'

Your unconscious mind's your 'artist/creator'. You can overcome limitations by asking your unconscious mind to imagine, for example, 'What am I like if I don't have the problem? How do I feel to be free?'

French psychologist Pierre Janet (1859–1947) first suggested the concept of dissociation, proposing that at times (as with hypnosis) a separation occurs between your conscious and unconscious minds. During this dissociation, the conscious mind lessens its grip over your behaviour, thinking and body functions and allows your unconscious to respond more directly to the hypnotherapist.

Dissociation occurs as you become able to relax or focus more inwardly. As you become more relaxed during the trance induction, your unconscious mind begins to respond to the hypnotist (or your own self-hypnosis suggestions), while your conscious mind retains the awareness of reality.

This can be very useful when applying hypnosis to areas such as:

- ✔ Eating problems
- ✔ Memory enhancement

✔ Overcoming physical reactions to fear and anxiety

✔ Pain management

✔ Self-anaesthesia (dental hypnosis)

✔ Stopping smoking (ignoring the urge for a cigarette)

Building on post-hypnotic suggestions

After you reach a comfortable level of trance (and that doesn't have to be deep), you (or the hypnotherapist if you want to have hypnosis done *to* you for your first time) can begin to give post-hypnotic suggestions.

Post-hypnotic suggestions are the component of the hypnosis session where the message for change or therapy occurs. These are the key messages that enable a shift in your behaviour or thinking to move you closer towards your goals.

The 'post' part of the term 'post-hypnotic suggestion' indicates that a suggestion's given *after* you're in trance.

Post-hypnotic are the words, suggestions or 'scripts' that are created to deal directly with and resolve your problem. Simple and concise single sentences work best when constructing post-hypnotic suggestions and in Chapter 6 we help you to do this.

Effective post-hypnotic suggestions involve clever use of language and logic mechanisms to help lure the mind into making changes. One example combines a truism – a statement too obvious to disagree with – with a post-hypnotic suggestion for change:

> 'As the sun sets every evening, so you're going deeper and becoming relaxed . . .'

Skilful hypnotherapists work with language in various ways in order to plant suggestions within your unconscious that facilitate your getting what you want.

Reassuring Yourself About Safety

One area of concern about hypnosis focuses on personal safety during the hypnosis process. This is understandable, as historically hypnosis has been surrounded by mystique and misrepresentation. Even someone like yourself, who has a genuine interest in this area, may also have concerns before becoming involved with hypnotherapy or self-hypnosis. In fact, if you search on the internet for 'Frequently Asked Questions + Hypnosis', you repeatedly see similar queries regarding the potential risks of hypnosis.

Here are some typical safety questions:

✔ Do I reveal my own secrets against my will?

✔ Can I open myself to possession?

✔ Can the hypnotherapist make me cluck like a chicken?

You're always in control when hypnotised and no one can make you do anything against your will. *You* cannot make yourself do anything against your will, for that matter.

Some people with particular religious or spiritual beliefs can be concerned about potential spiritual harm from hypnosis. However, this is a misconception. This is because self-hypnosis is simply a form of directing your mind away from feeling trapped by a problem and moving it towards the ability to generate new potential ways of achieving goals. See self-hypnosis as a way of harnessing your imagination for productive means. Additionally, when you are hypnotised, you are safe and able to be aware of everything around you. This means that you can safely come out of trance at anytime you wish. When these points are understood, we can free ourselves from any misinformed fears about the process of hypnosis.

The last question in the preceding list ('Can the hypnotherapist make me cluck like a chicken?') is one that first-time visitors to a hypnosis session actually want to ask, but rarely say directly. This fear's based on influences from stage hypnosis, where participants are often hypnotised for laughs and lightweight entertainment. Clinical hypnotherapy focuses only on helping you to achieve your goals by empowering you. No humiliating or demeaning behaviours are involved.

When approaching self-hypnosis for the first time, you may have similar safety apprehensions to those above, intensified by being alone.

The key concept to remember is that self-hypnosis is safe and that you're always in control. Self-hypnosis is like a daydream state where you're guiding the daydream.

Staying in control

One of the nicest things about hypnosis is that you're always in control. Many people expect that when they're hypnotised certain things happen that simply don't occur.

So be reassured by understanding that when you're hypnotised you're still able to:

✔ Hear or ignore what the hypnotherapist is saying to you

✔ Think your own thoughts

✔ Come out of trance when you choose (although if a hypnotherapist is conducting the hypnosis, chances are that you want to stay in trance for as long as possible)

The irony is that while people who are new to hypnosis sometimes focus on whether they lose control, those who are experienced with self-hypnosis understand how they're *increasing* their abilities to be more in control.

Deciding when to stop hypnosis

Generally speaking, you know when you've had enough self-hypnosis because you get bored or come out of trance. This experience varies for different people. For some people, brief periods of two to four minutes are enough. Others may choose to spend significantly longer periods of time in trance.

Initially, you could time yourself to ensure that you can maintain a trance state for around two to three minutes. But we would strongly recommend practising self-hypnosis by feel alone. Eventually, as you become more experienced and comfortable with self-hypnosis, there will be no need to worry about timing or other common fears like not coming out of trance. It is very similar to daydreaming. Even the most pleasant daydreams cannot be sustained for more than a few minutes. So you can be assured that you will never be 'stuck' in trance.

Knowing you always wake up

Another common safety question is 'Am I able to come out of trance?'

A useful way to reassure yourself about not getting stuck in trance is simply to think of the approach as like having a brief, pleasant daydream – you just can't avoid coming out of the daydream eventually.

People *always* come out of trance. Trance isn't a coma. In fact, people who are hypnotised by a hypnotherapist are often amazed at the end of the session that they were able to hear what was being said, or even not listen and yet still respond.

Keep in mind, however, that when you do self-hypnosis, you probably don't go into as deep a relaxed state as when someone else hypnotises you. In fact, depth of trance is irrelevant and is certainly *not the goal* of hypnosis.

The goal of hypnosis is to focus your unconscious to be able to help you to make changes. And this can happen even in very light trance states. This information should be very reassuring to you as you begin to practise self-hypnosis. You don't have to put yourself to sleep to make effective changes.

Chapter 2

Getting Your Mind and Body Working Together

....

In This Chapter

▶ Understanding the connection between your mind and your body

▶ Healing your body by using your mind

▶ Sympathising with your nervous system

▶ Visualising your solutions

....

*H*ave you ever had that wonderful feeling of being in love? Can you remember how your mind and body expressed those feelings of excitement?

On the other side of the coin, have you ever had the dreaded 'Monday morning' feeling? Especially if you were anticipating something unpleasant about your job/school/routine? Can you remember how your mind and body expressed those feelings of avoidance?

These are only two extreme examples – one positive and one negative – of how your feelings can affect you, not just psychologically but physically too.

At one time very few people were aware of the connection between emotions and thoughts, and how they can both affect health. Thankfully, time and understanding move on and today we have a much greater understanding of how our mind influences the way our body works. If we're being honest, though, we still have a lot to understand, because when we're unwell we still mainly focus on our biology, and forget to acknowledge how our thoughts and feelings – that is, our mind – may be contributing.

In this chapter we examine how you can use your mind to improve your health. Self-hypnosis can be a powerful aid in optimising your health and minimising physical discomfort, as we demonstrate in Chapters 11, 14, 15 and 16.

Self-hypnosis also works by indirectly changing the way your body physically responds, which means the mind and the body work together as a team: a team that you can cheer on as it wins the 'health improvement competition'! If you want to maximise your chances of winning, then read on to get a better understanding of how your mind and body work and how you can maintain better emotional and physical health.

Exploring the Mind–Body Conundrum

Understanding the connection between your mind and body has two main benefits:

- ✔ Understanding the connection helps you to be aware of your own mind–body signals that point to symptoms needing your attention.

- ✔ This understanding leads to greater emotional health. With greater emotional health comes the added benefit of naturally developing better behaviours that improve your physical health too – a great win–win situation.

If you wonder what we mean by 'emotional health', here are some of the indicators of people with good *emotional health*:

- ✔ They are self-aware.

- ✔ They can identify their emotions in most situations.

- ✔ They are aware of their thoughts as well as their feelings.

- ✔ They use a range of healthy strategies for coping with the stresses of daily life.

- ✔ They like themselves.

- ✔ They have good relationships in their lives.

- ✔ They have largely tamed their 'inner critic'.

- ✔ Thinking (head) and feeling (heart) work together.

Think about someone you admire for their personality. They can be a person you know or even someone you don't know, someone whose positive reputation you've heard of or perhaps a celebrity. Whether you actually know the person doesn't matter – the following exercise is more about what traits you perceive the person to have that you like, lack or even envy.

When you think about this admirable person, ask yourself:

✔ Which of the traits of emotional health in the list do they possess?

✔ What other positive emotional traits do they have that aren't in the list?

✔ How do you think you may feel if you have one of these traits?

✔ Where exactly do you feel this in your body?

Look again at the list of indicators of emotional health. Focus particularly on the point 'Thinking (head) and feeling (heart) work together'.

The phrase 'thinking (head) and feeling (heart)' implies something that therapists call 'congruence'. *Congruence* means 'agreement'. Congruence means appropriateness and suitability. It also means that therapists like to use big words.

You may use the expression 'My head said one thing, but my heart said another'. This feeling of being conflicted or pulled in different directions implies a lack of congruence. When you feel torn like this, depending on the seriousness of the subject, therapists refer to this as being *incongruous*. Being incongruous can be a minor thing, for example not knowing whether to purchase a pair of shoes that you like but don't really need. This doesn't necessarily affect your emotional health (unless you're a shopping addict!).

However, incongruity can become an issue as more serious conflicts arise, creating difficult mind–body splits. An example is a man who smokes cigarettes. On the one hand he enjoys smoking on his own or with his friends, and yet on the other hand he worries about what smoking's doing to his lungs. While he socialises and smokes, his body seems to enjoy the feeling of smoking. At one level his mind says 'Unhealthy!' but it may also suppress some of the following thoughts and feelings:

✔ Fears of the health warnings on the cigarette packet.

✔ Memories of a close relative or friend who smoked and died from lung cancer.

✔ Television commercials warning against smoking.

✔ Descriptions of smoking as self-destructive behaviour.

✔ The unpleasant feeling of wheezing and coughing.

The mind–body or fear–pleasure split evolves over time and may be minor to begin with, but can be a source of anxiety that's a good example of incongruence.

Mind–body conundrums appear within everyone from time to time. If you've got such a conundrum, you may feel torn or split. These words imply a type of internal tension, which can build up and, if serious and enduring, may affect your health.

As an example, a person who works in a high-paying job that causes regular anguish, leading to ulcers, body aches, frequent headaches or other illness, may be experiencing the most common form of mind–body split – his mind justifies carrying on with the job, while his body desperately tries to give him the hints that he ignores until he ends up in hospital.

Health professionals face another type of mind–body split – their different views about the best way to treat physical and emotional illness. We tackle this debate in the next section.

Approaching the Holistic vs Medical Debate

When you're sick, you may call your doctor, a therapist, an acupuncturist or a homeopath. Or maybe you use a homemade tonic recipe your great-grandmother handed down. For safety's sake your first port of call should always include your doctor, but many people choose to approach other professionals as well.

The debate about holistic healing versus conventional medicine isn't new. Down the centuries the two sides have banged their heads together. The debate's been around at least since the days of Hippocrates (460 BC–*circa.* 370 BC, otherwise known as 'the father of Western medicine' and on whose writings the Hippocratic oath all doctors take is based. In Hippocrates' day, medicine was intertwined with philosophy and the emphasis was more on the pursuit of truth and knowledge, rather than discovering a cure for cancer.

But even poor old Hippocrates had to take sides in the debate between the two opposing approaches to treatment:

- ✔ The rationalist approach – today called allopathic or conventional healthcare.
- ✔ The vitals approach – today called naturopathic or complementary/ alternative healthcare.

The rationalists felt that reasoning was the way towards truth and knowledge. The vitalists felt that truth and knowledge came from experience.

The vitalists are also called empiricists, due to their belief in a philosophical system known as 'empires'. The vitalists looked at how the environment affected the whole body. They felt that the job of medicine was to treat patients as individuals and to activate the body's own natural tendency to heal itself.

Today we call this a 'holistic' approach to medicine, one that looks at the patient's whole system of environment and individual body characteristics. The holistic approach downgrades the role of disease, and sees it as a symptom of disharmony between the person and their environment. A cure comes from understanding the unique nature of that disharmony.

In contrast, the rationalists focused on the concept of disease and how it caused illnesses across groups of patients. Allopaths or rationalists believe that illness occurs because a person gets a disease. The person and the environment are secondary to an understanding of the disease.

Allopaths/rationalists feel that if they can define certain conditions in advance, they can predict and therefore cure certain illnesses. To the rationalists the physician is the key agent in curing disease. This has become the dominant medical model.

These two camps continue to influence opposing approaches to medication, sometimes cynically called 'proper medicine' vs 'New Age medicine' – terms that we certainly don't agree with.

We thought about calling this section 'Approaching the Allopathic vs Naturopathic debate', but if you know what those words mean, then you probably already know what this section's about. In short, *allopathic* refers to what we think of today as conventional medicine, the medical professions and hospitals. *Naturopathic* refers to alternative/complementary medicine.

We can see healing from two perspectives. The conventional medical model of seeing a doctor is the most familiar. Increasingly, however, people seek the help of alternative or complementary practitioners, such as homeopaths and osteopaths for body treatments, and counsellors and hypnotherapists for emotional and mind-related treatments. This is especially the case when conventional medical treatments don't provide a cure or solve the problem.

The good news, though, is that many professions on both sides of the debate are coming together in a new understanding of the issues, working together under the new name of 'integrated medicine'. Congruence at last!

Helping the Mind to Heal the Body

Sometimes you may be so involved in an activity that you don't realise you've had an injury. For example, think of the following situations:

✔ You're so involved in work that only when you stop do you notice your finger bleeding from a paper cut.

✔ You're playing a sport. After the action stops you realise you've gained an injury.

✔ You have a list of items or tasks to complete and when they're done you suddenly feel exhausted.

These situations are examples of how your mind ignores pain or other discomfort when its focus is elsewhere. Unconsciously, you use a type of hypnosis to help you complete an activity or mental work that you have to get through at that moment.

If you're a fan of the 'Road Runner' cartoons (Beep! Beep!), think of the coyote who's so busy chasing the speedy bird he runs off a cliff and for a moment is unaware that he's running on the air. The laws of gravity come into effect only when the coyote stops chasing and realises that he's doing the impossible.

Although self-hypnosis can't help you to levitate, it can certainly help you to have greater awareness and, subsequently, greater control over the healing processes within your body.

Therapists use the word 'healing' to mean gaining emotional and psychological control over the way you feel about and respond to a specific illness. Healing doesn't mean curing an illness – we leave that to medical doctors. However, as we show throughout this book, when your emotions and feelings are healed, this helps your body respond in the best way when fighting an illness. Therapists call this healing the body.

Dr Ernest Rossi (see the nearby sidebar 'Using hypnosis to heal' for more on him) originally trained as a psychoanalyst himself, and expressed his respect for that tradition. But he stated that our minds and consciousnesses have evolved beyond the 19th-century mind of Freud and that a new model for healing was developing and needed to be explored.

Rossi is a big expounder on the concepts of how the mind could harm or heal. He proposed that when we experience stress we inhibit our immune system by blocking the same 'molecular messenger molecules' – as he termed it – that medical science is seeking to amplify in order to cure diseases such as cancer.

Using hypnosis to heal

Dr Ernest Rossi has done pioneering work in using hypnosis to heal the body. He worked closely with the 'father' of modern hypnotherapy, Milton Erickson, and Rossi himself has written over 20 books on hypnosis, with titles such as *Mind–Body Therapy, The Psychobiology of Mind–Body Healing: New Concepts in Hypnosis*, and, even more amazingly, on how hypnosis can potentially affect us at the genetic level in *A Discourse with Our Genes*.

Rossi quotes this as an example of how science and clinical hypnotherapy are working with two sides of the same coin. Science is seeking to use the same molecular messengers that hypnotherapists use to work with emotions, behaviour, memory and learning. Rossi proposed that these messenger molecules make up a complex system of mind–body communication that psychology is now beginning to understand and work with, particularly in the areas of solving emotional problems related to stress and trauma, such as post-traumatic stress disorders (PTSD).

As the two sides of the holistic and conventional medical debate come together under the integrated medicine umbrella (for more, check out the earlier section 'Approaching the Holistic vs. Medical Debate'), this has stimulated a great deal of research exploring how the mind influences the healing processes of the body. One of the repeating key factors – perhaps not surprisingly – is maintaining a positive mental attitude against difficulties. Optimism about the healing process is another key theme in mind–body research.

For example, the researchers Lydia Ievleva and Terry Orlick (1999) compared slow and fast healers. They defined athletes as 'fast healers' if their knee and ankle injuries improved in less than five weeks. They found that fast healers have certain characteristics, such as the following:

✔ Maintaining a positive attitude.

✔ Being determined and highly motivated.

✔ Taking responsibility for helping their own healing.

✔ Having more social support than those slower at healing.

✔ Being less worried about a repeat injury after being well.

✔ Using creative visualisation for healing purposes.

 As you use self-hypnosis to help you achieve your goals, try to remember these points to help heal yourself more rapidly – especially if your goals relate to personal health.

Engaging your central nervous system

We can put things into perspective with a little Neurology 101. All of your thoughts and all of your feelings and emotions are a direct result of what happens within your nervous system.

Your *nervous system* consists of your brain, spinal cord, nerves and chemicals called neurotransmitters. Found everywhere in your body, your nervous system is the electrical circuit that keeps you alive and connects all the organs of your body. Your brain is the master computer that keeps the whole thing going, and your spinal cord acts as a backup.

If you think something, your nervous system creates that thought. If you feel something, your nervous system sends out impulses to every part of your body. Without a nervous system you would be unthinking, unfeeling and, quite frankly, dead!

Evolution's a wonderful thing and over time the human nervous system has developed some wonderful characteristics that allow it to do more than just keep you alive through making your body work. The nervous system has two special survival instincts:

- ✔ **Reflexes:** You are happily walking down the street one day and you turn the corner and come face to face with a huge, snarling tiger. What do you do? Do you stand and consider whether the tiger's friendly or if it's going to eat you (by the time you've done this you're likely to be tiger food)? Or do you, without thinking, turn and run away? The chances are you turn and run away without thinking, as this is a reflex response that aids survival. In this situation thinking gets you killed and your nervous system takes over and allows you to take immediate action.

- ✔ **Emotions:** When you meet the tiger in the example above, the last thing you are is overwhelmed with feelings of love (unless you're very strange, in which case you probably need to read *Survival For Dummies*). Your nervous system produces the survival-based emotion of fear. This is an unpleasant emotion that stimulates your need to escape and works in conjunction with the 'run-away' reflex to rapidly remove you from the dangerous situation. On the other hand, love's a survival emotion that allows you to bond to significant others in your environment and then to procreate with them or protect them (more on this in *Sex For Dummies* and *Relationships For Dummies*).

For many years scientists viewed the nervous system as responsible only for thought, action and keeping you going, while giving your immune system the sole responsibility of protecting you against disease and illness. Your immune system is a collection of organs, structures and chemicals spread throughout your body that have evolved to protect you from disease.

As science has progressed, the fact has become increasingly obvious that the nervous system and the immune system are not so mutually exclusive in their roles. In fact, scientists now know that many of the chemicals involved in transmitting messages throughout the nervous system (called neurotransmitters) are also involved in helping protect against disease. Likewise, many of the chemicals involved in protecting your body (immunotransmitters) can play a role in creating emotions.An example of this is the scourge of every stressed person: adrenaline. Adrenaline's responsible for making you active, increasing your heart rate, and is part of the run-away reflex. Interestingly, adrenaline's also involved in producing immune system structures called natural killer cells. These cells are involved in protecting your body from viruses and tumours. On the other side of the divide are cytokines. These come from the immune system and are involved in creating inflammation. Cytokines also help you control how you experience pain and emotions.

This is all part of the marvellous way in which the mind and body work together, remaining congruent in order to keep you healthy in both mind and body. In this book we aim to help you maximise your ability to keep mind and body congruent with each other.

Being sympathetic to your nervous system

When people say that someone's unbalanced, they're generally being derogatory about his state of mind – and that's not a nice thing to do. However, when you look at someone who's ill, stressed, anxious or fearful, you can describe his biological and physical states as being out of balance with each other.

Increasingly medicine is recognising the importance of redressing this balance in order to maintain good physical and mental health. One of the things you can do to help this process is to be aware of how your nervous system is responding and be nice to it. Listen to what it's saying in the form of thoughts and feelings and then take action. Likewise, if you listen to what your body's saying you can have power over the emotions that creates. A first step in this direction is to learn to relax.

Relaxation's at the core of being nice to your nervous system. Relaxation calms you down and this is an important factor in redressing the imbalance between mind and body. Your friendly neighbourhood neurotransmitter adrenaline's a major player, among others, in keeping you alive – and in helping to kill you too. For example, adrenaline keeps your nervous system overexcited when you're stressed. If you allow this overexcitement to continue, you may descend into ill health for the following reasons:

✔ Too much adrenaline damages your immune system and reduces your immunity.

✔ Adrenaline puts undue strain on your heart by making it pump faster.

✔ Adrenaline can cause depression as the anxiety you feel from stress can result in you giving up hope.

✔ Adrenaline-induced emotions are partly controlled by cytokines, taking the cytokines away from doing their important job of protecting you against infection.

In contrast, when you relax, the following things may happen:

✔ Relaxation can boost your immunity by calming your nervous system and switching off adrenaline.

✔ Relaxation can help your heart to slow down and rest.

✔ Relaxation produces a positive state of mind.

✔ Relaxation lets your muscles relax.

Your nervous system divides into two parts: the central nervous system made up of your brain and spinal cord, and your autonomic nervous system comprising everything else. Your autonomic nervous system also has two parts:

✔ **Sympathetic nervous system:** This is responsible for activity and keeps you going throughout the day. When neurotransmitters like adrenaline are released, the sympathetic nervous system responds.

✔ **Parasympathetic nervous system:** This is responsible for inactivity. When you're resting, sleeping or relaxing, the parasympathetic nervous system's in control and turns off adrenaline.

One of the best ways to learn to relax is through self-hypnosis, as this has a direct effect on calming your nervous system. When you go into a state of hypnosis, you turn on the parasympathetic nervous system, which means you calm everything down and bring your mind and body back into balance. You can then begin to take control using the techniques we describe in this book to help maintain that balance.

Relaxation's very good at keeping you healthy, but to restore balance to your life we recommend you combine relaxation with exercise and good eating habits too.

Experiencing Visualisation

Visualisation is simple – even though we often feel we aren't 'visual types'. What comes to your mind with any of the following three questions?:

✔ How would you describe the way your face looks?

✔ What would you first buy if you suddenly became a millionaire?

✔ What colour is your front door?

If an image comes to mind with any of these questions, then congratulations – you have just visualised something.

So how does visualisation work with self-hypnosis? Well, the good news is that you don't have to visualise in detail or for more than a few seconds to make self-hypnosis effective. It is the same speed that you 'saw' the answer to any of the above questions when you visualised the answers. Self-hypnosis visualisation is the same – it *is* that simple and that quick.

So armed with this information, you simply visualise how things would be different if you changed a certain behaviour, or achieved a certain goal.

This can be done easily even without hypnotising yourself as we frequently visualise when we daydream. But when we use self-hypnosis we visualise the goal state – what we want – as if we already have it and feel the accompanying feelings of this success.

When visualisation happens in hypnosis, it can be referred to as a *post-hypnotic suggestion*, implying that we are giving ourselves a suggestion or command that our unconscious will begin to put into effect. The conscious mind will often be unaware that anything is happening and simply responds differently in ways that move us closer towards achieving our goals.

In the earlier section 'Helping the Mind to Heal the Body', we discuss key aspects of people who heal faster than others. One of the key differences between fast and slower healers is that fast healers use visualisation techniques for healing.

Visualisation is a type of self-hypnosis. However, you can make visualisation more effective and pleasurable by bringing it into self-hypnosis. Simply by using techniques such as creating images of health and healthy behaviours, you can change unhelpful thoughts and take more responsibility for reaching your goals. This has a direct impact on your body as it helps to create a positive state of mind, positively affecting the way your body works.

Your thoughts give birth to your emotions, not the other way around. If you think a bogeyman's under the bed, you're afraid to turn the lights off in the bedroom and a dark bedroom makes you fearful.

Humans are very creative in the way they think. The thoughts and emotions that go through your mind create your universe and your understanding of what's true or real. When these thoughts are unhelpful – for example 'I'm not feeling well' or 'I'm unloveable' – what you're thinking leads you to act in ways that confirm your reality – you actually feel sick, or act in ways that make others dislike you. Thankfully the same goes for positive thoughts and emotions. That happy-go-lucky person walking down the street that everyone seems to like is probably thinking 'What a great day' and 'How nice to be meeting all these people', which leads to behaviours that create this reality. And with some effort and the appropriate application of self-hypnosis, you can be that kind of person if you want.

Self-hypnosis can help you to challenge unhelpful beliefs and thereby change your perception of reality, as well as taking control of your emotions. Using your mind in this way directly influences your emotions and therefore your body.

Someone who's afraid of dogs experiences a faster heartbeat when he sees a large dog walking towards him, even if the dog's on a lead. The self-statements that tell the person how horrible this is create a scary reality. However, techniques that work directly on thoughts and emotions by associating dogs with pleasantness and affection can alter these physical reactions. In other words, the mind (the creation of positive thoughts and emotions) helps to heal the body (by having a normal heartbeat around dogs). Any therapist worth his salt also ensures that the ex-dog phobic treats all dogs with respect as he discovers their temperament. No need to get bitten and undo all the good work!

We cover many situations in later chapters where emotional or physical healing's the goal. Hypnosis can help to bring about a faster recovery than methods such as conventional talking therapy, as the use of images and feelings can maximise the way the mind and body communicate and bring about the balance, the congruence, that's all-important to health.

Seeing how everyone can visualise

Many people who are asked to visualise feel blocked and that this is something they're unable to do. They may have several reasons for thinking that visualisation's difficult – all of them completely unfounded.

Some people feel that a suggestion to visualise means they need to sustain a highly detailed image. This isn't what hypnotherapists mean and they aren't looking for high-definition (HD) imagination. Hypnotherapists look for brief impressions that satisfy the unconscious that you've registered the image, even on the most subtle level. A shape, an outline or a blur of colour's okay, as long as that means something to you. Of course, if you can imagine in HD that's great, but doing so isn't any more or less effective.

Some people are unnerved at the thought of visualising something because they feel they simply aren't a visual person, they can't imagine themselves seeing something. But you probably visualise things regularly, even though you may not be aware of doing so.

For example, quickly, without thinking, answer the following question: 'What colour is the front door of your home?'

As soon as you answer this question, you've visualised your front door. You didn't need a sustained, detailed image. You simply get a fleeting impression of the door and ping! You have the answer to the question.

This level of imagery's sufficient for the techniques you practise as you read this book. Using these techniques, you don't simply stick to pictures – you bring other senses into the mix too.

Adding extra senses to deepen your experience

You can make visualisations more powerful by using all aspects of your physical senses, not just your imaginative use of sight. For example, imagine being at the beach on a hot summer day. How many of your physical senses do you use? You can try some of the following:

- ✔ Feeling the hot sun on your body (sense of touch).
- ✔ Seeing the sand and sunbathers and swimmers (visual).
- ✔ Hearing the ocean waves as they reach the shore (hearing).
- ✔ Smelling the salt air from the ocean (smell).
- ✔ Tasting the sweat on your skin as your face perspires (taste).
- ✔ Feeling the sense of pleasure at being there (emotion).

You invoke multiple physical senses to deepen your experience of being on the beach. You go beyond the simple visualisation you did with the 'What-colour-is-your-front-door' example in the previous section.

By using these additional sensory experiences, you begin to induce a trance state. This may be a waking trance state that lasts only a few seconds, but it's a trance state nevertheless. Think of the three questions given in the preceding section on 'visualisation' and you will understand that what we are describing is something we do daily – especially when we daydream in an 'escapist' way about holidays or something we'd like to purchase or perhaps someone we fancy!

Another example of a waking trance is when we play any sport and engage with the intention to win. Think of being a runner at the start of a race, just before the race commences. When you hear someone say to you and the others in the race the words, 'On your mark, get set, get ready . . . ', at this moment you and the other racers are in a very focused alert trance state.

Feeling a pleasant emotion is one of the most powerful methods for invoking a trance. Ultimately, using all your senses leads to what we assume you want to achieve by reading this book – using hypnosis safely and effectively to imagine a problem gone or a goal achieved.

Creating a safe place in your mind and body

Your mind's a wonderful cauldron of creativity that brims with ideas, thoughts and feelings. When you practise self-hypnosis, doing so from a balanced perspective helps you maximise the effectiveness of the technique. To help achieve this balanced perspective, try creating something that hypnotherapists call a 'safe place'. The imagination you use to create this invokes a calming response in your nervous system, helping to contain and channel the contents of your mind in a beneficial way.

Enjoying your own personal bubble

You can think of your safe place as your own personal bubble of calmness from which you can enjoy working with self-hypnosis. Your safe place means something to you and has good feelings attached to it.

Your safe place can be:

- Somewhere you know
- Somewhere you want to go, but haven't been yet
- Somewhere you've invented

If imagining somewhere's difficult for you, then your safe place can also be:

- An emptiness of your mind
- A feeling of peace
- A sense of self-confidence
- Listening to yourself saying positive things

Whatever your safe place is, it should mean something special to you.

Invoking your physical senses to make your safe place real

Now think about your safe place and ask yourself the following questions:

- What does my safe place look like?
- What does being in my safe place feel like?
- What does it feel like to touch the objects in the safe place and feel their textures?
- What can I hear in my safe place?
- What can I smell in my safe place?
- Are there any tastes that come to mind when I think of my safe place?

Write down your answers to these questions so that you have a record of them and can use them when you practise self-hypnosis. In Chapter 6 we help you create suggestions based on your answers to maximise their effectiveness.

Don't worry if you can't answer some or all of these questions. Instead, try writing down your answers to the following questions:

- What do I want my safe place to look like?
- What do I want my safe place to feel like?
- What do I want to hear in my safe place?
- What do I want to be able to smell in my safe place?
- What tactile pleasures would I like to experience in my safe place?
- What do I want to be able to taste when I think of my safe place?

Try imagining that in your safe place you have complete control over who or what comes in or out by creating a boundary such as a strong wall or force shield. In this way the place really is your own personal bubble.

Working magic in your personal bubble

By creating your safe place you are creating hypnotic induction and deepener – a way of going into trance that is your wonderful own bubble. This can then allow you to easily imagine visualisation that is actually a post-hypnotic suggestion, all stemming from feeling the wonderful feelings of achieving your goals. So you can begin to prepare for this by making your safe place more real and vivid. You can make your safe place more vivid by allowing yourself to:

✔ Imagine you're going to your safe place

✔ Imagine what the journey's like

✔ Imagine what being on that journey feels like

✔ Imagine arriving at your safe place

✔ Notice what's around you, the colours and shapes

✔ Notice the feelings and sounds

✔ Perhaps notice the smells and tastes

Spend time really creating and then enjoying the magic of your safe place. When you're ready, you can begin to work on the issues that are important to you following our suggestions in Parts III and IV of this book, or using the self-hypnosis CD that comes with the book.

Chapter 3

Using Self-Hypnosis to Achieve Your Goals

In This Chapter

▶ Working out what you really want and how to get it

▶ Being realistic in your expectations

▶ Knowing what to do once you've got what you want

▶ Keeping the momentum going

Most people like to plan for the future. Your hopes and dreams probably run through your mind when you're excited about something or as you stare out of the window at work. This daydreaming is a natural form of self-hypnosis where you put aside your conscious awareness of the world around you and focus on some pleasant fantasy or thought. Daydreaming's a creative state of mind, albeit a very raw and unchannelled one. You've probably planned what to spend your lottery winnings on if you hit the jackpot. We've certainly planned who to give money to, what to spend the money on, the property to buy, and so on. A lot of time and pleasurable effort can go into the creation of this fantasy.

And that's the important thing to remember – a daydream's a fantasy. Though plotting what to do with your imagined winnings is fun, you can't create a plan that gets the megabucks into your pocket in the first place, because winning the lottery relies purely on chance.

But imagine what may happen if you harness the power of this creative mindset and focus it in a more productive way. Instead of fantasising about something that has very little chance of happening, you can put your mind to work in a fun and structured way so you get something you want. You may be reading this book because you want to achieve something in particular, such as a change in the way you respond to a situation or an improvement in your health. Whatever your goal, in this chapter we examine how you can plan for change and then make that change a reality.

Clarifying Your Goals

You probably think you know what you want. But do you really, really know? We ask this question of all our clients because we want to make sure that what you hope for is what you actually want. A cursory thought of 'I want this' or 'I want that' may seem appealing. But when you look closely, do you really know what 'this' is and do you really know how you're likely to feel when you have 'that'?

Clarifying your goals makes certain that the reality of achieving them's acceptable to you. By achieving any goal, big or small, your life changes – and we want to make sure that change is acceptable to you. We also want to make sure that what you want is grounded in reality and not in fiction, because the best way to fail is to go hell for leather after something that either isn't achievable or ultimately isn't right for you.

When setting goals, say what you want, not what you don't want. If you focus on the negative you may inadvertently get the negative. For example, if you work towards losing weight, stating 'I don't want to be fat' focuses on the negative suggestion 'fat'. Better to state 'I want to slim down to a healthy 12 stone', as this focuses your mind on the positive suggestion 'slim' and encourages you to think positively about ways to become slim. Skip to Chapter 6 for more on the use of language.

SMARTening up your goals

The title of this section isn't wrong – we do mean SMART rather than simply 'smart'.

SMART goals are clear goals. The acronym SMART is a very useful one to keep in mind whenever you're planning change. The theme has several variations, but in general the letters refer to:

- ✔ Specific
- ✔ Measurable
- ✔ Achievable
- ✔ Realistic
- ✔ Time oriented

To illustrate what we mean, think of something that you want to achieve. Now think SMART about that goal as you read the following explanation of SMART and then go through the questions that follow:

- ✔ **Specific:** Can you sum up your goal in one sentence? For example: 'I want to lose weight', 'I want to be a calmer person', 'I want to be confident about taking a plane when I go on holiday'. These are all specific statements that say what you want. Beware a statement that starts 'Maybe . . .' because this gets you nowhere – 'maybe' is too vague!

  Be aware of the words you use in your statement. If, for example, you say 'I want to be a calmer person', then think about the word 'calm'. What does that word *really* mean to you? Make 'calm' something personal and realistic to you.

- ✔ **Measurable:** This step further refines the *specific* nature of your goal. Perhaps you 'want to be a calmer person'. You know that 'calm' means being more relaxed and more approachable. Now start thinking about when you want to be calm, in what situations you want to be calm and so on.

- ✔ **Achievable:** Thinking about the lottery, is this *truly* achievable? We don't think so! On the other hand, if you think about being calm in a traffic jam, ask yourself if *that* is truly achievable? We hope you can say 'yes'.

- ✔ **Realistic:** Ask yourself in what situations behaving in the way you want to when you achieve your goal is *realistic*. Is remaining calm in the face of extreme adversity realistic, for example? The answer's usually 'no' – unless, of course, you're a continually cheerful Stepford Wife! In this case, ask yourself how you *want* to be responding, keeping the answer positive.

  Think around your goal. Think about what achieving it means and how you realistically want to be behaving in a variety of situations.

- ✔ **Time oriented:** Over what period do you want to be achieving your goal? When you can answer that question, make sure that the time you're thinking of is *realistic*.

  A patient contacted Peter to book therapy for a flying phobia. The patient did this at 8 p.m. and was flying at 7 a.m. the next day. Not very good time planning or realistic in our opinion!

  Another question to consider is: when do you want to start? No time like the present, as a 'mañana, mañana' attitude is a good way to go nowhere.

Make sure your goals are healthy and safe (perhaps we should talk about SSHMART goals). For example, the person who sets a goal to win the lottery has a serious risk of ending up a gambling addict if she's not careful. Likewise, if you want to lose 2 stone in weight over a month you may end up either failing spectacularly or making yourself seriously ill.

Now spend some time working through the following points to SMARTen up your personal goals:

1. **Define your goal in one sentence.**

2. **Write down what any emotional words in your goal, such as 'calm' and 'confident', really mean to you.**

3. **With regard to your goal, write down how you want to behave or respond in a variety of situations.**

4. **Is your goal realistic?**

5. **Review what you want to achieve with regard to your goal and make sure that you really can do this.**

6. **Write down the *realistic* time period over which you want to achieve your goal.**

7. **Think again about your goal. Is it safe and healthy for you to achieve?**

You can alter your goal as you work through the above questions. You're better to spend time adjusting everything now, than to realise later that you haven't properly thought things through.

Deciding on your steps to success

After you create a SMART goal, as we explain in the earlier section 'SMARTening up your goals', you can plan how to get there. All the imagination and self-hypnosis in the world gets you nowhere if you don't *plan* to be proactive in attaining what you want. Stepping up to success is straightforward if you know how.

Think about your goal and ask yourself the following questions:

✔ What do I need to do each day to make sure I'm working towards achieving this goal?

✔ What is my daily motivation to achieve my goal?

✔ What can I do *now* to start me on the path to success?

Doing daily tasks

Your daily tasks are realistic, proactive things you can and should do each day – the building blocks of your goal. Plan to be active in this! For example, that may mean that you plan the amount of extra physical activity you bring into your daily life as you lose those unwanted pounds. Or, if you want to be a calmer person, think of what you can say to yourself to help keep you calm when in the past you flared up inappropriately.

Don't be surprised if you can do several things each day. Goal setting rarely relies on minimum input and always thrives on positive effort. If having to change several things is daunting, self-hypnosis can play a strong role, as we explore in the section 'Achieving Your Goals' later in this chapter.

Dealing with daily motivation

Your goal must be something that's personal to you, something you want to achieve for *yourself*. The most effective way to sabotage a goal is to be trying to achieve it because somebody else wants you to. If the goal means nothing to you, then you're not going to put in the effort necessary for success.

Peter had a patient come to see him with regard to weight control. When he asked why she wanted to lose weight, she stated that her boyfriend wanted her to slim down so that he was proud to have her on his arm when they went out. Perhaps you can see the problem here! Apart from the fact that her sexist boyfriend probably needed therapy more than she did, this goal meant nothing to her and built up frustration. In fact, she stated that she was very happy being the size she was. Consequently she was going to get nowhere.

Getting started now

Reading this book doesn't count here! You may want to throw out all the unhealthy food in your fridge to start your weight control goals, or book yourself in for a massage if you're managing your stress, or sit down and listen to the CD that accompanies this book as a means of getting things going. Don't just think it – do it!

Scoring the self-exploration goal

As you take a look at the big picture and think about what you want to achieve, ask yourself how that feels. Feelings are an important part of motivating you to succeed, so the feelings you have with regard to your goal need to be positive. Don't worry if some negative thoughts and feelings pop into your head and you feel daunted or a little scared – we can all feel worried about succeeding or frightened of the path we choose to take to success. Help's at hand in the form of Chapter 4, Resisting Resistance and Avoiding Relapse.

Striking the problem-solving goal

Perhaps you're working towards a goal that relies on solving a particular problem. Maybe you have a relationship difficulty or a work-related issue. No matter the problem, you can find a way to work it through. Of course, you have to be SMART about what you want to achieve. You may be able to tick all the SMART boxes, but when you're exploring the things you need to do each day in order to achieve your goal, you may find your way blocked by a rather talented goalkeeper: your own mind.

Being stuck in a mindset

Mindset is a term that psychologists and others use to describe a set way of thinking that a person or a group of people uses. You're stuck in a mindset when you feel you can't think about something any other way. The important thing to remember here is the phrase 'you feel you can't think about something any other way'. In this book we share with you ways and means of overcoming this and altering your mindset.

Try looking at the problem from a different perspective. As Albert Einstein said, 'You cannot solve a problem with the same mind that created it.'

When you have a problem you often go to others for advice. You may talk things over with a family member, a friend, a work colleague or a therapist. You get an opinion about the problem based on someone else's perspective. The important thing to note here is that listening to another's opinion opens up new perspectives for you, regardless of whether you agree with what the person says. As your perspectives widen you can start to examine your problem and the options for resolution in a different light.

You want to tell the world about your problem, and that's fine. But this book's about self-hypnosis and so we hope to show you ways of helping yourself.

If you struggle to find a way of resolving your problem, we recommend you visit your doctor or hypnotherapist.

You can help yourself by stepping into the mind of another person. Before you think we've gone barking mad, we want to point out that we're not advocating some form of esoteric mind transference. Instead, we're asking you to think the way someone else thinks. Parents often try to 'step into the mind of their child' in order to understand why she's behaving in a certain way. In self-hypnosis you can use this principle to imagine asking people you know, want to know or admire considerably to help you come up with solutions. By listening to their imagined answers, you help yourself to shift from one-way thinking to open perspective thinking. And that helps you find the solution you're looking for.

Here's how you can do it:

1. **Create your SMART goal.**

2. **Guide yourself into self-hypnosis, as we explain in Chapter 5.**

3. **Imagine going on a journey to somewhere nice, perhaps to your 'safe place'. (Flip to Chapter 2 for more on your safe place.)**

4. When you reach your safe place, spend time enjoying the sights, sounds, smells, feelings and even the tastes that you find there.

5. Think of someone, or a group of people, whom you particularly admire and trust, people you think are able to help you to get a better understanding of your problem and then work out a solution. Remember you're using your creative imagination, so these people can be anyone you want: family members, friends, celebrities, historical figures etc.

6. Invite this person or these people to come into your safe place.

7. Greet your guests and ask them to make themselves comfortable.

8. Tell your guests about your problem and your desired outcome (if you know it).

9. Ask them for their assistance in helping you to find the steps that you need to take in order for you to resolve your problem.

10. Listen to what they have to say. Be open to what comes into your mind – thoughts, feelings, colours, sounds etc. Just let those impressions flow.

11. You may want to get into a dialogue and debate some issues. Do whatever you feel is appropriate for you.

12. Thank your guests for their help. Not reaching a solution doesn't matter, as you can reconvene in another session.

13. Imagine returning from your safe place to where you're practising your self-hypnosis.

14. Wake yourself up, as we explain in Chapter 5.

15. Immediately write down the thoughts and impressions you now have with regard to your problem and its resolution.

Waving a Magic Wand to Manage the Magic of Goal Setting

For some people, the process of setting goals is magical and straightforward. Other people need a little extra magic to get that transformation to success going. Whether you need to or not, everyone can benefit from waving the 'magic wand question'.

The question in question has very little to do with Harry Potter and a lot to do with a form of therapy called solution-focused therapy. A technique used in that therapy known as the 'magic wand question' can help you further enhance the creation of your goal.

Focusing on solutions

Solution-focused therapy was developed in the USA during the 1980s by Steve de Shazer and Insoo Kim Berg. This approach to family therapy focuses on solutions rather than problems. One of the main theories put forward by de Shazer and Berg is that a problem is not a constant. Even though you may think that your problem is with you 24/7 there will be times when it will have lessened, or perhaps won't be there at all. A solution-focused therapist will help you identify these 'exceptions', as they call them, and to then discover what you are doing at these times that make the situation better. They then help you take these solutions and reinforce them,

applying them more consistently to your day-to-day life. Another big part of solution-focused therapy is the idea that you get more of what you focus on. When you have a problem, you focus on having the problem, and that in turn keeps the problem in its place. A solution-focused therapist focuses you on solutions (the give away here is in the name) with the idea that you are more likely to achieve what you want if you are thinking about it in a positive and constructive way. Since its development, solution-focused therapy has been increasingly used outside of family therapy and applied to one-to-one therapy with a single client.

The magic wand question helps you gain a variety of perspectives on what you're trying to achieve. By answering the question, your mind focuses on different aspects of the reality of your goal, helping you to make the goal real in your mind and to confirm that this is truly what you want (for more on making sure you've got what you want see the section 'Ensuring you've got what you want' later in this chapter).

Here is the question: 'If I can wave a magic wand and suddenly I've achieved my goal, what's different?''

Questioning the magic wand question

As with all things therapy, to get the most out of the magic wand question you need to really question what you're saying. Ask yourself the magic wand question and then ask yourself the following questions as well:

1. **What am I saying to myself that lets me know I've achieved my goal?**

2. **What am I saying to others that lets them know I've achieved my goal?**

3. **If I'm a fly on the wall watching myself, what do I see myself doing differently?**

4. **How does a close friend know that I've achieved my goal?**

Thinking through these questions stimulates the goal-setting process if you're stuck, or enhances what you've already created if you aren't stuck.

Freeing yourself with the magic wand

The human mind has a rather unfortunate habit of focusing on problem thinking when it encounters a difficulty. You've probably switched more than once into a mindset that thinks 'Why has this happened to me?', 'This is terrible' or 'I can't get out of this'. Such thinking binds you into the problem. The more you use approaches such as the magic wand question – or the time travelling that we discuss in the section 'Travelling in time' later in this chapter – the more you begin to think positively.

Positive thinking frees up your mind so that when you encounter a problem your mindset switches to solution mode; for example, 'this is how I'm going to change the situation', 'I'm now taking control of the situation and doing something about it' or 'I'm now going to plan my way out'. In effect, you train yourself to be a problem solver rather than a problem maker.

Achieving Your Goals

By planning and preparing, you create the building blocks to help you achieve your goal. This planning process is therapeutic, as you move from thinking about your desired outcome in a superficial way to buckling down to look at it in detail. In the detail you can find the power to change. Check out the sections 'Clarifying Your Goals' and 'Waving a Magic Wand to Manage the Magic of Goal Setting' earlier in this chapter for the lowdown on planning.

By breaking down your goal into its constituent parts you're already getting those successful outcomes into your mind. This is a form of waking hypnosis, which we explore further in Chapters 7 and 8. To really take advantage of your planning and preparation endeavours so far, and to enhance the likelihood of a positive outcome, you can take the next step of firming everything up in your mind using self-hypnosis.

By working through the following three steps you cement your goal into place in your mind:

1. **Imagine your goal.**

2. **Imagine overcoming the saboteurs to success.**

3. **Make your goal a reality by imagining it happening to you now.**

In this chapter we focus on your goal. However, don't forget to look at your problem too and explore what makes it a problem for you. If you know the nature of the beast, you can gain power over it. We recommend you use the relevant chapters in Parts III and IV in combination with this chapter to maximise your chances for success.

As you look at the exercises in this chapter, you may feel you have a lot to remember in order to do everything we say. A little practice helps you overcome this. Or try reading Chapter 6 and become your own recording star as you record your answers to the exercises to listen to later in self-hypnosis.

Keeping your success in mind

The clearer your goal is in your mind, the more powerful its influence is on the way you behave. And those behaviours are directed towards helping you get what you want. When you think of your goal, try to take the following steps:

1. **Notice how you want to feel.**

2. **Notice how you want to think.**

3. **Notice how you want to behave.**

4. **Notice the positive images and sounds in your mind.**

5. **Focus on creating a very clear and sharp image that's pleasing to you.**

6. **Do anything else you want to improve that image.**

Repeat this process for each of the steps that we suggest you take in the sections 'SMARTening up your goals', 'Deciding on your steps to success', 'Striking the problem-solving goal' and 'Questioning the magic wand question'. Think about your goal itself, the steps you need to take in order to achieve your goal, and what you can do today to kick-start this goal into action. For each, create a strong and positive image that you can use in self-hypnosis, or even when you simply have nothing to think about – or perhaps want a distraction and fancy daydreaming!

Jumping the hurdles

Confront the saboteurs! That means plan for every eventuality – or at least as many eventualities as you can think of. You may be thinking that this bit of advice is a little negative as, after all, everything's going to be nice and smooth because you've created such a clear goal. At this point we need to remind you of the 'realistic' in SMART. You're realistic to expect that your path to success has the occasional pothole and rock in the way. If you anticipate some small hazards, then you can do something about them. For example, if you're controlling your weight and you're invited out for a meal in a restaurant that you know has the most delicious, calorie-heavy desserts, you have several options: you can pig out on those desserts and risk jeopardising your new healthy eating behaviours (not good), you can refuse to go to the restaurant (a little anti-social), or you can prepare in advance with self-hypnosis so that you can have a great evening, enjoy eating healthily and have a strategy in place that helps you resist the desserts and choose something healthier instead.

If you find that the saboteur's coming from within yourself, then we suggest you read Chapter 4, where we give lots of tips on resisting resistance.

In the section 'Keeping your success in mind', we suggest six steps to take as you think about your goal. Take those same steps now and apply them as you create an image for each anticipated hurdle. In the case of the enticing desserts you may do the following:

1. **Notice how you want to feel:**

   I feel confident as I order something healthy.

2. **Notice how you want to be thinking:**

   I think to myself 'Well done. You're doing well!'

3. **Notice how you want to be behaving:**

   I pay more attention to enjoying the company I'm with than the menu.

4. **Notice the positive images and sounds in your mind:**

   I imagine myself healthy and slim, hearing words of praise for my achievement.

5. **Focus on creating a very clear and sharp image that's pleasing to you:**

   Turn up the brightness, bring the image closer, put a big smile on my face etc.

6. **Do anything else you want to improve that image:**

   I imagine myself looking good and feeling good as I happily ignore the unhealthy desserts.

Try to think of a few positive things to say to yourself at times of temptation or when you find things challenging. This immediate resource can help you stay on the straight and narrow.

Travelling in time

Your unconscious mind responds to whatever reality you create within it. If you always think of failure, you may be more likely to unconsciously create behaviours that lead you to fail. If, on the other hand, you think about realistic success (think SMART!), then you unconsciously create behaviours that move you towards that success.

As you take an active hand in creating your goal using your conscious mind, you have a double-barrelled approach to achievement – both parts of your mind work together as a very effective team.

Part of the process of making something real is to imagine that it *is* real. Whether you imagine taking the steps to achieving your goal or you imagine the goal itself, try to imagine yourself travelling forward in time. In this way you give your unconscious mind every opportunity to respond by stimulating unconscious positive behaviours.

 Hypnotherapists call the process of imagining yourself in the future 'pseudo orientation in time' or 'hallucinated time progression'. This is a very powerful and motivational technique that they can use in every session to help a patient move to a solution.

Putting Everything Together

If you've read the earlier sections in this chapter, you may want to read through the following checklist, using it as a guide to remind you how to achieve your goals. As you work through the list you may notice quite a bit of repetition. Repetition is effective as it reinforces the positive images and thoughts strongly and effectively in your mind.

1. **Spend time creating your SMART goal.**

2. **Spend time working out the daily steps you need to take as you work towards achieving your goal.**

3. **Decide what you can do *today* to get you on that path to success.**

4. **Think about the challenges that may come your way as you move towards your goal. Spend time thinking about how you're going to meet and overcome those challenges.**

5. **When you're ready, guide yourself into self-hypnosis (turn to Chapter 5). Don't rush to get to this step, as good preparation makes the following steps much more meaningful and effective.**

6. **Imagine the goal you created in step 1. Create one image that encapsulates that goal. Make a strong, clear image. If you want to alter anything then change it in order to improve the image. When you're ready, put the image to one side, somewhere in your mind.**

7. Imagine the daily steps you need to take that you created in step 2. Create one image that encapsulates those steps. Make a strong, clear image. If you want to alter anything then change it in order to improve the image. When you're ready, put the image to one side, somewhere in your mind.

8. Imagine what you're going to do today, the action you decided on in step 3. Create one image that encapsulates that action. Make a strong, clear image. If you want to alter anything then change it in order to improve the image. And keep that image where it is, there in your mind.

9. With the image you've just created in step 8 still in your mind, bring back the image you created in step 7 and merge the two together, creating one new unified image.

10. Make the unified image strong and clear. If you want to alter anything then change it in order to improve the image. And keep that image where it is, there in your mind.

11. With the image you've just created in step 10 still in your mind, bring back the image you created in step 6 and merge the two together to create one new image.

12. Make this new unified image strong and clear. If you want to alter anything then change it in order to improve the image.

13. Take this new image and let it become a part of your mind. Imagine your mind absorbing the image as it becomes a guiding force within you.

14. Now, imagine travelling into the future in any way you wish. Travel to a time when you've not only achieved your goal but have kept that goal going.

15. Imagine that you're fully a part of this image and notice the positive feelings and thoughts. Notice the positive way in which you're thinking.

16. Step back a little and notice how good you look. Perhaps notice the positive things others are saying to you.

17. Now, gather up all these thoughts and feelings and bring them back with you to the present.

18. Again, imagine what you're going to do today that you decided on in step 3 and spend a few minutes focusing on this.

19. When you're ready, wake yourself up (more on how in Chapter 5).

20. Go off and *do that task* you set up in step 3!

Maintaining Your Goals After You Achieve Them

After you achieve your goal, you need to maintain what you've accomplished and keep the momentum going. With just a little planning and forethought this is simple to do.

Ensuring you've got what you want

As you work towards your goal, you may find that when the reality gets closer you begin to realise that the goal isn't in fact what you want or perhaps is no longer relevant. If so, don't be afraid to change your goal. Trying to maintain something that you have no use for only causes resentment and frustration and leads to failure. Many people come into our therapy rooms complaining that they can't achieve their goals. On close inspection of those goals, they realise that the goals are unwanted or irrelevant – a major stumbling block to success.

If your goal isn't what you want, then have the courage to go back to the beginning and plan a new goal. Doing so's worth the effort in the end.

Staying positive

A positive mental attitude helps you to keep things going. If you've set your goal properly, then those behaviours that made the goal a reality become a natural part of your day-to-day life. A little tweaking here and there is all you need to keep the momentum going. Just revisit the steps that took you to your success and modify them in a way that allows you to maintain your goal. Once you've done this, you can set that change up in your mind using self-hypnosis.

Practising to make perfect

Be proactive in maintaining your goals. That means making a conscious effort to keep things going. The smoker who succeeds in quitting the coffin nails knows that she has to keep vigilant and not bow to temptation when offered a puff. The more she says 'no', the easier saying no is. Practise, practise, practise and saying no – and meaning it – becomes natural.

Creating new goals

Setting goals is a good habit to get into. Doing so helps to make you more productive and can certainly enhance the quality of your life as you're learning to take control. You don't have to wait to achieve one goal before you embark on setting another. Goal setting can be a very fluid process, with one goal aiding and influencing the success of another. Remember, by goal setting you can sometimes achieve what you may have always thought impossible. So, keep thinking forward to what you want and keep setting those SMART goals for success!

Chapter 4

Resisting Resistance and Avoiding Relapse

Almost everyone has emotional and psychological blind spots. You may have personal problems or faults that:

✔ You're unaware of

✔ You're aware of but play down as you think they're not that much of a deal

✔ You're aware of but don't know how to change

✔ Your loved ones have tried to help you with but now don't dare speak to you about

In this chapter we look at how you may block making the changes you need to make. Before you can effectively apply self-hypnosis techniques, you need to understand why you may sometimes resist or give up.

Resistance is therapy talk for how you may keep yourself stuck by refusing to change unhelpful behaviours, thoughts or beliefs. In a sense, resistance is those times when you self-sabotage, a bit like the Radiohead song 'You do it to yourself'.

By understanding your own resistance style and self-destructive patterns, you can begin to alter entrenched problems. This can make the self-hypnosis techniques that you practise as you read this book contribute to long and lasting change.

Understanding How You Block Your Own Needs

Imagine you're in a large rectangular room with two doors on either side – call them Door A and Door B. You stand at Door A and you desperately want to walk across the large room and reach Door B. However, you feel quite hopeless and frustrated about your chances of reaching Door B. The problem is that another you – a stronger, cleverer, more powerful and crueller version of you (cue dramatic music) – is blocking your way and preventing you from reaching Door B. We call this obstacle version of you your 'inner critic'.

No matter how hard you try, your inner critic successfully blocks you through a series of tricks including:

✔ Making you feel confused and unsure of yourself.

✔ Lying to you about not being deserving enough to reach your goal (Door B).

✔ Distracting you with daydreams or fears that make you forget about your goal.

✔ Making you feel selfish and indulgent for even thinking about achieving your goal.

By understanding your inner critic, you can see how your own attitudes may be your biggest problem. When you think the source of a problem's someone else, try to be honest – you may well have a role to play.

Although we often play a role in events that happen to us, please *never* blame yourself if you're the victim of unprovoked violence or childhood abuse or neglect.

The idea of taking responsibility for your role in certain problem situations shouldn't be a source of greater self-blame. Instead, taking responsibility can help you feel empowered. By understanding how you may have contributed to certain unwanted situations, you have the potential to change matters for the better.

The secondary gain conundrum: The 'benefits' of keeping the problem

It's not unusual for us to become used to living with a personal problem. After a while, the problem can even begin to feel normal and define who we are. You may have come across people who say things like:

> 'I can't stop eating chocolate . . . especially from this specialist chocolatier'.

> 'I'm a shopaholic when it comes to designer shoes...even though it keeps me in serious debt'.

> 'I'm claustrophobic, so I can't ride on public transport . . . I'm afraid we'll have to drive'.

You may even have said similar things yourself. With these examples, difficulties result from keeping the problem. Becoming overweight through eating fancy chocs, going deeper into debt through buying shoes like Imelda Marcos, or causing inconvenience at times when public transport may be easier for others.

Additionally, in these examples you can begin to see how the problems might make the speaker feel that they are special or more refined. Yet paradoxically, holding onto the problem creates frustration as it makes you suffer, or makes your life more difficult.

We regularly work with people who come for counselling or hypnotherapy to solve a problem, but begin to resist when we challenge their problem behaviours. We don't challenge them because we're being deliberately difficult, but rather because on some level the person perceives a benefit – conscious or unconscious – by keeping that problem. Problems that provide some sort of respite from physical and emotional pain are called *secondary gains*.

An example of a secondary gain is 'the lonely widow':

> A lonely elderly widow who lived alone longed to see her children, who had all grown up and rarely visited her, even though they lived nearby. One day she became ill with serious flu symptoms and her children all rushed over and took turns looking after her, cooking, cleaning and spending 'quality time' with her.

> As the woman recovered, her children gradually returned to their lives and their visits decreased, until the old pattern of neglecting their mother returned. As the old woman's loneliness returned, she unconsciously

made herself ill again. The illness was eventually 'rewarded' as her children began to visit her again, taking turns to look after her.

After a while, the woman developed an unconscious need to become ill, as this kept her children constantly close to her – but they found this increasingly a strain and their loving feelings became feelings of obligation and some unstated resentment.

In the example above, the old woman's illness becomes her secondary gain. Her illness gives her a very good payback – being nurtured by those she loves the most. However, the story does not have a totally positive outcome, as her children's loving feelings deteriorate into obligation and resentment.

A healthier way to get the love she seeks is to be more assertive and simply ask her children to visit and spend more time with her.

Secondary gains are a common form of resistance that you need to identify and overcome as you work towards achieving your goals.

Pedalling through the cycles of awareness and addiction

When we repeatedly do something that is self-destructive – such as smoking, overeating or drinking too much alcohol – we can find that it soon becomes a habit. We may at times have brief periods of stopping the behaviour for a while, but when we suffer stressful times these habits return. This cycle of stop/start with repetitive self-destructive habits is referred to as a *cycle of addiction*.

The type of addiction may vary – drugs, sex, alcohol, destructive relationships – but certain predictable behaviours tend to apply across these areas.

A cycle of addiction typically begins when a person is upset emotionally or in chronic physical pain. This pain or upset may result from any challenging life experiences that exceed the person's ability to cope, including:

✔ Personal rejection in a family, romantic or work relationship

✔ Significant bereavement

✔ Serious illness or long-term pain

✔ Deep issues of shame or guilt

Different people's individual coping skills vary. If two people experience similar hardships, one person may cope sufficiently, while the other may feel total despair and helplessness.

The coping person may fare better than the not-coping person for a variety of reasons. Possibly he:

✔ Has more of a support network of friends, family and helping resources

✔ Has an early upbringing that involved a solid, supportive childhood

✔ Is financially better off

No one completely understands why some people can cope better than others with stresses that lead to addictive behaviours. Keep in mind that as you begin to learn self-hypnosis, you will place less emphasis on 'why' the problem exists, and begin to move towards increased focus on how it feels to be problem-free. This shift in focus will enable an unconscious shift in your behaviours and thoughts to enable you to free yourself from the problem without overanalysing it.

Figure 4-1 shows the cycle of addiction. The cycle begins with some sort of stress factor or factors, which ultimately lead to an addictive behaviour. This may initially make the person feel better (not good), but at some point leads to the opposite state of feeling worse (so not good) and increasing self-loathing (mega not good). This cycle repeats and repeats and repeats . . . and unless help can stop or reverse the cycle, can go on indefinitely with all the nasty consequences that can bring.

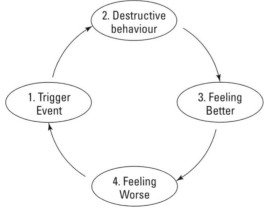

Figure 4-1:
Cycle of
addiction.

The word 'addiction', as we use it, means any problem pattern you have that repeats and you find difficult to change.

You can start to resolve addictive patterns with the following approach. Take a broad definition of 'addictions' and choose a personal problem. Apply that problem to the cycle of addictions in Figure 4-1, and then try to understand what your trigger events are by asking the following questions:

- ✔ What sets off the problem for you?
- ✔ What destructive/unwanted behaviour do you engage in?
- ✔ How does this temporarily make you feel better?
- ✔ How do you later feel worse?

You may find this a bit daunting, but the first step's having the courage to apply the model to yourself. After that, you've taken a big step towards resolving your issue as you're beginning to take control.

If you have a serious problem that may threaten your health, please seek professional help. After you resolve your problem professionally, you can use self-hypnosis to maintain your feelings of confidence and success.

Helping yourself to remove obstacles

How do you block your own goals? By considering this question you are on the road towards removing your obstacles. For example:

- ✔ If you want to be more confident, consider what beliefs cause you to be shy.
- ✔ If you are overweight from bad eating habits, consider why you snack on unhealthy sweets and comfort eat when you are not even hungry.
- ✔ If you get angry too easily, consider what beliefs you hold that make you feel that you can't communicate effectively in a calm way.
- ✔ If you are not assertive enough, consider the negative, unhelpful beliefs you have about people who _are_ assertive.

An additional approach to remove obstacles is to think of an emotional problem that you have managed to resolve. Try to remember how you overcame the problem, whether you conquered it on your own or with help, and what obstacles kept you feeling stuck before you were able to move on.

Removing obstacles typically involves these key assessments:

✓ **Changeability assessment:** How good do you feel about change? Do you fear it or are you okay about changing? Can you implement change in small bits in order to achieve your goals?

✓ **Perfectionism assessment:** How unrealistic are your goals? Can you get by with change that results in an outcome that's okay and not perfect? Perfectionism's one of the biggest enemies of change. If you have to have perfectionism or no change, you're really avoiding tackling the problem.

✓ **Risk assessment:** How threatening is the problem? What's the cost of doing nothing?

Look at the cycle of addiction in Figure 4-1. Think of your emotional problem in the context of this model, even if your problem's not strictly speaking an addiction.

Now consider the following points as you identify how you can begin to remove your obstacles:

✓ Become aware of the events that may trigger your problems and prevent you finding new, healthier ways to respond to them.

✓ Try to identify whether you're maintaining your problem by feeling excited or by reducing tension or both.

✓ If you're having problems leaving the excitement of a problem, consider how frightened you may be of being 'ordinary' and how uneasy this makes you feel. Being ordinary's often a constructive therapeutic goal, even if it doesn't flatter your ego!

✓ Can you become better at living with painful emotions? You have to live with some problems, especially those involving painful memories of the past. Problems arise when you try to get rid of these.

Obese people who overeat commonly do not consider themselves to have a food addiction. However, those who do think of themselves in this way can begin to come to grips with the seriousness of their problem, seek help and develop a strategic approach to understanding and overcoming their issues.

For example, one of my clients (Mike) who significantly reduced his weight did so by learning to be constantly vigilant about his eating habits and ensuring that he was receiving support from a local support group, where he met others who were facing a similar struggle. This is similar to the approach of successfully staying in recovery used by those have experienced alcohol or narcotics addictions.

Self-hypnosis can be useful in giving you a sense that you can overcome your personal addictions and remove the obstacles that keep you feeling stuck.

Countering Your Inner Critic

We all have a little voice inside us when we think about things. When we think about ourselves. That voice can be either helpful or critical. When the voice is critical, we refer to it as our *inner critic*.

When the voice is supportive, we refer to it as our *inner coach*. Or simply our *healthy voice*.

The relative kindness or severity of our self-thoughts and self-talk form both our self-esteem and our body image. So one key way of dealing with the critic is not to ignore it – this is virtually impossible. And sometimes the critic can deliver the odd helpful message, but it's consistently harsh in its delivery. However, it's important to not believe in the critic too completely and even to increasingly challenge its negativity. It's especially important to challenge its intimidating style and fear-based messages. At the same time, by speaking more to your coach, you can feel more positive and this sets the foundation for being able to make changes with self-hypnosis. So, yes, we are encouraging you to talk to yourself, but in the healthiest possible way!

And keep this in mind – most of this 'dialogue' will be silent and internal to your mind – you talking to your critic or coach. No one should notice that you are doing this!

In this way, you will increasingly connect to the part of you that provides encouragement and will enable you to change in new and surprising ways.

Listening to your healthy voice can be challenging when you are having a bad day. Using self-hypnosis can make it easier to tune into your inner coach. Even on bad days.

Imagining your inner critic and speaking its language

Your inner critic Is the sum total of all the negative messages you've ever received and taken to heart. Think of someone beating you with a metaphorical big stick, which you then grab hold of, saying 'Hey, give me that big stick, I can do a much better job' and continue to beat yourself! And the worst part is that you're often beating yourself with this big stick unconsciously, without even realising you're hurting yourself.

Much of your self-criticism's unconscious. By reading about your inner critic, you help to make the self-criticism more conscious.

Try the following exercise with or without self-hypnosis. You're creating a mental filing cabinet to organise the key critical themes that you repeat.

To soften your inner critic's harshness, it's useful to understand its style of attacking you first. By initially listening to and categorising the types of messages it gives you, you become more consciously aware of the hurt that it is causing you – often at an unconscious level. This helps to see these messages as variations that eventually lose their 'sting' and can even become laughable due to their predictability. Here is one exercise that can help with doing exactly that.

1. Imagine an office filing cabinet with three pullout drawers. On the front of each of these drawers is a blank label, on which you write three key critical themes that you continually say to yourself. Phrase these in the first person, for example 'I am (some critical message)'. Here are some common key critical themes:

   - 'I am bad'.

   - 'I am ugly'.

   - 'I am stupid'.

   - 'I am unloveable'.

   - 'I am clumsy'.

   - 'I am powerless'.

   - 'I am inept'.

   Remember this exercise isn't initially about stopping the thoughts, just organising them so you can be aware of how you criticise yourself.

2. Write your three key themes on the drawer labels with a black felt pen. For example:

   - Drawer 1: 'I am bad'.

   - Drawer 2: 'I am unloveable'.

   - Drawer 3: 'I am powerless'.

3. As you pull out each drawer, notice several folders inside. These folders have tabs, which you can also label. The individual files represent the variations on each of your three key themes. For example, in Drawer 3: 'I am powerless', you may have files that read:

   - File 1: You didn't get the job.

   - File 2: Your ideas were rejected at yesterday's meeting.

   - File 3: You failed to be assertive yesterday.

These three files all represent different ways of saying 'I am powerless'. This is a graphic representation of what you're doing to yourself all the time. The unfortunate genius of the inner critic is that it can create infinite variations on a theme. But once you have become aware of each of your key themes and their variations, you have made a formerly invisible (that is, unconscious) process very visible, very much within your conscious awareness, bringing these negative messages very much within your control. Hold on though, don't rush to control them just yet. You're only in the organising stage. In 'Using Your Critic to Achieve Success', later in this chapter, we discuss what to do with your collection of negative key themes and their variations.

Be creative with the way in which you represent the critical themes and messages. For example, imagine a computer containing documents with critical messages. The key themes may be the names of directories and the variations could be the different sub-directories.

Empowering yourself

Power has a bad reputation. We've noticed that people who come for hypnosis often mistakenly view their own power as something negative and shy away from using it. But accessing your personal power is important in order to achieve your goals. Overcoming problems also requires that you empower yourself to overcome stuck patterns that you may be experiencing. So in the therapeutic context power is not about dominating or manipulating others, but about generating new behaviours and challenging unhelpful beliefs that will help you to be successful with self-hypnosis.

Power's a funny thing. You frequently don't realise how much power you have, and when you use it you may go way over the top and feel ashamed. A good example is when people are learning to be more assertive. The distinctions between assertive (using power effectively) and aggression (using too much force) need to be learned through trial and error in order to learn how to get the balance right of how much of your personal power to apply. Importantly, you need to become aware that you often have more power than you think – even when you feel the world's against you or that the situation you're in is impossible.

In situations where you feel helpless, you often feel so because you've given your power away by entering 'victim mode'. Here are some thoughts that indicate you're in victim mode:

- ✔ 'I can't win'.
- ✔ 'Everybody hates me'.
- ✔ 'He always gets his way. I never do'.

✔ 'I'm between a rock and a hard place'.

✔ 'I can't cope'.

✔ 'I'm no good in this situation'.

✔ 'Poor me . . .'.

✔ 'What if I fail?'

The minute you begin to recognise these patterns, you're becoming aware of being a victim. Simply being consciously aware of this type of 'poor me' thinking begins to empower you. People often recoil in horror or become angry if somebody tells them they're self-pitying. This horror or anger can set you free and motivate you towards seizing your own power.

By imagining how you would be if the problem were gone and you had already achieved your goal, you immediately begin to activate your unconscious to generate possible new behaviours or more supportive thoughts. Throughout this book we will give examples of how to do this with self-hypnosis.

To recap, empowering yourself involves two key stages:

✔ Identifying how you disempower yourself by the obstacles and victim thinking.

✔ Imagining how it would feel with the problem gone. Developing self-hypnosis skills to enable you to spontaneously behave as if you had solved the problem.

Creating good images for body themes

You may remember a commercial featuring a photograph of a happy, naked infant. The caption read something like: 'When was the last time you felt good about your body?' This simple message was answered by the photograph, as few of us are completely okay about our entire bodies, whereas infants are not self-conscious about theirs.

As adults we compare our bodies unfavourably with others and use this as a big stick to beat ourselves with in numerous ways, including thinking we're:

✔ Too fat

✔ Too thin

✔ Too tall

✔ Too short

✔ Possessing body parts that aren't 'good enough'

Being good enough, not perfect

Therapists use the phrase 'good enough' as shorthand for an antidote in thinking against unhelpful perfectionist tendencies. This nifty phrase came from Donald Winnicott (1896–1971), an English paediatrician and psychoanalyst. In his work with young mothers, Winnicott contrasted the phrase 'good enough mother' with 'perfect mother'.

The *perfect mother* never fails, and perfectly looks after her newborn child immediately, whatever the child's need. This, of course, ultimately creates problems for the infant, who never discovers how to do anything for himself.

Contrastingly, the *good-enough mother's* behaviour involves understanding how to live with feelings of failure. However, this is good for the child. The fact that a mother can't always attend to the infant's every need instantly leads to that child knowing how to interact with everyday life.

By understanding how insidious or unconscious these messages can be, you can move on to using self-hypnosis techniques to give counter-messages about your body. One of the key messages to give yourself to counter-balance your critical body image messages is the general message of being 'good enough'.

Being good enough means that you're able to cope better and accept certain things, like a less than perfect body. Being good enough doesn't mean giving up on getting fit or healthy, just not letting your critical thoughts lead you into depression, despair or other victim-like thoughts.

There are a number of ways to overcome problems with your body image:

- ✔ Reduce your self-critical comments and thinking: replace critical self-talk with encouraging comments. Instead of putting yourself down for what you've eaten or how your body looks, use self-hypnosis to imagine gaining more self-control or seeing yourself wearing new clothes to celebrate the weight loss that you will achieve very soon.

- ✔ Hypnotise yourself to see images of a 'STOP' sign whenever you begin to admire media images of a too thin model. See the same 'STOP' sign when you hear yourself criticising any part of your body as being too fat or not right in any way.

- ✔ Imagine (hypnotise yourself) to begin to feel greater self-love, especially towards your body as it looks currently. This is not to avoid setting goals for weight loss, but simply to be kinder to yourself.

- ✔ Educate yourself about healthier options: hypnotise yourself to find learning more about healthy eating and enjoying mild forms of regular exercise.

Countering 'I am bad' themes

A common self-critical theme is 'I am bad'. Your inner critic is like your own little inner demon – it uses half-truths to create a persecutory voice, which you accept as truth. This is a tendency you must challenge, particularly with the 'I am bad' theme and its own variations.

The 'I am bad' theme increases feelings of shame, guilt and self-loathing. All of these can contribute to feelings of depression and self-destructive thoughts and behaviours. Ultimately, given enough pressures and a severe enough onslaught of critical thoughts, this may even include suicidal thoughts.

Try the following self-hypnosis technique using a judge and jury metaphor.

1. Imagine that you have the 'I am bad' critical message looping around in your thoughts for some time. You want to stop these messages, but you don't know how.

2. Now imagine that you're before a judge and jury – both are thankfully kind and understanding and on your side (much kinder than your own critic). Imagine the judge asking you the following questions and how you answer:

   • What 'crime' have you committed? (What makes you so bad)

   • How have you already punished yourself for this badness?

   • How much time have you already served? (How long have you been punishing yourself, telling yourself that you're bad?)

   • Have you served enough time? (Keep in mind that even the worst criminals serve a finite sentence and can be let off early for good behaviour.)

   • When are you going to allow yourself to be pardoned?

The last question about allowing yourself to be acquitted is a type of hypnotic suggestion. The suggestion's in the phrase – 'allow yourself to be pardoned'. At some point you must show yourself mercy and when the words come from a judge, this grants you an official pardon. So go on – accept forgiveness with pleasure.

Using Your Critic to Achieve Success

Rather than letting your inner critic put you down, you can transform your critic into a coach, mentor and friend. In this section we show you how you can use your critic to your benefit by questioning your negative thoughts and choosing healthier, more positive options.

Try the following exercise:

1. **Imagine the same critical voice that used to yell at you and make you feel bad becoming your best friend. This voice wants you to listen, and even though its approach is destructive, you're now a small step away from changing it into a more constructive source, if you can view this voice as an overprotective friend.**

2. **Begin to alter its messages by entering into a dialogue with it. Examples:**

   - 'Okay, I messed up, now I need your help.'

   - 'What should I do next?'

   - 'We've been here before, haven't we? What do I need to know?'

3. **This voice becomes so surprised and pleased that you're seeking its advice that it begins to respond in a totally different way that is no longer hurtful, but helpful. Even though you may feel weird talking about your own thoughts as if another person is inside your head, believe us, under hypnosis, you can easily do this.**

Other ways of helping your inner critic turn from destruction to construction can include imagining:

- ✔ Your toughest school teacher suddenly becoming a gentler, softer voice

- ✔ An angry marine drill sergeant suddenly gifting you kind advice

- ✔ Your childhood bully becoming your childhood protector

These images all represent a part of your harshest self becoming more of a guiding and positive internal force.

Challenging unhelpful beliefs

Your thoughts and beliefs generate your perception of the world. If, for example, you believe that the world's a dangerous place, you become a fearful, paranoid person. However, if you believe that the world's a place of wonder and amazement, other people probably think of you as a lucky person. Remember, your thoughts create your experiences.

NLP: A brief description

Neuro-linguistic programming (NLP) is a system that focuses on how you think, how you perceive things and communications. The idea being that you can change your behaviour by observing your predictable patterns. NLP aims to increase your self-awareness and your ability to achieve goals by noticing the helpful and unhelpful patterns of your behaviours, thoughts and speech. It is especially popular with hypnotherapists and life coaches as an effective form of therapy. For more information on this see *Neuro-linguistic Programming For Dummies* by Romilla Ready and Kate Burton (Wiley).

The area of therapy called Neuro-linguistic programming (NLP) describes how you maintain your unhelpful beliefs by twisting reality in the way that your inner critic dictates by using the following erroneous thinking patterns:

- ✔ **Distortion:** Removing details from your memory in order to narrow your focus and prove the Inner Critic's view is fact, when it's not. i.e., 'Mother has never said one single positive thing in her life to me.'

- ✔ **Generalisation:** using one experience and applying to others – usually in a limiting way. That is, 'I failed once, so I'll never try that again.'

- ✔ **Deletion:** Omitting important details in order to focus on a specific point. That is, forgetting about past successes to maintain feelings of failure.

By becoming increasingly aware of the three unhelpful belief approaches, you begin to think, feel and speak in ways that help facilitate your making the changes that you want in your life.

Using your mistakes to your advantage

One of the best ways to develop is to make mistakes, so that you never have to repeat them. Through making mistakes you see how to do things better and how to avoid making more mistakes.

Ever had an annoying memory that keeps repeating in your mind? For example, some embarrassing moment where you did or said something you deeply regretted?

ABCs of controlling the inner critic

You can use three positive tools to shrink the influence of your critic:

✔ **A**mplify your successes. The critic does the opposite by focusing on failures.

✔ **B**elieve that you will achieve your goals. The critic's mantra is 'give up – you'll never change'. Yours can be to continually use self-hypnosis to imagine the feeling of achieving your goals.

✔ **C**ategorise: your critical messages. As in the filing cabinet exercise in the earlier section

'Imagining your inner critic and speaking its language', if you become aware of three or four broad critical themes that your inner critic uses, you will quickly see that all of the messages tend to be variations on the big themes. This can help reduce its influence as you become more aware of this as a sort of cruel game that is now coming to an end.

By increasingly applying these three helpful approaches you will begin to think, feel and speak in ways that help you make the changes you want in your life.

When we cringe about a past gaffe, we are invoking an unhelpful trance state in which we make ourselves feel worse, or set the unwanted event to recur at some future point. These events form 'memory loops' that the inner critic can replay to make us feel worse about ourselves. The following exercise will help to break those loops so that we do not feel bound by the past.

1. **Imagine a mistake you've made in the past that you regret. Imagine the episode from beginning to end as if you're watching an old black-and-white movie.**

2. **Imagine the beginning of the same memory, but this time in colour.**

3. **Imagine that instead of making the mistake, you do something entirely different and better, so that everyone involved feels good.**

This helps you to influence your critical inner voice directly so that you can imagine a future of not repeating this mistake *and* not condemning yourself for the past.

Finding healthier alternatives to problems

In the previous section we described how to break revisiting past regrettable memories that your inner critic uses to constrain you and make you feel bad.

Next, you need to replace any negative views you have of yourself with healthier alternatives. For example:

- ✔ If you see yourself as clumsy, do self-hypnosis to see yourself as graceful.

- ✔ If you view yourself as fat, see yourself in your ideal body weight celebrating significant weight loss by buying some new, smaller-sized clothes.

- ✔ If you see yourself as shy and having poor social skills, hypnotise yourself to see yourself being socially impressive and the centre of attention as you smile confidently and see others smiling back, nodding their heads as you speak.

As you control your critic, you can counter obstacles so that you're able to break out of unhealthy cycles. Like every skill, this takes effort and dedication to achieve. The more you practise the techniques in this book, the more effortless and natural you will find the process of creating healthy alternatives to your problems.

Part II
Training Your Mind with Self-Hypnosis

The 5th Wave   By Rich Tennant

"You can use these scented candles along with self-hypnosis to help curb your appetite. There's rotting shellfish, country outhouse, and vomit medley."

In this part . . .

Time to get technical. In this Part we open the self-hypnosis toolbox and take a good long look at self-hypnosis techniques. We explore the ways in which you can enter the trance state, and take a tour through the language used in hypnotherapy, helping you to get the most out of each session. We help you to become conscious of your unconscious, and provide you with the tips you need as you learn to harness its power for your benefit.

Chapter 5

Entering a Hypnotic Trance with Traditional Self-Hypnosis

. . . .

In This Chapter

▶ Understanding traditional approaches to self-hypnosis

▶ Using your own words

▶ Easing gradually into a deeper trance state

▶ Evoking the feeling of your favourite places

. . . .

*E*ntering self-hypnosis is an art. Thankfully it is an art that everyone can master quite easily if they want to. Guiding yourself into trance is far more than simply closing your eyes and finding that you are there, deep in your own inner world, enjoying self-hypnosis. There are many ways of going into self-hypnosis and coming out of it, the ones we believe are most effective are explored in this chapter.

The poet William Cowper once wrote that 'variety is the spice of life, that gives it all its flavours'. What's true of life is also true of entering self-hypnosis. There are many ways of going into self-hypnosis and coming out of it, and in the pages of this chapter you will find a variety that we believe will make your experience of self-hypnosis more effective and rewarding. Some approaches you may like, some perhaps you won't. That's a very common experience, and with a little experimentation you will be focusing on the ones that appeal most to you.

Practice makes perfect! Self-hypnosis is a skill that everyone can acquire. Like all skills, the more you practise, the better you get and the easier the skill becomes.

Because we are individuals, we respond better to therapy approaches that are personally meaningful. So we begin this chapter by discussing the way self-hypnosis was traditionally taught to everyone. We then engage your creative mind and move on to helping you modify these time-honoured techniques in ways that not only help you to go deeper into trance, but make doing so more fun, enjoyable and personal to you. In this way you not only gain more from the experience of self-hypnosis, you get more rapid results.

Looking at Traditional Self-Hypnosis Techniques

Over the years hypnotherapy has had its fair share of developments as it has evolved. Some of these developments have been left by the wayside and many others have made it into the standard cannon of hypnotherapy and self-hypnosis. However, there's nothing like going back to your roots, where tried-and-trusted traditional techniques can be found that are still useful, relevant and very effective. These techniques make a good starting point in discovering how hypnosis works. Later you get to know how to modify these in ways that allow them to work even better for you.

Using your mind to help with problem solving can be one of the most liberating feelings imaginable. Curiously, we tend to look for external cures first and only resort to using our own inner resources as a last, desperate measure.

Setting the scene

The environment in which you practise self-hypnosis should be as comfortable as possible. Here are some tips to help you:

✔ Make sure that you practise at a time you know you're not going to be disturbed.

✔ Turn off your mobile phone and turn down the ringer on any landlines.

✔ Find a comfortable chair to sit in, preferably one that supports your head.

✔ You can lie down, but be aware that you may fall asleep.

✔ Make sure that the temperature of the room's comfortable for you.

✔ Go to the toilet. A full bladder isn't conducive to relaxation!

✔ Tell yourself how long you're going to practise for – 10–15 minutes is a good time to begin with. As you progress, you can shorten or lengthen the time as you see fit.

✔ If you're worried that you may fall asleep or lose track of time, then you can set an alarm (making sure that the alarm has a gentle tone when it goes off).

✔ If you practise in bed at night don't bother to wake up. Let your experience turn into a natural sleep (great for insomniacs).

The Father of Hypnotherapy

In a sense, this is exactly how the use of traditional self-hypnosis began. In the 1840s Scottish surgeon James Braid developed what was arguably the original self-hypnosis technique. Such was the impact this technique made on the fledgling world of hypnotherapy that many luminaries in the field moulded, developed and emulated the approach over the next century. Braid had already pioneered the use of hypnotherapy with patients, and in fact invented the word 'hypnosis'. For more on Braid and other pioneers as well as a potted history of hypnosis, see our previous book, *Hypnotherapy For Dummies*.

With his development of hypnotherapy Braid wasn't simply being altruistic. He had another, more personal interest that led to him developing self-hypnosis – he suffered from severe, painful rheumatism in his upper body. He initially tried to alleviate the pain with medicine, but this didn't help. Eventually, Braid resorted to using his own mind, and for nine minutes practised self-hypnosis to remove his pain. To his surprise, he successfully improved his condition and found himself pain free. He continued to practise and was so impressed with the results that in 1844 he published a paper detailing what he'd done, effectively giving the world the first template for self-hypnosis. We refer to this technique as traditional self-hypnosis.

Traditional self-hypnosis involves the following procedure:

I Preparing for self-hypnosis

1. **Sit in a comfortable chair with your feet flat on the floor, hands resting on your thighs, and close your eyes.**

2. **Breathe gently through your nose.**

3. **Begin to slow your breathing and relax your body.**

II Inducing self-hypnosis

4. **Breathe in deeply. Hold your breath until you feel the need to breathe out (don't make yourself uncomfortable, though).**

5. **As you begin to exhale slowly, repeat the phrase 'sleep now' in your mind, firmly and with intention.**

6. **Enjoy the feeling of release as you emit a deep sigh and allow your body to slump comfortably down into the chair like a limp and loose doll.**

7. **Repeat steps 4 to 6 three times to help you relax even further.**

III Deepening your hypnosis

8. Count slowly and silently from 10 to 0. Count on every second out breath and imagine that each descending number is helping you to become 10 per cent more relaxed as you do so.

IV Using hypnotic suggestion

9. Give yourself the suggestion that you want your mind to receive for the therapy result. Simple suggestions such as the ability to experience increased relaxation and confidence are the most common. Allow plenty of time. Don't rush. (Turn to Parts IV and V for more help.)

V Wakening from hypnosis

10. Tell yourself that you're going to wake up.

11. Tell yourself that when you wake up you're going to be full of energy and alert.

12. Count from 1 to 10, one number a second. Tell yourself that your eyelids are going to flutter open on the count of 8 and that you're going to be fully awake on the count of 10.

13. On the count of 8, open your eyes. On the count of 10 give yourself a big stretch and enjoy feeling the positive feelings and anticipation of the transformation to come . . .

Focusing on eye fixation

Have you ever stared absent-mindedly at something and found yourself 'spacing out'? This often happens if you watch television and are no longer interested in the programme, or are sitting bored indoors and looking out of the window, staring at the flames of a log fire or reading a book and finding your mind drifting and wandering.

These are common examples of a technique called 'eye fixation'. This has many variations, but eye fixation's one of the easiest ways to do self-hypnosis – especially for nervous beginners.

Eye fixation's probably the best known of all ways of inducing hypnosis – 'look into my eyes' is the classic approach used in film and television. No, we aren't going to suggest that you stare at yourself in a mirror or look intently into the eyes of your best friend. In this section we explore how you can take your natural ability to relax when you stare at something and turn it into a pleasant way of entering trance.

You can buy a wide variety of computer programs and devices that give you something to look at as a means of helping you into trance. These products usually come at a price, so unless you're dripping with money you may want to find equally effective (and free) objects to stare at in your own home.

If you wear contact lenses, you may prefer to take them out, and if you wear glasses you may want to take them off. This helps you feel more comfortable and if things seem a little blurred that doesn't matter.

This is a simple eye fixation exercise for you to try:

1. **Sit comfortably in a relaxing chair, look upwards and find a spot to stare at on the ceiling.**

2. **Continue to stare at that spot for maybe one or two minutes as you breathe more slowly. Remember to blink!**

3. **Keep your body as still as you can and relax.**

4. **Be aware of a degree of *slight* discomfort from the steady upward staring.**

5. **Hold on to this feeling of discomfort. Take a slow, deep breath and release it and the discomfort as you close your eyes and let your head slowly move towards your chest.**

6. **Take a deep breath, hold the breath for a few seconds and breathe out slowly. As you exhale, give yourself the suggestion that your body's becoming more and more relaxed.**

7. **At this stage, you're likely to have induced a very light trance state and this is a good time to give yourself your hypnotic suggestions (for more on hypnotic suggestions, see 'Setting the scene', earlier in this chapter).**

8. **Once you've given yourself suggestions, tell yourself that you're going to wake up.**

9. **Follow the waking procedure that we describe in 'Setting the scene', earlier in this chapter.**

That's just one way of looking at eye fixation. You can add variety to the approach, keeping what you do fresh and enjoyable. You may like to try the following variations:

✔ Fixate on a beautiful picture, imagine stepping into it and exploring the scenery.

✔ Look at the second hand of a clock go round as you listen to the sound of ticking.

- ✔ Watch the rhythmic left-to-right sway of a metronome.
- ✔ Focus on the flickering flames of an open fire.
- ✔ Stare at the intricate structures that create the head of a flower.

The possibilities are endless. If you can look at something, you can use that as an aid to entering trance.

As soon as your eyelids begin to feel heavy and tired when using any eye fixation approach, let them close. This is just your body and mind saying 'time for trance'.

If you don't like eye fixation as an approach, that doesn't mean you can't do self-hypnosis. Vision is only one of your five senses – you can also use hearing, smelling, tasting and feeling to induce self-hypnosis. For example, sit comfortably in a chair and close your eyes. Then:

1. **Listen to the sound of a ticking clock as you begin to imagine yourself relaxing deeper and deeper into the trance.**

2. **Imagine that you can smell the most wonderful aroma, one that makes you think about relaxing. Focus on that smell and the relaxation it brings as you drift deeper and deeper into the trance.**

3. **Imagine what the taste of relaxation is like. Imagine really enjoying that taste, rolling it around your tongue, as you relax deeper and deeper into the trance.**

The next section, 'Relaxing progressively', is a good example of using the last of your five senses: feeling.

When hypnotherapists talk about the sense they use to guide someone into trance they call it 'modality of representation'. Everyone has their own preferred modality of representation, with some people favouring vision over feelings over sound, for example.

Relaxing progressively

When you let out a sigh of relief, your body relaxes. This is because you usually tense up as you inhale and then relax as you exhale. This happens naturally and unconsciously, but you can also use the idea deliberately and consciously to lessen anxiety and to induce a trance state.

The goal of progressive relaxation is progressively to create an overall feeling of comfort from head to toe.

Progressive relaxation

Progressive relaxation can help reduce anxiety by relaxing your muscles. After all, you can't be anxious and relaxed at the same time. In the 1920s American physician Edmund Jacobson originally developed the technique to ease muscle tension. During practice, he noticed that people's anxiety was reduced and so relaxation was increasingly applied to manage anxiety. As a by-product, progressive relaxation proved a great way of helping to reduce blood pressure and slow down the heart rate – a very good thing for those with cardiovascular disease.

One of the easiest ways to begin to induce a trance state for self-hypnosis is to gently tense physically and then relax each group of muscles in your body.

Try taking the following steps to see how progressive relaxation works:

1. **Find somewhere comfortable to sit. Crossed arms and legs lead to tension and discomfort, so make sure that both your feet are flat on the floor and your hands are resting gently on your thighs.**

2. **Close your eyes and slow your breathing. Breathe through your nose. Make each out breath slower and longer than the next until you can feel yourself becoming more comfortable. Feel with each breath that you are exhaling bodily tension, helping you to deepen the relaxation even further.**

3. **Gradually relax each of your muscle groups, either working your way from head to toe or from toe to head, depending on your preference.**

4. **Suggest to yourself that you're steadily relaxing all your muscle groups. You can imagine in your own way what these muscles relaxing is like. Don't worry about being perfect. Forgetting to relax a specific body part – the muscles around your knees, elbows or toes, for example – is only natural. Your unconscious helps you by relaxing any parts you forget to focus on. After all, if you're worrying too much about relaxing you never relax in the first place!**

5. **As you feel your whole body relaxing, give yourself your pre-chosen hypnotherapy suggestions, which we explain in 'Setting the scene', earlier in this chapter.**

6. **When you're ready to wake up, follow the steps in 'Setting the scene', earlier in this chapter.**

You can spice up your progressive relaxation in some interesting ways. You may like to try the following:

✔ As you relax, give yourself suggestions such as 'I am becoming more comfortable and relaxed'.

✔ With each out breath, imagine breathing out the colour of tension and then breathing in the colour of peace and tranquillity while feeling your body relax.

✔ As you breathe out and relax, mentally say the word 'relax' in a gentle way. If you do this often enough, you become conditioned to relax every time you think about relaxing. Very useful when you feel under pressure!

Investigating Different Ways to Induce a Trance

As you become comfortable with the basic forms of trance induction that we explore in the earlier sections of this chapter, you may realise that you can take yourself into trance in so many ways. After regular practice, you can begin to improvise induction methods that feel right to you.

For example, you may choose to enter a trance in some of the following situations:

✔ Sitting in the bath.

✔ Waiting for a bus on a busy street.

✔ Watching television adverts and waiting for the main programme to return.

✔ On the train on your way into work to help set yourself up for the day.

✔ Having a conversation with your most boring friend!

One of the old-fashioned ways of achieving trance used to be to look at objects that spiral or sparkle – think of the stereotypical hypnotherapist in movies and television programmes spinning a black-and-white spiral or holding a shiny fob watch and asking the patient to stare.

Staring at a spiral or shiny object is certainly one way to go into trance, but this is a bit unoriginal and gimmicky and, because of this, possibly less effective than ways that are more meaningful and personal to you.

You have no limits to the ways in which you can achieve trance. The best ways are the ones that come naturally and unconsciously to you, almost without thinking of them as techniques.

What does 'being hypnotic' look like?

Milton Erickson was a fine example of someone who was naturally hypnotic. Ironically, Erickson's seeming naturalness came from his painstaking observations about people from an early age.

Today hypnotherapists study Erickson's case studies to emulate his style in order to be hypnotic. What exactly *did* Erickson do that made him hypnotic? Lots of things: he told stories, he used images that were meaningful and came from his patients' own phrases, and he used subjects that interested the people who spoke

to him. In fact, no subjects were too boring; the more mundane, the better.

One of his most famous cases involved talking to a patient about his keen interest in gardening. Erickson used growing tomatoes as a metaphor for personal growth in a way that enabled the gardener to make the changes he sought without actually doing talking therapy on specific issues. Yet those changes occurred nevertheless. By using your own images and emotional feelings of growth, change and success, you too can be hypnotic.

Being hypnotic

Most people who discover self-hypnosis begin by reading scripts. This book offers many examples that can get you started. The aim is that after repeated practice, at some point you don't need the scripts and you begin to be able just to go into trance without even realising that you're taking yourself 'into the zone'.

In his book *Treating Depression with Hypnosis*, American clinical psychologist Michael Yapko writes about the need to move from *doing* hypnosis to *becoming* hypnotic. Although he wrote his book for training hypnotherapists, his advice applies equally to anyone finding out about self-hypnosis.

Being hypnotic means moving beyond reciting other people's methods and scripts of trance induction and doing hypnosis your way. Use your own metaphors and images to induce trance based on ideas that are meaningful to you so that you can achieve your personal goals. Here are some examples:

- An artist may imagine relaxing *images* to go into a trance.
- A musician may *hear soothing sounds* to become more relaxed.
- Someone who enjoys reflecting on things may simply remember a past hypnosis session that worked particularly well.

Ultimately, being hypnotic implies that you've reached a certain level of familiarity with the feeling of trance based on practice and confidence with self-hypnosis.

Scripts are certainly not meaningless and arbitrary. Scripts are essential for finding out how to induce trance and phrase hypnotic suggestions in a meaningful way (for more on how to be hypnotic with words, have a look at Chapter 8). They are where you *begin*. With experience, you can then apply Yapko's advice and even take the advice one step further. Scripts are the *beginning* of your discovery of hypnosis.

It is realistic to be aware that as you journey down your path of discovery there can be challenges to how effective self-hypnosis is for you. The 'sin of literalism' implies all the things that can get in your way, like:

- Being too literal and serious-minded.
- Being too concerned about getting things right.
- Forgetting to have fun doing self-hypnosis.
- Expecting that you must go into a deep trance for hypnosis to work (not true).
- Relying blindly on scripts without introducing any personal content.
- Using scripts with phrases or approaches that you don't even like.

Being hypnotic simply means absolving yourself of the 'sin' by adapting your self-hypnosis approaches in ways that feel comfortable and produce the results that you want.

Remembering past relaxed states

You have a wide variety of past experiences filed away in that vast storehouse of your mind in the form of memories. When you recall these memories they can produce a whole variety of emotions, many of which are truly lovely and a pleasure to experience again. You can use these happy memories and their resultant feelings as an aid to trance (we spend more time exploring the use of memories in Chapter 8).

Try the following exercise to relax into a good memory:

1. **Sit comfortably with both feet flat on the floor and your hands resting on your thighs.**

2. **Close your eyes and think of one of the most relaxing moments that you've ever experienced.**

3. As you think about this wonderful moment, try to make the experience even more vivid by bringing to mind any other sensations, such as accompanying pleasant sounds and smells, the feel and texture of things around you, and most importantly the positive emotions that come from remembering this situation.

4. Imagine yourself there, once again fully experiencing this place.

5. When you're ready you can begin to deliver to yourself the suggestions you want to work with, as we explain in 'Setting the scene', earlier in this chapter.

6. When you're ready to wake up, follow the steps in 'Setting the scene', earlier in this chapter.

For example, if you think of the beach holiday you had last summer, you may begin by remembering the wonderful fresh smell of the sea air, the sound of the waves as they break onto the beautiful golden sands, the pleasant feeling of a cool breeze brushing against your perspiring skin and the sense of sublime relief you felt enjoying this wonderful change of scenery.

Feeling relaxed? Good. Of course, variety and creativity are the name of the game and things are more interesting if you can come up with a selection of pleasant memories of relaxed times to enjoy.

If you can't remember a specific time when you were relaxed, simply invent a time. Let that creative mind of yours go to work. You may even want to have a combination of remembered relaxed times and invented relaxed times at your disposal. Always remember to use as many of your senses as possible.

Understanding Vogt's fractionation

Fractionation is a scary-sounding word, but you may be relieved to know that this isn't turning you into a Humpty Dumpty-type character, where you shatter into pieces and have to be put together again. Instead, fractionation's a term in hypnotherapy that means stopping and starting.

Vogt's fractionation technique is a traditional hypnotherapy technique where the hypnotherapist does a series of rapid consecutive inductions, hypnotising and then awakening the client, then asking the client to recount the sensations she's just experienced.

In this way the new (and often nervous) client is able to 'relax' into the experience of first-time trance induction. This technique's particularly useful for people who are slightly afraid of being hypnotised and losing control (we discuss the issue of control – and how the hypnotised person keeps it – in

Chapter 1). Vogt's fractionation method allows the client to understand the often used phrase that 'all hypnosis is self-hypnosis', meaning that you can only be hypnotised if you relax enough to allow the hypnosis to happen.

Vogt's fractionation's also a very good way to explore your own unique response to trance in self-hypnosis. Basically you can find out what works for you and reject what doesn't. The process of stopping and starting can allow you to access some very deep and very pleasant levels of hypnosis.

The following exercise shows how fractionation can bring you together in trance:

1. **Adopt the position that we suggest in other sections of this chapter: sit comfortably with both feet flat on the floor and your hands resting on your thighs.**

2. **Close your eyes and just let yourself experience whatever you're experiencing.**

3. **After about 20 to 30 seconds, open your eyes and look straight ahead.**

4. **Identify what you enjoyed or found positive about that brief time with your eyes closed. That's the first fraction completed – on to the next one.**

5. **Close your eyes again and think about what you enjoyed. See what else comes into your mind.**

6. **Again, after about 20 to 30 seconds open your eyes and look straight ahead.**

7. **Identify once more what you enjoyed or found positive.**

8. **Close your eyes and think of all the things you've enjoyed or found positive so far and then see what else comes into your mind.**

9. **Keep repeating steps 6 to 8 above until you're in trance. Don't be surprised if you find opening your eyes more and more difficult each time. This just shows that you're nicely trancing out.**

10. **Work through our suggestions in 'Setting the scene', earlier in this chapter, to deliver your suggestions and then wake yourself up.**

If you apply this approach appropriately, you may be pleasantly surprised to find that you become skilled at a form of rapid self-hypnosis. You may need only one or two fractions before you're deep, deep, deeeeeeply in trance . . .

Rising to the challenge with arm levitation

This section isn't about magic and mystery. Nor is it about flying carpets or levitating assistants. Rather, this section's about using your natural ability to do things automatically in response to thought. You have probably experienced a time when you were resting and one limb or another twitched at a certain thought. Perhaps you were thinking of something pleasant and found that a smile spread to your lips without your being aware. You may find this happening when you practise any of the techniques that asks you to remember something happy or create something positive. Who says you can't go into trance with a smile on your face?

Ideo motor response (often shortened to IMR) is the name hypnotherapists give to the process whereby a thought leads to an automatic movement of a muscle or limb. These movements can be very useful in therapy, as they can allow a very pure route of communication to the unconscious mind. To find out more about the use of IMRs in therapy, have a look at our book *Hypnotherapy For Dummies*. We tell you more about how to use IMRs to induce trance in this section.

When you do something automatically, running on autopilot, then your mind becomes 'split' or dissociated (turn to Chapter 1 for more on this interesting subject). This is a very efficient way for your mind to work as you need less conscious processing time and things run more smoothly. If we take away conscious interference, then dissociation can also become a very effective way of going into trance. You're only doing something that's natural.

Arm levitation techniques have led to some of the mystique surrounding hypnosis, as your arm seemingly rises up of its own accord as you enter trance. What really happens is that when you think that your arm's lifting automatically, small and unnoticed micro contractions of your biceps muscle begin to carry out the action. Mystery solved!

Unconscious automatic movements are slight, hesitant and jerky. Smooth uninterrupted movements are usually under conscious control.

Arm levitation techniques are a very pleasant and interesting way to enter trance that allows you to find out more about the way the mind and body communicate.

The following exercise helps you lift up to trance:

1. **Adopt a comfortable seated position. Make sure that both hands are resting gently on your lap.**

2. **Lift one of your hands (which one doesn't matter) and rest it so that your fingertips are just touching your thigh.**

3. **Look at that hand.**

4. **Notice the rise and fall of your chest as you breathe.**

5. **With each in breath, imagine that your arm's getting lighter and lighter. Imagine that your arm wants to lift.**

6. **As you breathe in, notice any slight movement of your arm. You can encourage movement by silently saying to yourself 'lifting', 'lighter' on each in breath.**

7. **If you want, you can close your eyes and begin to imagine helium-filled balloons attached to your wrist making your arm lighter and lifting it up. You can also imagine that someone you care for and trust is gently raising your arm up too.**

8. **Once your hand has lifted you can (if you haven't done so already) close your eyes.**

9. **Continue to let your arm move upwards as you repeat the suggestions and imagery in steps 5, 6 and 7.**

10. **Once your arm's at a comfortable level, imagine and suggest that it slowly and gently returns to your lap.**

11. **As your arm moves towards your lap, tell yourself that you're becoming wonderfully relaxed.**

12. **When your hand touches your lap, allow yourself to relax completely and drift deeper into the trance.**

13. **Tell yourself that all normal feelings and weight are now returning to your arm as you prepare yourself for your suggestions.**

14. **Work through our suggestions in 'Setting the scene', earlier in this chapter, to deliver your suggestions and then wake yourself up.**

Don't worry if nothing happens at first. Persevere and you can succeed. If still nothing happens (and that can apply to the most experienced self-hypnosis practitioner), then this can simply become a variation of the standard eye fixation induction we talked about way back at the beginning of this chapter.

Picturing your favourite place

We all have favourite places that we like to visit, or places we want to visit. As children (and this applies to some adults too) we made up worlds in our mind where we played fantastical games and felt positive and good. The good news is that if you've forgotten how to do this you can once again enjoy these flights of fantasy.

Favourite places are useful as they're associated with positive feelings. These can range from relaxation (something we explore in 'Remembering past relaxed states', earlier in this chapter), excitement, confidence, safety and so on. Using your mind to recreate, create or be creative with your favourite place is an excellent way for you not only to enter trance, but also to set yourself up for therapy, as you're already accessing some of the psychological resources that can help you change.

Psychological resources are those thoughts, feelings and ideas that help you cope with the day-to-day trials and challenges of life. In therapy we can find out what resources are needed to help a person overcome an issue in his life and then move on to helping him access them.

Try the following exercise to open the door to your favourite place:

1. **Sit in a comfortable position and close your eyes.**

2. **Imagine that you're about to take 10 or 20 (or as many as you want) steps down a beautiful path or corridor.**

3. **Imagine the path, bringing in all your senses. What does the path look like? How do you feel on the path? What pleasant aromas can you smell? What can you hear? Does the air have a taste?**

4. **Begin to count down from 10 to 1, thinking each number on every out breath. As you count, imagine taking one step along the path with each number.**

5. **When you get to the number 1, imagine (with all your senses) that you're standing in front of a gate or a door and that on the other side is your favourite place.**

6. **Imagine opening that gate or door and stepping through into your favourite place.**

7. **Spend time exploring with all your senses – this helps to make the experience so wonderfully real, just like a pleasant dream.**

8. **You can make adjustments to your favourite place. For example, put a protective boundary around so that you control who or what comes into the place, keeping yourself wonderfully safe.**

9. **Enjoy the experience of being in your favourite place and when you're ready, find somewhere to rest and begin to work on whatever you want to work on. Parts IV and V of this book can be your guide here.**

10. **When you've finished working, imagine yourself back in your favourite place. Imagine leaving the way you came in (knowing that you can return whenever you want). And retrace the steps you took along the path or corridor.**

11. **Wake yourself up following the steps in 'Setting the scene', earlier in this chapter.**

You can enjoy visiting your favourite place as often as you want. Maybe you can be creative and find entrances to other favourite places hidden in your current one.

You can simply enjoy going into trance without having to work on anything in particular. Doing so helps you relax and shut off from a tiring day.

Chapter 6

Working with Words: Becoming Your Own Recording Star

. . . .

In This Chapter

▶ Working out what to say in self-hypnosis

▶ Being positive with the words you use

▶ Being expressive with your voice

▶ Recording your own words to listen to later

. . . .

*H*ypnotherapy is a talking therapy and during a trance session the hypnotherapist plans and uses words and sentences carefully and precisely. After all, in therapy trying to convey one idea when the listener is interpreting what you're saying in a completely different way isn't a good idea. The result's probably that nothing happens. That's why training in hypnotherapy is more than knowing how to hypnotise someone. As you may have found already by hypnotising yourself, that's the easy part. The skill of therapy comes from the words you use during the session and the way you express them.

Talking therapy is any therapy that uses conversation, questioning or listening to another person speak as its main tool. Hypnotherapy's one of the talking therapies. Other examples are counselling, psychotherapy and psychoanalysis.

Words convey information and meaning. Making sure that the correct information and the appropriate meaning are delivered to your unconscious mind during a therapy session is therefore important, allowing you to make the changes you want to make.

In this chapter we explore how you can create your own hypnotherapy sessions for self-hypnosis and how to record your sessions for future use.

Your unconscious mind only accepts suggestions that fit in with your personal moral and ethical way of thinking. That means that if we give you the suggestion in trance that 'the next time you see a taxi you think you're Lady Gaga and perform 'Poker Face' in the middle of the street', you may immediately wake up from trance and ask us what on earth we're doing – unless you really do want to be Lady Gaga, that is!

Scripting Your Success

Planning and forethought in therapy help you maximise your chance of getting the outcome you want. That's why hypnotherapists use scripts. Just as in a play where a script directs the action and makes sure that the story flows, in hypnotherapy you script a session in order to maximise the effective outcome by focusing both the therapist and the patient in the right direction.

Sometimes spontaneity can be very effective too. But we therapists are devious so-and-sos, so what may seem spontaneous to you is often based on our past experience and actually has planning behind it!

Formulating your focus

You may be asking: 'Where should I begin my planning?' The answer's simple – find your focus. That means deciding what you want to achieve and how you want to go about achieving it. Working on one thing at a time is important. This means that you maximise your focus and therefore the potential for a positive outcome.

If you have several issues you want to work on, then prioritise them. Start working on the most important and when you've resolved that, move to the next on your list.

To help you really focus in the right direction, have a look at Chapter 3 to explore how to set your goals and get what you want. If you're working on an issue such as weight, you can also narrow down your focus of attention and create scripts for specific aspects of weight control, as we explain in Chapter 16. For example, you can create one to help you focus on healthy eating, one to help you focus on exercise and so on.

After you set your goals and fine-tune your focus, you can work on what you want to say. The starting point for that is to determine the structure of your script.

Ericksonian hypnotherapy

You may have been to a hypnotherapist who delivers a script during therapy that jumps around all over the place. What he's doing is using Ericksonian hypnotherapy. That means that the seemingly disjointed nature of what you're listening to is meticulously planned. This is a therapy technique that takes skill in order to maximise its therapeutic impact.

Ericksonian hypnotherapy was developed by Milton Erickson. He was a medical doctor trained in traditional hypnotherapy who eventually moved away from the way he was taught and put his own individual spin on the practice. Colleagues and friends noticed that he was having a lot of success and so with him started to study what he was doing, all leading to the development of the style of hypnotherapy that now carries his name. For more on Milton Erickson, read our book *Hypnotherapy For Dummies*.

Attending to structure

Structure's important when you create a hypnotherapy script. The impact of a script is reduced if its focus keeps jumping around all over the place, turning it into a confusing mess. Just as you find listening to a disjointed story distracting, so your unconscious mind is distracted by listening to a jumbled hypnotherapy script. The name of the game here is focus.

A successful hypnotherapy script comprises several factors that make the script meaningful to you, helping your unconscious mind pay attention to the words that you're saying and the change in behaviour that you're encouraging:

- ✔ **Storyline:** This holds the structure of the script together. For example, if you want to sleep better at night, then try thinking about what you do as you go to bed each night. You may feel tired, go up the stairs, brush your teeth, get undressed for bed, climb into bed and pull the duvet cover over yourself . . . culminating in waking up refreshed at the right time in the morning. This is the storyline that you want to follow. It has a beginning, a middle and an end. Now you need to add something to that storyline to make it more therapeutic: direct suggestions.

- ✔ **Direct suggestions:** These help program your mind to respond in different, more positive ways. You add these to the storyline to make the script more meaningful and to encourage change. Building on the example above, you may want to add suggestions of 'feeling so wonderfully tired and relaxed' as you go up the stairs, perhaps adding that 'your eyes can hardly stay open as you climb into bed' etc. We explore how you create suggestions in 'Creating key phrases', later in this chapter.

✔ **Imagination:** Your imagination is the fertile ground in which many of your previous successes have grown. However, often your imagination is responsible for maintaining many of your problems too. A good hypnotherapy script harnesses your ability to imagine and use imagery to create a positive and motivating state of mind that enhances the therapy. Again, taking the example we've been working with, you can throw imagination into the mix: 'imagine what you feel like to be so wonderfully tired and relaxed as you go up the stairs to bed', 'see yourself so wonderfully tired and ready for sleep as you find your eyes can hardly stay open as you climb into bed' etc.

Getting help with what to say

If you don't know what to say, don't panic and assume that this means you can't benefit from self-hypnosis. You can find ideas to help you create a meaningful script in many places, this book being one of them. Many books of hypnotherapy scripts are on the market. Most of them are designed for use by professional hypnotherapists and are quite expensive. However, you can also find several books that aren't budget busters and that you can use as sources of ideas for your own script. Check out the Appendix where we point you towards some relevant books.

The internet is a good, cheaper alternative to books (we can feel our publisher scowling at us as we type). Swarms of websites are devoted to providing scripts for professionals and patients alike, such as www.choose hypnosis.com/scripts.htm and www.hypnosis.com/scripts.aspx. Most of these websites are free, so have a look and select something that appeals to you.

You can simply use a script straight from a book or website. However, the recurrent theme in this chapter is focus. A script that you take lock, stock and barrel from another source may be good, but that script was never designed to focus specifically on *you* and your individual needs. We suggest you use the script as a source of ideas and then adapt it to focus on you – we show you how to do this in 'Modifying scripts to suit your needs', later in this chapter.

Creating key phrases

Whether you create your own script from scratch or modify a script from a book or website, your script contains direct suggestions. These direct suggestions are important keystones of successful therapy. Direct suggestions help to re-program your mind to respond the way you want it to. The suggestions are designed to refer to specific parts of whatever problem you're working on, helping you change that aspect of the script. You can add to your key phrase a standard phrase that helps maximise its impact: 'as soon as'. Those three little words help condition the way you respond to a situation. In the case of a phobia of spiders, in the past *as soon as* you saw a spider you ran out of the room. Now after therapy, *as soon as* you see a spider you remain calm and relaxed. Sometimes the most simple phrases can lead to big changes.

If you think about what makes your problem a problem for you, you can begin to create your suggestions:

1. **Think about how you want to respond to whatever triggers your problem:** For example, in anger management you may have the suggestion: 'As soon as I see my ex-partner I instantly and immediately become calmer and more relaxed'.

2. **Think about how you want to behave just before the problematic behaviour starts in order to prevent that behaviour:** For example, when becoming more assertive: 'As soon as I open the door to my boss's office I stand up straight, take a deep calming breath, and confidently walk in'.

3. **Think about what you want to think just before the problematic behaviour starts in order to prevent that behaviour:** For example, with a flying phobia: 'As soon as I step on to the plane I think about really enjoying my holiday'.

4. **Think about how you want to feel just before the problematic behaviour starts in order to prevent that behaviour:** For example, with sporting enhancement: 'As soon as I step up to the ball I feel a strong sense of confidence, calmness and focus as I prepare to take the penalty kick'.

5. **Think about how you want to feel in the problem situation:** For example, with smoking cessation: 'As soon as others step outside to smoke I feel proud of myself as I remain confidently behind'.

6. **Think about how you want to think in the problem situation:** For example, with weight control: 'As soon as I'm confronted with a bar of chocolate I instantly and immediately think of how good I feel to be in control of my eating'.

7. **Think about how you want to behave in the problem situation:** For example, in an exam situation: 'As soon as I turn the question paper over I remain calm. I focus on answering the question'.

In order to maximise the impact whenever you make a suggestion to yourself, imagine carrying out what that suggestion's asking you to do. For example, if you suggest that you 'enjoy being a non-smoker at parties', then imagine what that looks like and feels like, and what positive things you're saying to yourself and others as you enjoy being smoke free.

Speaking 'Hypnotese'

Hypnotherapists can sometimes appear to be strange creatures. If you listen to what we say and how we say it during a therapy session, you notice plenty of pauses, changes in intonation and changes in speed of delivery. Also you become aware that we're very particular about the words we use. This isn't because we really are strange, but simply because we're speaking 'hypnotese'. In your average daily conversations you include all of these pauses and changes in speed and intonation, but with much less emphasis and probably much less awareness of the words you're using. In hypnotese we like to keep things positive, positive, positive! After all, to create change encouragement's a far better approach than admonishment.

Being positive with what you say

Many people who try to diet keep telling themselves 'I don't want to be fat', 'I must get rid of this fat', 'I mustn't eat chocolate'. Unfortunately, these negative statements only serve to focus your mind on being fat and on the food that makes you so. If you keep focusing on these then the consequences may lead you to put weight on. In Chapter 3, we explain the importance of being positive as you decide what you want. In fact, from this concept one of hypnotherapy's many mantras comes: 'Ask for what you want, not what you don't want'.

By becoming aware of your language and taking heed of the mantra, you can make your suggestions more positive and consequently more effective for yourself. As examples:

- ✔ 'I don't want to be fat' becomes 'I look forward to controlling my weight'.
- ✔ 'I must get rid of this fat' becomes 'I am becoming slimmer'.
- ✔ 'I mustn't eat chocolate' becomes 'I enjoy eating healthy food'.

Avoiding the 'must' trap is also important. The word 'must' ties you into doing something at all costs and doesn't allow for flexibility. If you think about the phrase 'I must be calm before going into a meeting', the word 'must' is adding undue pressure to respond. Therefore, instead of you becoming calmer, your anxiety can increase. The word 'must' can also have the unfortunate effect of reminding you of rather strict people who've demanded things from you in the past, leading your mind to rebel against what you're trying to achieve. These two examples demonstrate a phenomenon hypnotherapists call the 'law of reversed effect'.

The *law of reversed effect* states that the harder you try to do something that you want, the more likely you are to get the opposite of what you ask for. The best example of this is an insomniac who desperately wants to sleep. The harder he tries to get to sleep, the more awake he becomes. For more on insomnia, and how you can use the law of reversed effect for your own benefit, turn to Chapter 13.

By removing the 'must' and replacing that with a word or phrase that's more acceptable and empowering, your mind more than likely responds in the right way (goodbye, law of reversed effect): the demanding 'I must be calm before going into a meeting' becomes 'I confidently enjoy greater calmness before going into a meeting'.

When you think about creating suggestions, maximise their effect by sticking to phrases that are positive and empowering, such as the following:

- ✔ I am enjoying more . . .
- ✔ I am becoming more . . .
- ✔ I look forward to becoming more . . .

Reframing your words

Words convey meaning in many different ways. A specific word has a specific meaning, but the same word can also convey a wide variety of feelings, perhaps triggering different memories too. Take the word 'pain', for example. Pain conveys the meaning of an unpleasant aversive feeling. The word can also remind you of having been in pain in the past, not something you particularly want in your mind when you're trying to manage your pain. You need to recognise that the pain's there but, keeping in mind what we say in the previous section about positivity, you're much better to use a word that doesn't have such a negative focus. Instead of pain you can use 'discomfort'. Discomfort acknowledges that you have an unpleasant feeling, but also focuses your mind away from the negative intensity of that feeling. Another example is exchanging the word 'problem' for the word 'challenge'.

Taken from the work of family therapist Virginia Satir and hypnotherapist Milton Erickson, *reframing* has become an important aspect of many different types of therapy. The word literally means giving a more positive meaning to something by taking that thing from one frame of reference and putting it into another.

Are you a glass-half-empty person or a glass-half-full person? The glass-half-empty person looks at a negative situation and says: 'That's bad'. The glass-half-full person looks at a negative situation and reframes it by saying: 'I acknowledge the situation wasn't good. What positive things has that situation taught me?' By reframing situations you can become proactive, avoiding becoming embroiled in something similar again. If, for example, you reframe an exam failure, you may realise that you're wise to spend more time revising, or to seek further tuition, or even to spend time taking control of your exam nerves by practising self-hypnosis.

Excellent achievers are excellent reframers too. No matter the situation, they always look for the positives that experience has given them.

With practice, reframing can become a natural part of your thinking. As you think about creating your scripts, ask yourself the following questions. The answers to these questions can then form the basis of more direct suggestions to build into your script:

✔ Can I think of a more positive word to use instead of the one I'm currently using?

✔ What has that situation taught me about myself that allows me to improve?

✔ What other positive development can I take from that situation?

Being specific

Creating your own personal self-hypnosis script is fun. It also has the added benefit of being therapeutic too as you get to be creative with your thinking, chipping away at your problem whilst creating solutions. If you've read some of the earlier sections in this chapter, try taking all the building blocks we've discussed, pulling the specifics together and creating your own personal script following the steps we list here:

1. **Decide what you want to work on.**

2. **If appropriate, decide what aspect of step 1 you want to work on (for example healthy eating, exercise, temptation etc.).**

3. **Set your goal (for more turn to Chapter 3).**

4. **Think about trigger situations, times of temptation and the time just before your problem starts, and develop positive suggestions to help you cope at these times. Base these key phrases on how you want to be thinking, feeling and behaving.**

5. **Develop positive suggestions that help you cope during your problem situation. Again, base these key phrases on how you want to be thinking, feeling and behaving.**

6. **Create a storyline that takes you through your problem situation. Remember to include what's happening before the problem starts, during the situation and after it's ended.**

7. **For each stage of your storyline, add the appropriate direct suggestions.**

8. **Follow each suggestion with 'now just imagine what that looks like' and pause. 'Now just imagine what that feels like' and pause.**

9. **Remember to be positive throughout the script and reframe your words wherever possible.**

10. **Take a look at the traditional self-hypnosis protocol in Chapter 5 and slot your script into the appropriate place (after the induction and deepener and, rather obviously, before the awakening).**

Modifying scripts to suit your needs

You may need inspiration to help you create your own script and you can glean that from looking at what others have done before. When you look at any script, even the ones in this book, think to yourself: 'How can I make this mean something more to me?' Take the following excerpt from a script:

> *You forget about eating unhealthy food . . . and enjoy eating the right amount of healthy food that you know's right for you . . . so you lose weight naturally.*

You can modify and personalise this short example in several places:

1. **Look at the first phrase, 'you forget about eating unhealthy food', and ask yourself what the unhealthy foods are that you eat?**

2. **Look at the second phrase, 'and enjoy eating the right amount of healthy food that you know's right for you', and ask yourself in what way you want to enjoy eating healthy food, what the right amount of food is to eat for you to lose weight, what the healthy foods are that you can be eating.**

3. **Look at the final phrase, 'so you lose weight naturally', and ask yourself how much weight you want to lose.**

With the answers to these questions you can create something that's much more meaningful:

> *You forget about eating chocolate . . . you forget about eating cakes . . . and you really enjoy the flavour and the texture of fruit and salads and wonderfully lean cuts of meat . . . you eat a little less than you normally do . . . feeling proud of yourself as you leave food on your plate . . . so that your body naturally loses the 8 pounds that you want to lose.*

Putting the effort into thinking about and then creating your own scripts is therapeutic and can help you take a major step towards overcoming your problem. By thinking things through positively, you lay even stronger foundations on which to build your practice of self-hypnosis.

Using Your Voice to Best Effect

Silently talking your way into trance in your mind is a very effective way of practising self-hypnosis for many people. All it requires is a comfortable place to relax and the use of your imagination. Others like to have a more external form of guidance, listening to a voice as it delivers the relevant suggestions that help take you into trance and beyond. This externalised approach needs a bit more planning than just finding somewhere to relax, as you need to source equipment such as a CD player or mp3 player and buy or record the relevant self-hypnosis CD.

There are several reasons why you may wish to listen to a recording. These include:

- ✔ You find your mind wanders when you practise on your own and feel that this is too distracting.

- ✔ You may be practising at the end of the day and feel that you don't have the energy to be creative.

- ✔ You feel that the flow of creativity just isn't there for you when you practise self-hypnosis on your own.

Whatever your reason for wanting to use a recording, our experience has been that the best ones to listen to are those that you have created yourself. This means that what you listen to will be very specific and personal to you, hitting the right buttons as you go about the process of change.

Before you take the step of recording yourself, we need to impart some words of wisdom about how you can use your voice to improve your listening experience and, more importantly, maximise the effect of your script. You don't need to be an actor or voiceover artist to be able to use your voice properly. Listening to your own voice can be a little disconcerting to begin with. We all have the reaction: 'Do I really sound like that?' However, after you've heard yourself a few times you certainly get used to the sound of your voice.

Making your voice interesting

In the olden days when hypnotherapy was being developed, opinion was that the best way to deliver scripts was with a flat and monotone voice. A major drawback to this, which soon became clear, was that the sheer monotony put many people to sleep. Tell a child a story and no matter how good it is, if you tell the tale without excitement and enthusiasm, the child soon loses interest and stops listening. With therapy, you may like to think of your unconscious mind as like a little child listening to a story. If what your saying's boring, your mind's unlikely to attend. Make your story interesting and vibrant and you've got your mind hooked!

Have the courage to be expressive with your voice. By following these suggestions, your voice can become the star of the show:

✔ **Vary the tone of your voice and emphasise important positive words or phrases:** When you're more expressive with your voice, your unconscious mind pays more attention to what you're saying and is more likely to accept the suggestions you're making.

✔ **Vary the volume of your voice:** Keep your unconscious mind interested by varying between being a little quieter and a little louder as you read a script. Of course, that doesn't mean shouting loudly or whispering so quietly that your mind can't hear you.

✔ **Don't be afraid to pause:** Pauses give time for your mind to absorb what you've just said, and also serve to emphasis what you're about to say. In scripts you highlight these pauses using '. . .' Typically the pauses are no more than . . . a couple of seconds long.

✔ **Make your voice congruent with what you say:** Congruence means being in agreement with. If you're talking about the excitement of being a non-smoker, sound excited. If you're waking yourself up, speed up your delivery and become a little louder. As you count yourself down into trance, slow down your delivery and become quieter.

Listen to the CD that accompanies this book for examples of how your authors use their voices to full effect.

Choosing between authoritarian and permissive voices

To paraphrase Prince Hamlet, to be gentle or not to be gentle, that is the question. The terms authoritarian and permissive have specific meaning and are frequently applied to the way hypnotherapists use their voices.

✔ **Authoritarian:** This means using a more commanding tone when delivering suggestions. Commanding doesn't mean shouting, but that you bring a sense of authority into the way you're speaking.

✔ **Permissive:** This means that you bring a gentle tone into your voice as you deliver your suggestions. A permissive voice is slower and quieter than an authoritarian voice.

Authoritarian approaches are often associated with traditional hypnotherapy and permissive approaches are associated with Ericksonian hypnotherapy. Our book *Hypnotherapy For Dummies* has a more in-depth exploration of the differences between these styles.

Generally, when giving something up, be authoritarian – you're quitting something and don't want the opportunity to go back, so be commanding with yourself. When changing the way you respond to a situation, be more permissive – don't make an anxious situation worse by demanding change; you're much better to encourage it gently.

However, no absolutes exist. People are individuals and respond to different vocal approaches in therapy. That means you should decide what approach is right for you. If an authoritarian tone's too scary, be permissive. If a permissive tone's too wishy-washy, be authoritarian. Or maybe a mix of both styles hits the mark for you.

Recording Your Scripts Electronically

Stacks of pre-recorded CDs are commercially available for you to choose from should you wish to. Despite the fact that these can be effective, it is worth bearing in mind that as they are developed for a mass market these recordings are going to be generic and will not target your own unique requirements. It's also worth noting that after a week or so of regular listening you may find that you get bored with hearing the same thing over and over again and end up losing interest.

Recording your own scripts is by far the best way of making the most out of listening to a recording. This is because:

- ✔ You can make it personal and unique to you. That means that you will relate to it at a much deeper level, enhancing its effectiveness.

- ✔ You can create a variety of different recordings to play over time that will keep you interested and engaged with the therapy process.

- ✔ You can adapt your recordings to reflect your own personal progress and keep your listening experience fresh and relevant.

- ✔ It's considerably cheaper than spending a fortune on buying CDs!

Look back in this chapter at the section 'Being Specific' as this will give you an excellent template for your recordings. Create several recordings using different inductions that can be found in Chapter 5 whilst following the protocols we give regarding treating to your problem found in the appropriate chapter from Part III or IV of this book. You should listen daily, varying which recording you use to keep things interesting. Once your problem is resolved, you can put your recordings into your very own sound archive and get on with enjoying the new you.

You've written the script, you've had enough rehearsal. Okay, Mr DeMille, I'm ready for my close-up! Today you have a good choice of inexpensive and simple-to-use recording equipment to help you record your self-hypnosis scripts. Do you remember how old-fashioned cassette tapes broke after a few dozen plays and became unusable? Thankfully, with modern digital recording equipment you no longer have to depend on analogue cassettes. Another advantage of digital recorders is that with a computer or laptop, you can do a lot of other things with them.

Let's say that you've digitally recorded your self-hypnosis script. You've even saved it as an mp3 file (more on this later). Some of the ways you can potentially play your digitally recorded self-hypnosis scripts include:

✔ Playing them on your computer or laptop.

✔ Putting them on your iPod or other mp3 player.

✔ Burning CDs of your script.

✔ Combining separately recorded music to play in the background of your script.

✔ Incorporating parts of the recording in other programs, even word processors, PowerPoint or websites (advanced and probably unnecessary!).

Finding the right equipment

If you do an internet search on 'digital voice recorders', you may find a range of suitable products. But avoid searching on the phrase 'digital recording equipment', as the inclusion of expensive, professional-level, multi-channel digital recorders for bands and orchestras may well confuse you. These more expensive recorders are made for recording multiple sound sources simultaneously – much more sophisticated than your humble requirements for self-hypnosis recordings.

For recording your own self-hypnosis scripts, you only need the simplest equipment available. In fact, good news: you probably already own a digital recorder in the form of your mobile phone. If your phone can record sound – and most can – then congratulations! All you need to do is to find your mobile phone operating instructions and get ready to record your first script.

If you don't have access to a phone with recording facilities, or if your phone has limited capacity because you want to do, say, a one-hour recording, then here are some hints for purchasing a suitable digital recorder:

- To make digital recordings, you also need to have access to a computer or laptop with a USB connection. If you want to make digital recordings and use them as CDs or in an iPod, you need to be able to send your recordings to some type of computer.

- When shopping, do not confuse 'digital recorder' with 'digital TV recorders'. We want the former, not the latter. The latter is for recording TV programmes, not your voice. This sounds obvious, but may be helpful when searching the internet.

- Most good digital recorders should have a built-in microphone so that you don't have to buy one separately. Make sure before you purchase.

- Avoid multi-channel recorders; unless you're technically inclined, a simple stereo recorder is sufficient.

- If you *do* feel confident and can handle multi-channel recorders, choose something small and portable (such as the Boss Micro BR Digital Recorder we describe later).

Good mail order sources for purchasing digital recorders include:

- Amazon (`www.amazon.co.uk` or `www.amazon.com`)
- GAK in the UK (`www.guitarampkeyboard.com`)
- Musicians Friend in the US (`www.musiciansfriend.com`)

But also check out your favourite electronics shops, though their range may be smaller. See shops like Maplins (`www.maplin.co.uk`) in the UK.

The Olympus is one of many types of voice recorder. Sony also makes quite a few and sometimes they're called digital dictation voice recorders. Avoid purchasing the cheaper models as they may not come with a USB connection. If you don't have a USB connection, then you can't connect the device to a computer to make CDs or send recordings to other mp3 players.

The Boss Micro BR Digital Recorder is one of the easiest-to-use four-track digital recorders if you want to go the inexpensive route for multi-channel recording. This model's small and powerful and has a built-in microphone, or you can attach a more expensive microphone. If you're a musician and want to record your own music, the recorder accepts an input for musical instruments or a CD player. So you can make your own backing track with this as well!

Using recording equipment

Using digital recording equipment is simply a matter of reading the manual. Some players may have the feature of including extra memory for longer recording times. You usually do this by inserting a small memory card, usually a Flash memory card for a voice recorder or an SD card (like those in digital cameras) for a multi-channel recorder.

Make sure that you have the volume at which you are recording at the normal level range. This means looking at whatever sound-level meter your recorder includes to ensure that you don't speak too softly or too loudly. If the level of a digital recording is too loud, this results in distortion that makes the recording unusable.

If you want particularly crystal-clear recordings, you may want to invest in a microphone with a small desk stand to attach to your computer. You get what you pay for in the quality of your microphone. However, the cheapest solution is something like the Logitech USB microphone that can be bought for a price that won't break the bank.

A slightly more expensive microphone that can yield excellent, broadcast-quality results is a USB condenser microphone.

Keep in mind that most microphones are directional. This means that they pick up the voice that's in front of them. If you want to record several people in a room sitting in front of, to the side of and behind the computer, you need to invest in a more expensive microphone that has multiple directional settings. This is the type of microphone that recording studios use. Even some of these can cost very little and the upper prices can go into the thousands. Again, a microphone more expensive than the consumer types like the Samson USB isn't really necessary.

Also keep in mind that if you own a computer, you can record directly into the computer without a separate voice recorder. However, if you do this, you should be careful not to record background sounds from the computer fan.

Using recording software

After making your recordings, you can use software for different purposes.

✔ **Audio editing:** Audio editing software can make quiet recordings louder. You can also add effects such as reverb to produce a more professional sound. Restraint and understatement are the rules of thumb when applying effects to avoid unwanted results. 'Audacity' is free, downloadable, audio editing software that can do everything you need.

Go to `http://audacity.sourceforge.net/download/`

✔ **Mp3 burning software:** Mp3 is the standard sound format for creating sound files. Most computers come with some form of basic software that can play such files. By searching on the internet you can often find free mp3 burning software such as CDBurnerXP (`www.cdburnerxp.se`), or you can invest in paying for software such as Roxio Toast with a few additional features. Most have similar functions.

The most common free mp3 burning software may already be on your computer. If you are a PC user Windows provides its own free mp3 burning software via 'Windows Media Player'. If you turn on this software you will see the option that says 'BURN'. Once you have turned on Windows Media Player, if you press F1 (for 'Help') and type in the word 'Burn', you will see helpful suggestions that will give you step-by-step instructions on various topics. By reading these you will be able to learn how to burn a CD or DVD, for example.

Similarly Apple computers come with installed audio software called 'Garage Band'. This software can actually record and burn audio and will do the job. In fact with Garage Band, you could conceivably record your voice and have a track of background music at a lower volume than your voice, thus creating a very professional approach. And of course, iTunes that works on both PC and Apple computers has a facility to burn CDs too.

Chapter 7

Consciously Directing Your Unconscious

*F*rom a hypnotherapy point of view, the most common problem with the nervous system is that it tends to do its job *too* well. This can result in your body stressing itself and creating a new problem such as panic attacks, phobias, skin disorders, eating problems or physical illness.

In this chapter we focus on how you can manage the symptoms of nervous system problems by breath control. Breathing can be an important part of your self-hypnosis toolkit. You may not think very often about interesting ways to use your breathing. In fact, many people don't think about their breathing at all and they just breathe. But consider some of the following everyday expressions connected to breathing as a calming influence:

✔ 'I just need to catch my breath'.

✔ 'To me that's as simple as breathing' (to imply something's automatic or effortless).

✔ 'A healthy mind has an easy breath'.

✔ 'Take a deep breath'.

✔ 'You can exhale now' (to imply a sense of relief).

We show you that by linking the effortlessness of breathing to self-hypnosis, you develop a skill for life that helps you cope better with anxiety, problem solving and increased creativity – all of this in a way that becomes something that's automatic or effortless. To you, this is just like breathing!

Understanding Your Nervous System

Talk about slave labour – your nervous system works 24/7 and never gets holidays or a pension. You probably never stop to think about all of the things your nervous system does for you around the clock, including:

- ✔ Controlling your breathing.
- ✔ Transmitting signals between different parts of your body.
- ✔ Controlling your muscles and glands.
- ✔ Maintaining bodily functions.
- ✔ Preparing the body for emergency responses, for example fight or flight.

By reframing your stressed-out nervous system, you can begin to understand the control you can have over your nervous system through self-hypnosis techniques.

The term 'reframe' is an essential technique within counselling and hypnotherapy. Reframing's simply choosing a more helpful way of viewing a problem in order to manage or eliminate that problem. A common example's the 'half-empty vs. half-full' glass of water. Metaphorically speaking, if you view the glass or situation as half empty, you feel sad, angry or possibly even self-loathing, as this focuses on what you've lost. Changing this perspective to seeing the glass as half full helps you to feel more positive, as your focus is on what you still have.

An example of reframing is in the area of hypnosis for childbirth. Hypnotherapists often help clients manage their childbirth experiences by teaching expectant mothers to eliminate the word 'pain' and to substitute more helpful words such as 'discomfort' or 'pressure'. While the conscious mind may initially feel doubtful or cynical, this approach is often effective due to the unconscious mind's strong desire to have an enjoyable childbirth experience.

Reframing can empower you to see new options, to generate new behaviours and to eliminate unhelpful beliefs. By changing the beliefs that keep you stuck, you can let yourself have greater hope and optimism for change, which in turn allows you to move forward more easily. Think of changing unhelpful beliefs as similar to unblocking a pipe that has become blocked. See Chapter 4 for more on removing obstacles.

Appreciating your autonomic nervous system

Imagine an intelligent, self-operating robotic machine that you may read about in a science fiction book. This futuristic automaton works perfectly without any programming or any instructions from an external source. No one has to tell the machine what to do. It maintains its own system, diagnoses and heals itself. Perhaps this sounds far-fetched and a little ridiculous. We hope not, as we're simply describing your body, and in particular the part of the body that carries out these functions: your *autonomic nervous system*.

Your brain and spinal cord form the central nervous system, while the peripheral nerves that run from your spinal cord and connect to every organ form the autonomic nervous system.

When your body's healthy, the nervous system's the personification of a perfect machine. Your nervous system effortlessly multitasks many life-sustaining functions, continuing to function even while you sleep.

The system ensures that blood and oxygen flow continuously to your brain and vital organs, whether or not you're conscious of this happening. In many ways, this provides a model of what you want to aim for with self-hypnosis: a self-maintaining system.

Following the unconscious connection to your nervous system

Your unconscious mind's very sensitive to the needs of your body and works with the autonomic nervous system to regulate your essential functions. One example's the production of a variety of hormones that maintain the everyday functions and activities that keep you alive.

Meanwhile, your conscious mind's blissfully unaware of all of this activity and deludes itself that it's the most important part of you – 'I think therefore I am', and so on.

Your unconscious mind can work with your nervous system and through self-hypnosis you can train your body to work towards alleviating those symptoms that appear as a direct result of the action of the autonomic nervous system.

Looking at the Importance of Breathing

Human beings are natural born hypnotists – we just don't realise it. We regularly put ourselves into trance by carrying out ordinary activities such as daydreaming, reading, becoming engrossed in television or cinema experiences.

Beginner hypnotherapy students discover many different trance induction techniques. Below are a few such methods for beginning to establish trance:

✔ Imagining being in a safe, cosy place.

✔ Slowing the breathing.

✔ Staring at a particular point.

✔ Tensing and then relaxing all parts of the body from head to toes (also known as *progressive relaxation*).

In this section we focus on breathing as a trance induction method for self-hypnosis. Self-hypnosis is all about being relaxed – and an important key is breathing correctly.

Breathing your way to relaxation

Voice coaches and hypnotherapists think similarly about how breathing can help you achieve your goals. If you've taken singing lessons, your voice coach may have asked you not to breathe by flexing your rib cage but to breathe by flexing your diaphragm. The diaphragm's the main muscle involved in breathing, as we show in Figure 7-1.

You can see from Figure 7-1 how elastic your diaphragm is. If you place your hands below your ribs, you can feel the diaphragm moving as you breathe in and out. But please be careful not to hyperventilate as you check your breath!

Whether you're singing or practising self-hypnosis, your goal's the same: to breathe from your diaphragm. Sometimes diaphragmatic breathing gets confused with other terms such as 'belly breathing' or 'deep breathing'. The distinction is that breathing from the diaphragm means that the breath comes from the part of your body that's just below your ribs.

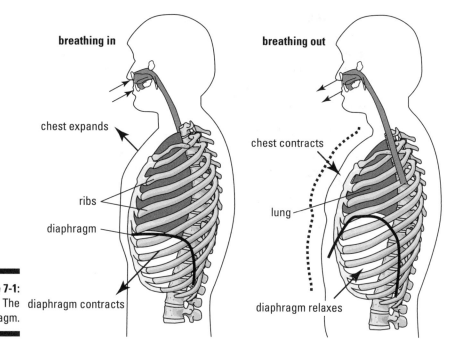

breathing in

chest expands

ribs

diaphragm

diaphragm contracts

breathing out

chest contracts

lung

diaphragm relaxes

Figure 7-1:
The diaphragm.

To get the full benefit of this technique, you need to become comfortable with:

✔ Breathing from your diaphragm (*not* your rib cage)

✔ Breathing increasingly more slowly

✔ Breathing through your nose (if this isn't possible, you can also breathe through your mouth with no problems, although nostril breathing's preferable)

Diaphragmatic breathing begins by breathing in and out of your lungs. You can tell when this is happening because your stomach begins to expand rather than your chest. Below is an exercise that will help you to ensure that you are breathing from your diaphragm and not from your chest.

1. **Lie down somewhere wearing loose, comfortable clothing.**

2. **Place one hand on your stomach, the other on your chest.**

3. **Slowly breathe in from your nostrils (or your mouth if your nose is blocked).**

4. **On the inhalation breath, you should feel your hand rise with your stomach.**

   (If the hand on your chest is rising you are NOT breathing from your diaphragm and need to retry steps 1–4 to ensure only the hand on your abdomen is rising.)

5. **Slowly exhale through your mouth.**

6. **Relax and repeat the exercise.**

As soon as you can become relaxed 'on demand', you can empower yourself in numerous ways, including:

✔ Being able to lessen anxiety

✔ Being able to calm your emotional state

✔ Being able to induce trance

As you develop your breathing technique, you begin to feel calmer and more relaxed throughout your body and more in control of your thoughts. Gradually, you develop a way of breathing that's slower and deeper and this eases you into a naturally more relaxed state.

Some of the beneficial changes that occur as part of this type of relaxation are reduced heart rate, reduced blood pressure, increased blood flow to your extremities and muscular relaxation.

You can develop this type of breathing in a way that actually triggers a trance state – one that you can use even with your eyes open, while you're going about your daily activities or even while you're asleep! (We discuss this in more depth in the following section, 'Slowing your breathing to trigger trance'.)

Contrast this slower, deeper breathing with the way you breathe when you're stressed, anxious or frightened (which is usually either breathing shallowly or panting). In this anxious state, your body experiences the adrenaline-fuelled 'fight or flight' response. If you sustain this condition for a long enough period, we call this 'stress'. The slowed breathing, in effect, becomes the antidote for the anxious state.

Slowing your breathing to trigger trance

Once you're comfortable with breathing more fully from your diaphragm, as we explained earlier in this section, you feel increasingly more relaxed. You can use this type of breathing as a trance induction method.

Breathing to induce trance

Try this breathing exercise to induce trance by relaxing your entire body:

1. **Slow your breathing and gradually shift your focus on to different parts of your entire body.**

2. **Imagine that you are breathing through each body part from your head down to your toes and each part begins to loosen and relax as you do.**

3. **Begin by imagining that as you breathe through your head , all the muscles in your head are relaxing. Then the same with your face muscles – your eyes, nose, mouth and jaw loosening as you breathe through the skin on your face.**

4. **Continue downwards, imagining breathing through your body, focusing on your neck, then your shoulders, your torso at the back and front, your arms and hands, your bottom, your upper legs, lower legs and down to your feet.**

No strict rules exist about how to use your breathing to induce trance, but here are two tips to begin:

- ✔ If possible, breathe through your nose. (If you have a cold or blocked sinuses, don't worry – just breathe through your mouth.)

- ✔ Breathe with your hands resting on your lap and your legs uncrossed. Your muscles should be as relaxed as possible.

Simply by breathing slowly and in a controlled way you begin to go into a trance state. We often misunderstand the concept of trance and assume that this is always a deep, sleep-like state – but a trance state can mean you're very alert, like an athlete preparing to run a race.

As you begin to breathe deeply and slowly from your diaphragm, you find yourself going into a trance state more rapidly – and yet you may feel that you're relatively alert. This is normal and you shouldn't expect to be deeply asleep or dreamy. A general relaxed state's all you need to go into a trance state.

When you do self-hypnosis, you don't need to go into a deep trance – a very light trance similar to a daydreaming state works just as well.

Conceptualising Your Unconscious Thermostat

Self-hypnosis can work extremely effectively when your conscious mind is unaware that it is occurring. In this section we consider turning on self-hypnosis automatically.

A good metaphor for this automatic self-hypnosis is the thermostat in your own home. In the winter, you set the thermostat to come on when the room gets too cool. At that point the room temperature rises, and then stops rising at a predefined point that you decide. Similarly, in the summer you can set the thermostat for air conditioning to come on when the room gets too warm. Then the room temperature drops and stops dropping at a predefined point that you have set.

In the same way, you can set self-hypnosis to work like a thermostat, using a post-hypnotic suggestion and then forgetting all about it. This means being able to hypnotise yourself without realising that you have done so, thus maintaining a level of calmness that provides you with a foundation from which to make significant changes.

The thermostat metaphor for self-hypnosis gains further importance in Chapter 8, when we introduce a radically new self-hypnosis concept – *unconscious self-hypnosis*.

What follows is a more detailed description that will help you to better understand the thermostat/self-hypnosis metaphor.

If you have a central heating thermostat at home, when the room temperature gets too cold the thermostat automatically turns on your heating and raises the temperature. When you adjust the temperature dial, you're telling the circuit switch inside the thermostat at which temperature you want it to switch on or off.

Imagine that you have a mental or emotional thermostat. Instead of turning the heating on or off by adjusting the temperature, your mental thermostat turns your anxiety on or off by adjusting your calmness. Self-hypnosis can help you to adjust your calmness so that when you get too anxious or upset, you slow down your breathing.

Imagine your emotional thermostat has a dial with three settings – top, middle and bottom:

- ✔ Top = anxious
- ✔ Middle = calm
- ✔ Bottom = asleep

Figure 7-2 gives an idea of what your mental thermostat might look like.

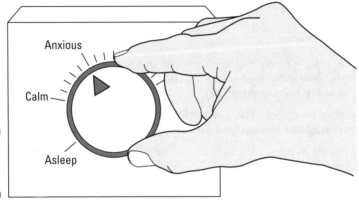

Figure 7-2:
Your mental thermostat.

By using this description, we've created a visual image for your unconscious to play with. This can be a powerful metaphor for your unconscious as it involves a physical sensation (touch). Remember that invoking physical sensations is an excellent method for inducing trance. In this case the dial is meant to be able to increase and decrease emotions. So for example, you could 'dial down' anxiety or 'dial up' feelings of optimism and hope.

This immediately gives your unconscious the concepts of:

- ✔ A range of experiences that can help to increase or decrease the emotion you are experience
- ✔ The potential to control the experiences or emotions, depending on your goal.

Your goal's to set your thermostat somewhere in the middle to indicate having calm emotions. This is especially useful if you become too 'hot', for example angry or anxious.

In Chapter 8 we discuss the power of using other metaphors in self-hypnosis in order to activate an unconscious form of self-hypnosis.

Adjusting your unconscious thermostat when you're stressed

The thermostat metaphor for hypnosis has many potential applications. The main concept is that with any feeling or belief you can increase something you want more of or decrease something that you want to be free of.

For example:

1. **Identify a recurring problem for you to apply the concept to. The problem should be one that affects your happiness or ability to cope in some area of your life.**

2. **Imagine being in that specific situation and allow yourself to feel the unwanted emotion that you typically experience.**

3. **Imagine using your thermostat to 'dial down' the anxiety from 'anxious' to 'calm'.**

Alternatively, if you feel that the solution for you is to gain *more* of something – say motivation – you could modify step 3 and imagine turning the dial up to increase your feelings of excitement and optimism.

As an example, let's say that you're going to the Monday morning staff meeting with competitive co-workers and an unkind boss. You're worried about the meeting and want to decrease your anxiety. Just before you walk into the room, you picture your imaginary thermostat. You see it as being set to 'hot!!!'. This acknowledges your current high anxiety level. You imagine touching the dial and adjusting the level very gradually downwards.

As you make the slow adjustments on your way into the room, by the time you take your seat, imagine you've now adjusted the thermostat dial to the 'calm' position.

Just as a room temperature can rise and fall, with a real thermostat making automatic adjustments, allow this to happen throughout the meeting. In other words, if you're put on the spot or a heated argument arises, your thermostat may drift upwards from calm towards hot. That's okay – you just imagine dialling the thermostat back down to calm again.

When you start to get hot again, picture the heat going back up and you turning the thermostat dial down, which is a metaphor that results in a real change to your body initiated by slowed, deep breathing.

As with many of the new concepts that you will come across throughout this book, your unconscious mind may offer some initial form of resistance, such as doubt, scepticism or simply a voice that says 'give up'.

However, please persist and with regular practice, you will quickly succeed in seeing signs of progress.

Some examples of the type of resistance your conscious mind may throw at you include:

- ✔ Telling you that you're failing and that you should just give up.
- ✔ Getting confused about the technique and worrying that you're not doing the approach correctly.
- ✔ Not relaxing into the technique and giving up too soon.
- ✔ Forgetting to use the technique at the appropriate moment.

Even though your conscious mind may *initially* try to sabotage your success, you can fairly easily distract it and this leads to your self-hypnosis practice becoming natural and spontaneous.

If you find the thermostat exercise easy to do, then try enhancing it. For example:

- ✔ Imagine becoming very interested in what others have to say and actually enjoying the meeting.
- ✔ Imagine helping to calm someone else down who's become too anxious and actually helping them to feel more relaxed.
- ✔ Imagine yourself having forgotten that you were even anxious until hours after the meeting's ended.

Controlling your health thermostat

Interested in a bit of home maintenance? Us neither, but you can usefully extend the thermostat metaphor by adapting the concept and linking it with a common piece of equipment found in every modern-day home – the radiator thermostat. Or, as more technically minded readers know it, the *thermostatic radiator valve* (TRV), which we illustrate in Figure 7-3.

You can apply the TRV metaphor to a range of issues, including your general health.

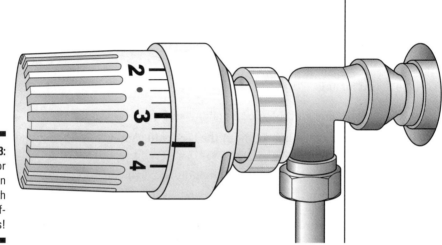

Figure 7-3:
This radiator
valve can
help with
your self-
hypnosis!

The TRV device individually controls each room temperature by controlling the hot water that moves through the radiator to which it's fitted. The TRV consists of two parts:

- A *valve* that regulates the hot water flow by opening and closing.
- A *sensor* that controls and adjusts the opening of the valve based on room temperature.

Still awake? If like us you're not interested in this stuff, we apologise if we've put you into a trance prematurely! But this concept can help with your general health.

In the previous section we used the metaphor of a dial for an increase or decrease. With the TRV metaphor we are now offering a variation on the dial example, which is a metaphor for a device which once it is set, turns itself on and off without help and increases and decreases the flow within an enclosed system, i.e. you!

The body's 'microcosmic orbit'

The energy flow diagram comes from Taoist practice, where the body's natural energies have been cultivated for centuries. This is called the body's 'microcosmic orbit'. The energy that circulates around the body goes by many names in different cultures, such as 'chi' or 'qi' or, in yoga practices, 'prana'. These terms all refer to the body's vital energy and are used in a range of applications, from healing practices to martial arts.

Figure 7-4 is based on prehistoric Chinese sources such as the I Ching and Taoist yoga systems. The fourth-century BC Chinese philosopher Chuang Tzu wrote, 'Use your mind to carry the vital energy along . . . constantly.'

Modern author Mantak Chia has written about the microcosmic orbit. In this system, *both* hot and cool energies are running *simultaneously*: hot energy through the rear both up and down the body, and cool energy through the front of your body, again both up and down. Follow the arrows in the diagram.

This simultaneous flow creates a flow of male/yang (hot) and female/yin (cool) energies. However, we're not giving you details of the microcosmic orbit, but rather simplifying the model and comparing it to a human radiator system for the purposes of self-hypnosis.

Table 7-1 gives examples of how you can apply the cool/calm or hot/energy flows.

Hopefully, you've now firmly established an image in your mind of a device that self-regulates the flow of emotions and thoughts within your mind and your body.

A practical example could include migraine sufferers who are able to decrease the physical pain they feel by imagining their hands become hot. This is a standard hypnotherapy treatment. What happens is that the excessive blood causing headaches actually begins to flow downwards, thus relieving their headaches. So our metaphorical radiator begins to have potential real physical benefits. Especially for anyone who has ever practised pain management using self-hypnosis and imagery involving the shifting of blood flow! Personalising a self-regulating device within yourself as part of your mind and body, you have:

- ✔ A valve that regulates the flow of calmness or energy by allowing and blocking that flow
- ✔ A sensor that controls and adjusts how much calmness or energy you need

With normal radiators you only get one choice of what's flowing, hot water. In the metaphorical TRV, you get two choices – hot or cool. The reasons for choosing a flow of either cool (calm) or hot (energy) through your radiators (your mind and/or body) vary depending on what you want to achieve.

Imagine a healing flow of calmness (or energy) moving through all parts of your body in a directional flow as we picture in Figure 7-4.

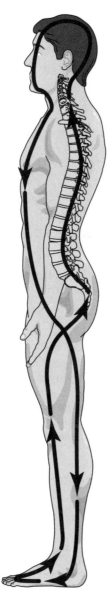

Figure 7-4:
The flow of health through the body.

Table 7-1	Examples of Body Thermostat Applications
Cool/Calm	*Hot/Energy*
To decrease anxiety	To increase stamina
To increase concentration	To improve health
To soften difficult emotions such as bereavement or anger	To increase sexual energy
To increase restraint in the case of addictions (eating, drinking, substance misuse etc.)	To increase confidence

Chapter 8

Using Unconscious Self-Hypnosis

In This Chapter

▶ Understanding the importance of forgetting

▶ Hypnotising yourself constantly

▶ Using metaphors for self-hypnosis

▶ Working with scripts

▶ Creating your own self-hypnosis suggestions

*I*n this chapter we look at a new way of doing self-hypnosis that provides you with a powerful tool for life. This chapter teaches you a new technique called *unconscious self-hypnosis* that we developed after seeing how clients' self-hypnosis improves when there is less chance for the conscious mind to criticise, sabotage or analyse their techniques. We explain unconscious self-hypnosis as a way of hypnotising yourself as and when you need to, but at an unconscious level, so that you are often unaware when it is occurring.

Introducing Unconscious Self-Hypnosis

By practising unconscious self-hypnosis you can begin to develop an automatic process for regulating your anxiety. This helps you to continually generate new behaviours and beliefs, which make achieving your goals easier. You can continue to modify your goals and shape the outcomes in the directions you want to proceed in over time.

When I (Mike) have taught this technique to clients, they often have two questions about unconscious self-hypnosis:

✔ How will I know if or when self-hypnosis is happening if it's unconscious?

✔ How will my unconscious mind know what suggestions to give on a moment-by-moment basis without help from the conscious mind?

The answer to the first question, 'How will I know if or when...' is easy: you won't know when it is happening! This is deliberate. The whole point of prac- tising self-hypnosis in this way is to allow your unconscious unobstructed opportunities to generate spontaneous behaviours or to respond to issues that are directly related to the areas unconscious deems as priorities. The traditional way of practising self-hypnosis is to very consciously use tech- niques like slower breathing and visualising success. But in the beginning stages, the conscious mind can really sabotage and criticise this and make people give up too quickly. With unconscious self- hypnosis, I (Mike) have repeatedly seen clients spontaneously generate results that surprised us both. These usually involved a lessening of anxiety in the areas connected to the goals or problem issues.

The second question is about a need to develop a growing trust that your unconscious will work in your own best interests to help you. Generally, hyp- notherapy works more with the unconscious to make the leaps in behaviour and cognitive changes.

In the past I (Mike) have helped clients with self-hypnosis the old-fashioned way: he demonstrated what to do in a session, and then asked them to go home and practise daily for a week. He frequently noticed that when they returned for the next session and he asked 'How did your self-hypnosis prac- tice go last week?', nine times out of ten clients replied sheepishly that they 'didn't have time to practise' or that they 'forgot to practise'.

This wasn't because they were lazy or even resistant. In most cases, their conscious mind sabotaged their efforts and told them that they weren't prac- tising properly or that the level of trance wasn't deep enough (remember, even light trance states are effective). This led Mike gradually to develop a different way of imparting the skill of self-hypnosis.

Understanding Amnesia

We often 'forget' unpleasant memories. We may even conveniently forget to do chores that we don't really want to engage in. But are we really forgetting these things or doing a sort of unconscious self- hypnosis that allows us to escape our unpleasant duties and opt out of them? The point is, we naturally and regularly practise an induced form of amnesia on ourselves. But in this section we will make amnesia work for us in a way that is helpful and allows us to practise self-hypnosis at a deeper level.

A common technique for inducing amnesia is to use metaphors or direct sug- gestions to forget. A metaphor might include a story where certain things were left behind and never missed. A direct suggestion might be the hypnotherapist saying to a client 'Your conscious mind can forget to remember or your conscious mind can remember to forget.' Very many ways exist to induce amnesia using hypnosis.

Ever seen one of those movies where someone bumps their head and forgets who he is? You probably view this as something you don't want, as the amnesia's based on some unfortunate accident or medical condition where memory's either confused or lost entirely.

Amnesia takes several different forms:

- ✔ **Functional amnesia:** Memory loss resulting from some type of change in the brain, but not necessarily due to brain damage or injury. This form of amnesia produces more memory loss than normal forgetting explains.

- ✔ **Organic amnesia:** Memory loss resulting from brain deterioration, such as dementia or injury.

- ✔ **Pathological amnesia:** Amnesia resulting from mental illness. This can include conditions such as multiple personality amnesia or functional retrograde amnesia. Functional retrograde amnesia is the type you see in movies and novels, as the term refers to loss of personal identity and large sectors of one's personal past.

- ✔ **Non-pathological amnesia:** This includes the more common 'forgetting', such as not being able to recall dreams or childhood events. This also includes our current topic of hypnotically induced amnesia.

You're probably reading this book because you want to find out about self-hypnosis, not how to forget things. You may even want to use self-hypnosis to improve your memory, so forgetting may initially seem counterproductive.

As you begin to understand more about the purpose and practice of hypnotically induced amnesia, you're able to use the technique in very innovative and effective ways by yourself. You can even forget that you used to have a poor memory!

Hypnotically induced amnesia can serve several useful purposes:

- ✔ We tend to follow suggestions we don't remember.

- ✔ A forgotten suggestion can feel like a spontaneous, original thought.

- ✔ We're more willing to follow an original idea.

- ✔ By forgetting, we're allowed to move on from problems and change unhelpful beliefs.

In general, hypnotherapists avoid using amnesia for the following reasons:

 ✔ They feel that inducing amnesia isn't clinically appropriate.
 ✔ They feel that they're not capable of inducing amnesia.

Making someone forget a painful event that's part of their life isn't clinically appropriate. Importantly, they need to be able to work safely through the thoughts, beliefs and emotions associated with the event so that they can properly integrate it into their mind. But this isn't the type of amnesia we advocate. The kind of unconscious self-hypnosis we describe in this chapter uses amnesia suggestions to change unwanted behaviours effortlessly, by the person being hypnotised forgetting to use the unwanted behaviour or belief and substituting a more helpful behaviour or belief. This isn't the same as erasing memories.

Here are two quick examples of how to induce amnesia:

 ✔ Think of someone from your past whose name you can't remember.
 ✔ Think of any other things that you've forgotten.

As you begin to think of other things you've forgotten, you prepare your mind to forget the problem (so you can focus increasingly on the solution).

Keep in mind that amnesia in a self-hypnosis context simply implies that almost no thought is given to the matter. The matter is not actually 'erased' from your brain, but rather you give little or no conscious thought to the matter. So self-induced amnesia becomes more like a continual distraction from thinking about whatever the matter is. It *does not* imply that the thought would never surface again. It's possible that it would, but that you ignore it, give it little or no mental energy and/or quickly forget about it again.

It is possible to induce amnesia for reasons that are therapeutically sound. Some methods for inducing amnesia are as follows:

 ✔ **Directly induced amnesia:** Giving yourself suggestions to remember something, or to do something unconsciously, for example 'Without even realising it, you will leave food on your plate'.

 ✔ **Indirectly induced amnesia:** This can include a range of approaches, such as the use of metaphor, where you make up a story during self-hypnosis in which something covertly that on the surface seems unrelated to your situation actually has strong parallels to a solution you are thinking of. This becomes an indirect suggestion to yourself.

 ✔ **Distraction techniques:** This may involve changing the subject after coming out of trance. This can be done by distracting yourself by thinking of food, a humorous or arousing situation, or physical activity. The point is to do anything but ruminate over the problem or the self-hypnosis you have just completed.

Speaking to your unconscious

It's important to be able to communicate quickly, concisely and directly to your unconscious. Simplicity is the key. Keep in mind that your unconscious is the first stage in communication. It produces the images, sensations and feelings that *subsequently* are used by your conscious mind to create words, phrases and sentences. This means that to speak to it, you want to also use images, sensations and feelings. For example, *imagining* or *feeling* the problem gone or success achieved.

The more hypnosis you do, the more you begin to trust your unconscious to help you achieve your heart's desire. Think of your unconscious as your inner genius – the part of you that knows what you want even before you can form the words to think it.

Imagine your unconscious mind as a friend who comes to stay. This friend is both telepathic and an intellectual genius. You want this friend to do a small errand for you: to run down to the local shop and buy you a newspaper, a carton of milk and some eggs. Because your friend's telepathic, he already knows your request. Because your friend's a genius, you don't have to repeat the request after you say it once. After your friend agrees to do the errand for you, you worry about whether he can remember all three items correctly or whether he may get the wrong type of milk.

Because your friend's both telepathic and a genius, he knows what type of milk you want – your friend's your unconscious mind, the part of you that sees the image first and then forms the words to speak. When you understand this, you can begin to trust that your unconscious fully understands your heart's desire, as the unconscious is the home of that desire.

Remembering your dreams

Freud called the interpretation of dreams the 'royal road to the knowledge of the unconscious activities of the mind'. As you work increasingly with your unconscious, you may become more aware of your dreams. It can be helpful for a while to keep some notes, but beware of overanalysing dreams, as they are by their nature irrational and abstract. Focusing on the feeling that they give (for example 'mad', 'bad', 'sad' or 'glad') may be more fruitful.

Memory is largely dependent on your state and the context you're in. To transfer memory from one context to another (from trance to a normal state of consciousness, for example) requires a bit of an effort. For example, when you wake up from a dream, you may have some memory of what occurred during that dream. If you don't make an effort to remember, the dream fades from memory pretty quickly. The dream may even fade if you try to remember it. You need to make an effort to carry that memory from your sleeping to your waking state. If someone distracts you as you wake up, you have even less chance of remembering your dream.

If you want to remember your dreams, keep a pen and paper beside your bed. As soon as you wake up, write down the content of your dream. This helps fix the dream in your memory. One of us (Peter) woke up in the middle of the night having dreamed the meaning of life. He decided to write down his profound revelation in the morning. Morning came and he'd lost the meaning, which is a shame, as I'm sure our publishers would love to add to the range by including *The Meaning of Life For Dummies*.

Doing self-hypnosis without realising you're in trance

We want to make self-hypnosis as easy as possible for you, so here's a big hint: you're probably already doing self-hypnosis without realising you are. You're in a trance state as you read these pages – you're staring at ink on paper and yet making something happen in your mind.

Perhaps you hear the words on the pages as you read them. Maybe you read and think about what you want to achieve. Or perhaps you're half reading and half bored (we hope not!) and thinking about what to have for dinner.

You're in trance many times each hour of every day and evening and even while you sleep. But trance is the prelude to hypnosis – you're not 'doing' hypnotherapy on yourself just because you're in a trance.

You don't achieve change simply from trance unless all you want to do is relax more. In order to make change in trance you need to provide a hypnotic suggestion (which we explore in Chapter 6) in the form of:

- ✔ An image
- ✔ A metaphor
- ✔ An emotional or physical sensation of how achieving your goal feels

You may stop short of using a trance state to move into hypnosis. You may sabotage your own efforts without realising you're doing so, usually by employing critical or so-called sensible thinking. Your inner critic resides within your conscious mind, the part of you that creates rules and 'rational' (or limiting) thinking.

In Chapter 1 we explain that trance is a relaxed state that we experience, which provides the first step in conducting self-hypnosis. By slowing your breathing and relaxing your body, as we describe in Chapter 7, you induce trance. Your goal for hypnosis – the thing you want to happen – should be clear and unambiguous. This means you should really want the thing you think about! Mixed feelings = aborted hypnosis.

You may think that if you have a clear and realistic goal (go to Chapter 3 for more on this) and can induce trance, this is enough. However, you need to be clear of a few obstacles before you can be effective with self-hypnosis without realising you're in trance. Your biggest obstacle is yourself – your inner critic. We discuss your inner critic in Chapter 4, and Table 8-1 gives you some tips for dealing with it.

Table 8-1	Dealing with your inner critic
Inner Critic Thoughts	*Think Instead . . .*
'But how can it happen?'	'What if I can . . .?'
'What if I fail?'	'Getting what I want's going to be great'
'How long may this take?'	'I'm finding this gradually easier each day'
'I'm going to fail'	'I'm looking forward to succeeding'

As you begin to practise self-hypnosis, let your critic be critical but always be aware that this is the critic speaking. Not really the healthy part of you. This simply means turning the spotlight on your critic so that it can never again work from an invisible vantage point, attacking you. Instead, when you think a harsh, critical thought about yourself, just say to yourself with a relaxed smile, 'There goes my critic again. She must be realising that I'm beginning to make changes. Only a matter of time and I'm going to achieve my goal.'

Saying this or something similar is especially important when you feel defeated, depressed or as if you've failed. These are the times your critic tries to get you to give up. These are the times when you must act as if any setbacks are temporary blips and part of your plan of progress.

Beware of your inner critic, who may attack you when practising self-hypnosis using phrases with a cynical flavour, such as:

'That's too easy'.

'What you're doing's just positive thinking'. (It's not! It's goal-directed hypnosis.)

'Only an idiot buys into this flaky stuff'.

Daydreaming more often

As you settle into regular self-hypnosis, you gradually begin to forget about the critic. Your first few attempts at doing self-hypnosis are likely to be extremely self-conscious, and as you become increasingly more comfortable with the cycle of the critic's attack (which lessens as you persist), you simply begin to *daydream* more and for increasingly sustained periods about your goals.

Daydreaming's a core feature of doing self-hypnosis. After a while, you begin to notice that you're becoming more able to see, feel, hear, taste and anticipate your goal in an increasing variety of scenarios.

After you practise the techniques, we ask you to *forget* about them – even the slowed breathing we describe in Chapter 7 – and to increase your anticipation of the good effects of your goal being achieved. Now you're beginning to do self-hypnosis in an alert state. Of course, we ask you to practise these techniques a lot at first, and *then* stop using them. If you've practised the techniques for a few weeks, even erratically, you've probably engrained them into your unconscious.

Turning on Unconscious Self-Hypnosis

In psychoanalysis, *introjection* means that someone else's ideas are unconsciously incorporated into your own mind. A common example is the messages that your parents repeatedly told you about yourself – positive or negative – which really stick with you throughout life.

Similarly, you also introject cultural rules gained from your environment about who you are based on nationality, race, gender and so forth. Even if you rebel against them, the war's primarily within your own head. Someone just like you who hasn't introjected the rules doesn't have the same issues.

If your desire's strong enough, if you have a reason to do self-hypnosis, then you're probably introjecting some part of the new information you're discovering *at this moment*.

We're describing an innovative technique that one of us (Mike) has never read in any other books on self-hypnosis: how to hypnotise yourself unconsciously. Even if your conscious mind does not yet 'get it', think of some of the topics that we discuss in other chapters:

✔ Mind–body connections

✔ Achieving goals

✔ Identifying your own resistance

✔ The power of your words

✔ Directing your unconscious

✔ Slowed breathing, muscle relaxation

✔ Ignoring your inner critic

✔ Forgetting to remember

If you've read about some of these topics, they may be concepts that you *introject*. Even if you don't remember or you 'forget' them, keep this in mind: you have a photographic memory and only your critic tells you otherwise. This information remains within you, but you 'forget' it and begin to use it naturally, in your own style, as if you invented the ideas yourself. Seeing your goal achieved and feeling the feelings of 'mission accomplished' is all that you need.

One of the most useful ways to turn on unconscious self-hypnosis is to practise visualising your goal achieved and then quickly change the subject. Distracting yourself becomes one of your greatest tools for turning on unconscious self-hypnosis.

For example, imagine that you've been promoted within your organisation and, as part of your new role, you now have to speak regularly in front of groups. As you begin to do this and have a few difficult initial experiences, you begin to develop a dread that gradually becomes a phobia of public speaking. You can use the type of self-hypnosis we describe in this chapter. Simply imagine images of a reversal of your phobia: within the very near future, you've 'forgotten' about the problem and are enthusiastically anticipating your next speaking engagement, even seeing images of enjoying the discussions as part of your talks.

Before going further, we want to ask you a couple of questions:

> 'What colour's the front door of your home?'

And:

> 'What colour's your mother's hair?'

If you answered these questions, then good for you – you successfully distracted yourself from the topic we were discussing! This is modelling the technique of seeing the solution (being able to enjoy public speaking), then changing subjects abruptly and deliberately. Practising this frequently is rapid self-hypnosis.

Using Anchors to Secure Positive Thoughts

We want you to have many different ways to do self-hypnosis. In this section we describe a self-hypnosis technique that does not require you to even go into a trance state. This is called *anchoring*. It is simply done by associating a physical gesture – such as touching two of your fingers on one hand together in any simple way you want to – with an emotional state.

Anchoring's a very useful technique that, among other things, helps you to get in contact with positive feelings almost instantly, whenever you want them. You can also use anchoring as a way of not thinking too much that you're doing a covert form of self-hypnosis.

You can associate (or *anchor*) the positive feelings or images of what you're trying to achieve by linking these to a specific action – most commonly an action such as squeezing your thumb and index finger together. This becomes something you can do easily and without being noticed, whenever you want to call up the image or feeling that's your goal.

You make the association by imagining what you want to achieve and how good this can feel. When you're experiencing these feelings at their peak, you squeeze your thumb and index finger together. By repeating this pro-cedure several times, you begin to develop a conditioned response – or set an anchor – which allows you to achieve this feeling every time you squeeze those fingers together.

After you set the anchor, the next time you're feeling negative about some situation, squeeze your fingers and you give yourself an unconscious self-hypnotic suggestion to enjoy the inevitable success that you're beginning to feel in both your mind and your body.

Using metaphors to trigger unconscious self-hypnosis

Metaphors are a powerful method for suggesting change without being obvi-ous. In Chapter 5 we refer to the use of innovation of metaphor therapy pio-neered by the hypnotherapist and psychiatrist Milton Erickson (1901–1980). Erickson used storytelling to activate his clients' unconscious capacity for change.

However, the use of metaphors needn't be as sophisticated or as covert as Erickson's. Mike was able to help his seven-year-old daughter to overcome her fear of dogs by telling her a story about a boy her age who magically overcame his fear of cats. Mike told her this story in an open-ended way for two nights in a row just before bedtime. The next day, during a walk in the park, she was overcome with an urge to pet every dog she saw walking past her, even Rottweilers! During her sleep she somehow found the 'magic' solution that worked for her. Many years later, she's still unafraid of dogs.

So storytelling becomes one useful way to apply metaphors hypnotically. Another way involves using images. For example, a common way to use self-hypnosis for pain management is to visualise the pain in some symbolic way (as a spiky green ball, for example) and then make that image shrink or leave the body.

Another image commonly used in self-hypnosis can be applied to Irritable Bowel Syndrome (IBS). IBS is a stress-related problem that creates problems either in the form of diarrhoea or constipation. Images of blocked rivers (diarrhoea) or flowing fountains (for constipation) can help to overcome these issues – especially when you practise them in the bathroom!

Hypnotic metaphors use 'doing words' such as feeling, listening and going. Here are some good key phrases to use in your metaphors:

- ✔ I'm finding it easier to . . . *(the goal you want goes here)*.
- ✔ I'm becoming more able to . . . *(implies change is occurring already)*.
- ✔ I'm pleasantly surprised that . . .

Developing useful scripts

While there are many books on hypnosis scripts, your imagination will provide the richest source of hypnotic metaphors. Begin to listen to interesting phrases in daily conversations you overhear for potential metaphors that you can use for your self-hypnosis.

If you use the internet to search for 'hypnosis' and 'metaphors', you find some websites that ask you to pay for their hypnotic scripts. Please don't fall for this trick. Many of these scripts are rehashes of what's already in, for example, *The Handbook of Hypnotic Suggestions and Metaphors* and very little new is available on these pay-for-it sites.

As you begin to develop a repertoire of hypnotic metaphors, discover how to incorporate words that express what you want more of. In this way you think less about your problems and increasingly about your solutions. You train your mind to move more towards what you want and away from the fear, the problem, the stuck position and the unwanted. You find explaining your goal easier and you may be pleasantly surprised as you start to make the changes you want to achieve.

Part III

Improving Your Outlook with Self-Hypnosis

The 5th Wave   By Rich Tennant

TRANCE INDUCING PHRASES

"Wait'll you hear what my 2-year old did..."

"I had the craziest dream last night..."

"Welcome to Calculus 101."

In this part . . .

Searching for the elusive feel-good factor? Step this way: This is the Part for you. Here we give you the inside track on using self-hypnosis to calm yourself, reduce your anger, ease your pain and even sleep better. We also show you how self-hypnosis strategies can help with boosting your self-esteem, and achieving a more fulfilling life.

Chapter 9

Putting Paid to Panic, Anxiety, Phobias and Fear

. . . .

In This Chapter

▶ Understanding how anxiety works

▶ Calming panic and anxiety through breathing

▶ Conditioning yourself to relax

▶ Rationalising away your phobia

. . . .

Fear's your friend and anxiety's your ally. No, we haven't gone mad and we certainly aren't embracing the more charismatic approaches to therapy that ask you to make friends with your problem. Far from it. We're simply stating a fact that these unpleasant feelings are a part of your very important survival response. In this chapter we explore ways of helping you cope when fear and panic cease to be friendly allies and become ardent enemies.

Foiling the Fear Factor

Fear! Panic! Anxiety! Stress! These are all words that describe unpleasant responses to a variety of situations. However, as noxious as these feelings may be, they're *natural* responses that evolved in order to help us survive in a very hostile world.

Take, for example, your friendly neighbourhood caveperson happily strolling through the forest carrying home the spoils of his successful hunting trip. As he turns the corner by the big oak tree, a caveperson from a rival tribe leaps out with a big axe, completely intent on stealing dinner from his intended victim. In order to know that something's wrong and that he needs to take action to protect his dinner, the first caveperson needs to feel something.

This feeling is fear. He may have discovered the feeling of fear from a wide variety of similar situations that he encountered in the past.

The important thing is that the feeling of fear is a trigger that creates a reflex response to immediately do something in order to survive, or at least hold on to dinner and not go hungry that night. So our caveperson may fight or run away. Once he's successfully done either, he returns to his comfy cave and rests as the fear response fades and he considers the most appropriate Neanderthal garnish to accompany the dinner he worked so hard to hunt down and keep.

A reflex response is a rapid survival response to something that happens without thought. The reflex allows your body to respond almost instantaneously in order to protect itself from injury. For example, if you accidentally put your hand on a hot plate you don't think about drawing the hand away in order to prevent yourself from getting burned. You just take your hand away, as having to go through a process of thinking 'Hmm, that's hot. What should I do? I think I'd better move my hand away' isn't very efficient. By the time you go through that process, the damage is done.

Understanding your body's unique responses

Fear and panic are your friends, as they help you to survive. They set in motion a series of events that prepare your body for immediate action, the 'fight or flight response'. When you feel fear, a neurotransmitter called adrenaline's causing that feeling.

Neurotransmitters are chemicals within your nervous system that help your brain, nerves and organs to communicate efficiently and rapidly with each other. Many different types of neurotransmitters exist with a wide variety of effects that keep your body running like a well-oiled machine.

Your adrenal glands sit one above each of your kidneys towards the middle of your back. They release adrenaline which causes many things to happen that prepare your body for action, including:

- ✔ You feel fear as you need to know that the situation's a threat.

- ✔ Your heart rate increases as blood and oxygen need to be pumped to your limbs ready for immediate action.

- ✔ As your heart rate rises so does your blood pressure.

✔ You breathe more rapidly so that more oxygen gets to your limbs as they prepare themselves for immediate action.

✔ Your muscles become tense, again getting ready for immediate action.

✔ Your digestion slows down as you have no need to do something that takes up vital energy that you can use for that immediate action.

✔ You may find a sudden urge to go to the toilet. This may happen in order to make you lighter for when you run and also to leave a nice smelly poo that diverts the attention of any predator (our apologies if you're eating when you read that!).

✔ Blood clotting factors are released in case your body's damaged and in need of rapid repair.

✔ You start to sweat as this helps your body cool down when you're actively running away or fighting.

✔ Your brain's continually monitoring your environment for further threats.

In other words, your body's revving up just like a racing car on the starting line at the Survival Grand Prix as it readies itself to win the race. And when you do win the race (we hope), the adrenaline response turns off and your body returns to normal functioning.

Fortunately, we don't have such immediate threats to our survival as cave-people trying to snatch our dinner. We still have our fight or flight response, though, as we may still need to run out of the way of a speeding car. Unfortunately, nowadays the fight or flight response is triggered by things that aren't necessarily going to cause us physical harm, such as the pressure of deadlines or financial concerns. Many people don't know how to switch off the fight or flight response once something's triggered it. And that's the major problem. Fear and anxiety aren't pleasant to experience. The more we experience them, the more strain we put on our body.

Just like a racing car at the Survival Grand Prix, your body's a finely tuned machine that's designed to work under certain parameters. Imagine what may happen if you keep the engine of the racing car revving without ever taking your foot off the accelerator and brake. Eventually the car's engine fails. The same can happen to your body if your fight or flight response is always active:

✔ You can have panic attacks because you're continually hyperventilating.

✔ You risk heart attack or stroke because of the extra pressure that you're placing on your heart and blood vessels.

✔ You have an increased risk of heart disease such as hypertension.

✔ Because your muscles are always tense, you can end up having tension headaches.

✔ You can't concentrate as you're continually monitoring your environment for threat.

And so the list goes on. But the good news is that help's at hand in the form of this chapter to help you switch off that revving engine before you do any damage.

Even the most modest reduction in anxiety levels helps to reduce the risk factors. The more you know how to control your anxiety, the less the risk to your health.

Safely going into trance

You may be wondering whether you can relax into trance if you're anxious. The simple answer's that you can. In fact, by allowing yourself to go into trance you've won half the battle in combating anxiety and knowing how to switch the feeling off.

The physiological state you experience when in hypnosis is completely opposite to what you experience when you're anxious (flip to Chapter 2 for more information). Regular practice of self-hypnosis is an important part of managing anxiety.

Some anxious people feel anxious about using self-hypnosis. This is very understandable as the technique's something new. To help you feel confident about entering trance, bear in mind the following points:

✔ Hypnosis doesn't just happen when your eyes are closed, so if you feel more confident keeping your eyes open then focus your attention on a spot in front of you.

✔ Don't overdo self-hypnosis. Start off with short sessions, no more than a couple of minutes at a time. As you get used to how you feel then extend the amount of time you spend in each session.

✔ Breathe through your nose. This helps to regulate your breathing so that you can relax more effectively.

✔ Try having a session or two with a trained therapist who can help build up your confidence.

We can use the third point above as an effective method of entering trance. Taking control of your breathing is important, as anxious people often hyperventilate.

Hyperventilation is rapid and shallow breathing through your mouth. This overbreathing alters the way your body handles oxygen and carbon dioxide, resulting in an increase in anxiety and potentially a panic attack.

The majority of breathing techniques that help calm people usually encourage them to breathe in and out through their nose. This prevents hyperventilation, as physiologically speaking you just can't hyperventilate when you're breathing through your nose.

Breathing techniques are used the world over to help calm people down. By using the following simple breathing technique, you can help both your mind and body to become more predisposed to relaxation, while at the same time guiding yourself into trance. Take time to practise this technique. Even if you don't go into trance to begin with, you certainly calm down. Remember that you can record yourself to help guide you through the following steps, so have a look at Chapter 6 if you want to become a recording star.

Try following these steps to induce controlled breathing:

1. **Throughout the exercise, breathe in and out through your nose (we keep reminding you of this as the point's important).**

2. **Close your eyes.**

3. **Take a slow, comfortable and controlled deep breath in through your nose and hold it for ten seconds.**

4. **Slowly breathe out through your nose for about ten seconds.**

5. **Breathe in through your nose for a count of three.**

6. **Breathe out through your nose for a count of three.**

7. **As you breathe out, think the word 'calm' or 'relax'.**

8. **Repeat steps 5, 6 and 7 for about a minute (you don't have to be precise on the timing).**

9. **At the end of the minute, take a slow, comfortable and controlled deep breath in through your nose and hold it for ten seconds.**

10. **Slowly breathe out through your nose for about ten seconds as you imagine all the muscles in your body relaxing.**

11. **Breathe in through your nose for a count of three and imagine breathing in a sense of peace and calmness. Some people like to imagine the**

feeling, while some like to represent that feeling as a colour that they safely inhale. The important thing is to do what feels right for you.

12. **Breathe out through your nose for a count of three. As you do so, imagine breathing out any unwanted thoughts and feelings in what-ever way seems right for you. Perhaps you can imagine those feelings as a sluggish colour that's leaving your body and evaporating, or perhaps you can imagine the words of the unwanted thoughts safely fading away around you.**

13. **Repeat steps 11 and 12 as many times as you want until you feel more calm and relaxed.**

14. **Take a look at Chapter 5 to help deepen your trance.**

15. **Follow the relevant advice we give later in this chapter under 'Reducing Anxiety' or 'Overcoming Your Fears and Phobias' as you carry out your therapy.**

Awakening from the trance:

Flip to Chapter 5 to find out how to awaken yourself.

As you wake up, take a few slow and comfortable deep breaths in through your nose, remembering to breathe out through your nose.

Give yourself a nice stretch and then carry on with your day!

Simply practising the controlled breathing induction is therapeutic in its own right, as doing so helps you relax while at the same time teaching you to do what it says on the tin: control your breathing.

Reducing Anxiety

Just about everyone experiences anxiety to some degree. It's there to let you know that a situation needs paying attention to and is supposed to be a transitory feeling that fades once you have dealt with what you need to. However, some people find that the anxiety persists and that they need an extra help-ing hand to wipe it away. Self-hypnosis can be that helping hand because, as we mention in the previous section 'Safely going into trance', anxiety and relaxation are completely incompatible and if you make relaxation strong enough, then anxiety has to fade away. Once you are relaxed, then you can think of constructive ways of overcoming the situation that is making you anxious.

You may feel anxious about situations because you don't feel that you have any control over what's happening. Here the 'c' word's important to remember: control! You may not be able to control the situation that makes you feel anxious, but if you can start to gain a sense of control over the way you respond to that situation, then you can begin to reduce the anxiety you feel.

Therapists call gaining control over the way you feel and respond to situations internalising your 'locus of control'. People who have an internal locus of control tend to be less anxious and can positively reframe situations. For more on reframing wander over to Chapter 6.

Exploring methods to reduce anxiety

Controlled breathing's an important part of controlling anxiety. We want to give you a technique that you can use wherever you may be to help control your breathing and consequently your feelings. And by the way, this one doesn't put you into trance.

As with all such exercises, the 7:11 breathing exercise (nothing to do with the famous supermarket, we hasten to add!) is designed to calm you down. You can do the exercise in bed to help you sleep (you can find more on dealing with insomnia in Chapter 13), when you're walking, waiting to go into a meeting or whenever you need it.

1. **Make sure that you're breathing from your diaphragm by making your tummy rise with your in breath and fall with your out breath. Breathe in and out through your nose throughout the exercise.**

2. **Breathe in through your nose for a count of seven.**

3. **Breathe out through your nose for a count of eleven.**

4. **Keep repeating steps 2 and 3 until you feel calmer.**

The amount of time you spend doing this exercise depends on you and can range from a few minutes to anything up to 15 minutes. Of course, you can use self-hypnosis to stimulate you to carry out the exercise almost without thinking.

The more you practise the 7:11 breathing exercise, the more natural the cycle of breathing becomes until it forms an integral part of the day-to-day management of your feelings.

One of the problems with anxiety is that you can let the associated thoughts run riot within your mind, never giving you a moment's peace. Keeping those thoughts there without doing anything about them does nothing for your anxiety levels, as we're sure you're aware. Here are some ideas to help you grasp those unwanted thoughts by the proverbial short and curlies and begin to kick them into shape.

- ✔ **It's good to talk.** Share your thoughts with someone you trust. Talking things over often helps to give you more insight into your feelings while at the same time opening up more options for change.

- ✔ **Write a diary.** This is an excellent alternative to talking and allows you to get those thoughts down on paper where they can't do so much damage.

- ✔ If your anxiety stems from having too many tasks to carry out, put the tasks all down on paper. Then prioritise them into tasks that are urgent and immediate, tasks that are important but can wait, and tasks that you really can leave until much later.

- ✔ Talking and writing can help define the problem for you. Consider the following:

  - • Who or what's making me anxious?

  - • Why am I feeling anxious about this situation?

  - • Have I always felt anxious about this situation? If not, what's changed to make me anxious now?

  - • What negative statements do I make that keep me anxious? For example, 'This is a terrible situation', 'I can't cope' and so on.

Defining your problem's a good, though rather obvious, starting point. However, simply focusing on the problem isn't productive, as doing so keeps you where you are in the first place – with the problem. You need to focus on creating solutions as these move you on, away from your negative feelings. Take time to think about your solutions.

You don't necessarily have to come up with answers straight away. As you practise self-hypnosis and become more relaxed, so you find that the way you think about situations changes too. In effect your mind relaxes as your body relaxes and you begin to see things from a different perspective. As a starter, begin to consider the following:

- ✔ Can I think of a more positive way of thinking about the situation that's making me anxious (here we go with reframing again)?

- ✔ What positive things can I take from thinking about the way I respond to this situation that help me change the way I respond in the future?

- ✔ What positive statements can I make that help to make me calmer? For example, 'I'm discovering how to cope', 'I'm beginning to take control of the way I feel'. Check out Chapter 6 for more advice on changing negatives to positives.

✔ What can I realistically do to take control of the way I'm feeling?

Have a look at Chapter 3 for more advice on thinking in a more solution-focused way. You can also practise the self-hypnosis exercises in that chapter to help you take control of your anxiety. In addition, when you practise self-hypnosis:

✔ Imagine yourself carrying out the 7:11 breathing exercise whenever you begin to feel anxious.

✔ Imagine that you're becoming more calm and in control as you breathe in a more controlled way.

✔ Imagine handling the situation in a different, more positive way. Perhaps imagine that you're more relaxed, more assertive (consult Chapter 11 to discover how to become more assertive) and so on.

✔ Imagine saying more empowering things to yourself as you handle the situation more appropriately. For example, 'I'm calmer', 'I'm discovering how to cope' and so on.

✔ If you've been prioritising tasks, imagine effectively carrying out those important and immediate tasks and feeling good as you do so. Then imagine that when these are complete you calmly carry out those important tasks that can wait. Finally, imagine carrying out the tasks that can wait until much later (remember that they need to be done before they become urgent and immediate!).

✔ Imagine yourself as a much calmer person who feels more in control.

Monitoring your success

Change happens only if you put in the effort necessary to make that change. In other words, make time to relax each day. Make time to practise self-hypnosis each day. Make time to practise your breathing exercises each day. So if you are making the effort, how are you going to notice that things are changing for you?

You have many ways to monitor how you're getting on, the most obvious of which is that you feel better! However, spend a little time each day reflecting on how things are going for you. You may want to keep a diary that details the positive way you've handled situations that day. You may want to note the positive thoughts and feelings you've had. You can also make note of those situations that you didn't handle the way you wanted to and reflect on how you can handle them if they crop up again in the future. In this way you have a record of how things are changing for you, while at the same time you notice areas that you may want to work on using self-hypnosis.

Diary writing's a good way of taking control and monitoring your progress. But you may not be able to spend time each day filling in an entry. In that case, you can use a simple visual scale to record how you feel each day (something that can be a part of your diary). Figure 9-1 shows such a scale:

Figure 9-1:
A simple
visual anxi-
ety scale.

As you progress with changing the way you feel, you notice that you have more low-number days than high-number days. You can even reflect on what makes a low-number day like that. Then think about whether you can use this knowledge to turn a high-number day into a lower number.

Optimising your performance

You may also want to pay some attention to activities such as sleep, diet and exercise. A good night's sleep from which you wake refreshed each morning psychologically sets you up to be able to handle the day-to-day challenges you encounter. So if you're experiencing poor sleep, have a look at Chapter 13 to find out strategies for pushing up the zzzzz factor.

Food's the fuel that gives you energy to keep going during the day. With a motor vehicle, if the fuel you put in is of poor quality, then the performance the car gives is poor too. The same with your body. If you have a poor diet, eating fast food, eating at inappropriate times, skipping meals and so on, then you may want to peruse the menu of improving your dietary habits in Chapter 16. That chapter also helps you to improve your exercise habits. By exercising, you're using your body for what it's prepared for (remember the caveperson hunter), helping you burn away the hormones and neurotrans-mitters that are producing your anxiety.

A person who came to see Peter for therapy as a result of having a multitude of anxieties over home, work and health-related issues was asked to practise self-hypnosis daily. This gave the patient a psychological and physical 'check-out' time from his anxieties. He reported that as he relaxed into trance he could focus more constructively on resolving the domestic and work issues that were driving him nuts. On top of this, he found that practising self-hypnosis in bed at night helped him get a better quality of sleep. With a little encouragement from Peter he then focused on improving his lifestyle by eating healthily and exercising more. After about a month he reported that his levels of anxiety were significantly reduced and that he felt fitter and more capable of handling life than he'd felt in a long time.

Overcoming Your Fears and Phobias

'I know I'm silly, but I can't stay in a room if a loose button's laying on the table.' This is the type of statement we've heard so often about a special kind of fear: a phobia. Many people may think being scared of such a seemingly innocuous object is daft. But the thing about phobias is that they're irrational fears that can have an impact on your life. For example, despite having a love of nature, a person with a phobia of insects may be unable to feel comfortable being in the countryside for fear of bumping into one of the little critters.

This section helps you to counter the irrational nature of your fear or phobia. Not only that, it will help you put whatever it was you were scared of into a proper perspective so that you cope well and free yourself up to enjoy a dimension to your life that may have been closed to you.

Understanding the emotional component of your phobia

When whatever you're phobic about confronts you, you produce feelings in exactly the same way as any other form of anxiety. However, the phobic response is much more extreme. You may have a phobia for many reasons:

✔ You may have gained a phobia from a parent. For example, a child watching her father shriek in terror and run out of the room at the sight of a tiny spider scuttling across the floor thinks that if daddy's scared of a spider, so should she be.

✔ The phobia may be the product of a nasty experience. For example, being attacked by a dog can lead a person to fear all dogs.

✔ Your phobia may build up over time. Some flight attendants who experience years of turbulence as they fly may develop a phobia of flying (despite the fact that flying's one of the safest forms of transport, in case you're wondering).

✔ The fear associated with a phobia may transfer itself to an object that you can easily avoid. For example, a person who survives a car crash may transfer the fear she experienced to the orange that was sitting by her at the time of the incident, thus developing a phobia of oranges.

You can have a phobia about absolutely anything – even phobias (that one's called phobophobia). The nasty thing about phobias is that they're irrational.

Wherever a phobia comes from, the most important things to remember are the following:

✔ A phobia's an irrational fear of an object or a situation.

✔ Fear leads to avoidance of that object or situation.

✔ You don't discover how to cope with the object or situation because you avoid it.

✔ Avoiding the object or situation leads you to fear it more.

This rather unpleasant cycle keeps the phobia in place.

Unpackaging your fears

Okay – time to apply the rational to the irrational and dissect your phobia. A good starting point for taking control of your fear is safely to confront whatever you're phobic about. Don't worry. We're not suggesting that you go out immediately and put yourself into that phobic situation. What we're suggesting is that you pull apart your phobia by asking yourself some questions about it. In that way you gain knowledge that helps to put things into perspective and overcome the phobia.

When you think of your phobia:

✔ If your phobia's of a situation, what's the most worrying aspect of that situation? For example, sitting on a plane when it's up in the air or standing close to the edge of a tall bridge.

✔ What's the least worrying aspect of the situation? For example, getting on to the plane or standing close to the edge of a very low bridge.

✔ If you have a phobia of an object, does distance from the object change the way you feel about it? For example, are you better being in a room with a spider or outside a room that contains a spider?

✔ Does colour make a difference? For example, is a white cat more acceptable than a black cat?

> ✔ Does movement make a difference? For example, when you look at a picture of a snake, does that make you feel any different than looking at a snake moving on television?
>
> ✔ When you're approaching the object of your phobia, what thoughts are going through your mind? For example, as you walk towards the dentist you may be thinking, 'This is going to be awful. I can't cope.'

Take time to consider these questions. Come back to them every so often and reconsider them. Think of any other questions you can ask yourself about your phobic response and answer them. This process of pulling apart your phobia helps to place its various aspects into perspective. Instead of thinking that the phobia's composed of equally scary parts, you're able to understand what aspect of the phobia you really need to look at. In effect, you're taking the first step to desensitising yourself to your phobia and in the process becoming proactive and taking control.

If you find that you can't face up even to considering these questions, then it's a good idea to go and visit a therapist who can help you out.

Once you've unpackaged your fear, what next? You then repackage a more appropriate response. Reading Chapter 3 can help you out here. But to start with, for each of the answers to the preceding questions, think: 'How do I want to be?'

What realistic and safe outcome are you looking for? The emphasis here's on *realistic and safe*. For example, is wanting to be able to go up to any dog and pet it truly realistic and safe? We don't think so. Better to be calm when in the presence of a dog and choose to pet one when you know its temperament.

Successfully facing your fear or phobia

Having taken that first step of unpackaging your phobia in the previous section, you can now move towards successfully changing the way you respond. You can use two approaches and you can vary between them when you practise, as they complement each other.

Don't rush through these approaches. Take them step by step. If you feel the need to stop at any point, that's fine. Just take yourself back to your favourite place. You're far better to work only so far as you're comfortable than to push yourself too far. Take as many sessions of self-hypnosis as you need.

Approach 1: The cinema

1. Make yourself comfortable and use the progressive relaxation induction from Chapter 5.

2. Take yourself to the favourite place we describe in Chapter 5. Spend some time there as you really enjoy the feelings this place brings you.

3. When you've done this, imagine that you're going through a door or a gate and entering a wonderfully comfortable cinema.

4. Find a seat and notice what's on the screen.

5. Notice that someone who looks very similar to you is just about to experience whatever you're phobic about.

6. As you watch her go through that experience, notice how well she's coping. Notice how calm she is. Notice how she's coping in a way that's very similar to the way you want to be coping.

7. Spend time observing this film. You may want to rerun it a few times if you wish.

8. Invite the person on the screen to step out of the screen and sit next to you.

9. Talk to that person about how she copes so effectively.

10. When you've asked all you need to and that person's replied, ask her to step inside you and become one with you.

11. As she does, realise that the person is in fact you.

12. Notice how you feel with these new feelings inside you.

13. Leave the cinema and return to your favourite place.

14. Spend time enjoying the feelings you find in your favourite place before leaving it and waking yourself as we detail in Chapter 5.

Approach 2: Relax your phobia away

1. Make yourself comfortable and use the progressive relaxation induction from Chapter 5.

2. Take yourself to the favourite place we describe in Chapter 5. Spend some time there as you really enjoy the feelings this place brings you.

3. Imagine that you've found a really comfortable place to sit or lie down.

4. Tell yourself that you're calm and relaxed and let yourself feel so.

5. Begin to imagine that you're about to enter your phobic situation. Tell yourself that you're calm and relaxed and feel so. Spend a few moments doing this.

6. Imagine that you're back in your favourite place. Experience the good feelings that this place brings.

7. Tell yourself that you're calm and relaxed and let yourself feel so.

8. Begin to imagine that you've just entered the phobic situation. Tell yourself that you're calm and relaxed. Begin to feel so and spend a few moments doing this.

9. Imagine that you're coping with the phobic situation effectively. Feel calm and relaxed.

10. If at any point you feel any anxiety, then simply go back to your favourite place and enjoy the positive feelings you find there. Once any anxious feelings have subsided, go back to step 4 and continue.

11. Progress as far as you can in as many sessions as you need.

12. The ideal is to be able to imagine handling that phobic situation with the minimum of anxiety.

13. At the end of each session, return to your favourite place.

14. Spend time enjoying the feelings you find in your favourite place before leaving it and waking yourself as we detail in Chapter 5.

You can do all the wonderful work you want with your mind. But the proof of the pudding comes in the testing. At some point you have to confront your phobia. You can make what therapists call a 'contract of action' with yourself. That means that when you feel that you can think calmly about your phobia, you should then try things out in real life. Take it easy and don't overdo things to begin with.

If you have a phobia of heights, for example, consider going up in a lift to the top of a tall building and standing away from the windows that look out on the world below. If that feels okay, try moving nearer and so on. If you experience any anxiety, this is just a sign that you need to do more work with yourself. Remember that success happens if you take your time and pace yourself in a way that's appropriate for you.

A patient came to see Peter with a phobia of insects. He found that he could cope with this as he never went anywhere where there would be a significant risk of being exposed to anything other than a fly or an ant. The company he worked for opened a branch of their business in Southeast Asia and he was asked to travel to the area to oversee the development of their new offices. He feared that being in a tropical country meant he would more than likely bump into insects of a significant size and quantity of legs. In self-hypnosis he was encouraged to follow the 'Relaxing your phobia away' approach over a couple of weeks. During this time he felt increasingly able to go into his own garden and look for insects to test that things were working. By the time he got to travel to Southeast Asia he reported that even though he still didn't like insects, he felt calm about encountering them and knew that he would cope well should he come face to face with something.

Chapter 10

Signing Up to Self-Esteem

. . . .

In This Chapter

▶ Understanding your level of self-esteem

▶ Accepting who you are

▶ Knowing that you can change

▶ Becoming the person you want to be

. . . .

Self-esteem's a phrase we happily throw around every day without thinking about what the term really means. How often have you heard phrases such as 'She is full of her own self-esteem' or 'Well, that really knocked my self-esteem'? Many people make the mistake of assuming that a good sense of confidence is an indicator of high self-esteem. As we reveal in this chapter, this isn't necessarily so. The media often write about celebrities who apparently can take the world by the horns and lead the way in their chosen field, but complain that they lack self-esteem. In fact, many confident people have very little self-esteem.

Self-esteem refers to how you feel about yourself, how you value your role in your family life and in society proper. Self-esteem isn't simply one feeling, rather it's the result of bringing together a variety of negative and positive feelings and behaviours that include the following:

✔ Behaviours such as shyness or assertiveness.

✔ Personal beliefs such as 'I'm incapable' or 'I'm capable'.

✔ Emotions such as anxiety or happiness, shame or pride.

Your self-esteem isn't necessarily something that applies to every aspect of your daily life. You may hold yourself in high self-esteem with regard to your career but have very little self-esteem in relation to your role as a parent, for example. Even within these roles self-esteem can fluctuate day to day, even hour to hour.

This chapter helps you to explore your own level of self-esteem and gives you ways of boosting how you feel about yourself and the world around you. From this foundation you will be able to deal more effectively with the challenges that life has a habit of throwing in your way.

Developing Greater Self-Love

Loving yourself doesn't mean standing in front of a mirror whispering sweet nothings to your reflection, although if that's what rocks your boat, nothing's wrong with that. Loving yourself means that you develop greater understanding and respect for who and what you are. In order to develop a greater love for yourself, you need to begin to understand yourself. This gives you a baseline from which to work.

Morris Rosenberg developed the Rosenberg Self-Esteem Scale and published it in 1965 in *Society and the Adolescent Self-Image* (Princeton University Press). Psychologists and sociologists the world over use this measure of self-esteem.

Have a go at answering the questions in the scale, as shown in Figure 10-1. Have the courage to be honest with yourself as you do so. This is an information-gathering exercise that helps define the areas you can work on in order to help you become the person you want to be.

You may wonder why some of the scores are reversed on the Rosenberg Self-Esteem Scale. The answer has everything to do with statistics. If you look at the statements on the items without an asterisk, they're all positive. Those on the items marked with an asterisk are negative. Reversing their scores ensures that a high score indicates a higher level of self-esteem. For more on understanding statistics, have a look at Deborah Rumsey's excellent *Statistics For Dummies*.

This measure of your self-esteem is the baseline from which you're working. As you practise the exercises in this chapter, you can periodically rescore yourself and notice how the result rises. But for now, have a look at the individual scores for each item. Where you've scored low, this indicates an area you can focus on improving. Where you've scored high, this indicates an area where you can discover something positive about yourself and apply it to further building up your sense of self-esteem. Keep reading to find out how.

The Rosenberg Self-Esteem Scale

Instructions: Below is a list of statements dealing with your general feelings about yourself.

If you strongly agree, circle **SA**.

If you agree with the statement, circle **A**.

If you disagree, circle **D**.

If you strongly disagree, circle **SD**.

1. On the whole, I am satisfied with myself.
    SA   A   D   SD

2.* At times, I think I am no good at all.
    SA   A   D   SD

3. I feel that I have a number of good qualities.
    SA   A   D   SD

4. I am able to do things as well as most other people.
    SA   A   D   SD

5.* I feel I do not have much to be proud of.
    SA   A   D   SD

6.* I certainly feel useless at times.
    SA   A   D   SD

7. I feel that I'm a person of worth, at least on an equal plane with others.
    SA   A   D   SD

8.* I wish I could have more respect for myself.
    SA   A   D   SD

9.* All in all, I am inclined to feel that I am a failure.
    SA   A   D   SD

10. I take a positive attitude toward myself.
    SA   A   D   SD

Scoring: For items *without* an asterisk:

SA = 3   A = 2   D = 1   SD = 0

For items *with* an asterisk the scores are reversed:

SA = 0   A = 1   D = 2   SD = 3

Add the scores for the 10 items together. The higher the score, the higher the self-esteem. Scores below 15 suggest low self-esteem.

Figure 10-1: The Rosenberg Self-Esteem Scale.

Accepting yourself

Be yourself; everyone else is taken – Oscar Wilde

Pointing this out may seem obvious, but you may be reading this chapter because you want to develop greater self-esteem. That means that you have a desire to improve the way you feel about yourself (keep stating the obvious, why don't you?). You may not believe us, but simply wanting to improve the way you feel about yourself means that you've already taken the first step by recognising that you're a worthwhile human being who's capable of change. So why not thank yourself now . . . go on . . . say thank-you to yourself.

Now you've done that you've taken another step forwards. For some reason humans have an incredible ability to castigate themselves freely and frequently while at the same time being unable to say thank-you for doing the most simple and straightforward task. Frustratingly true, isn't it? As you work on the exercises in this chapter, you become empowered to reverse this trend. Instead of castigating yourself for perceived mistakes, you become proactive in gaining from them. Instead of being embarrassed about your successes, you embrace them and build on them for the good of yourself and those you care for.

Time to take another step forward. Take two pieces of paper. On one write the heading 'Bad Qualities' and on the other write the heading 'Good Qualities'. As scary as doing so may seem, under the first heading write a list of all the bad qualities you have. Under the second write a list of all the good qualities you have. If the bad outweighs the good that doesn't matter, as we show how you can look at the so-called bad list in a very different light.

Put the bad qualities list to one side and pick up the good qualities list. Spend time and take a good looooong look. Now work through the following steps:

1. **Guide yourself into self-hypnosis.**

2. **Spend five minutes reflecting on all your good qualities.**

3. **Enjoy the feelings that these qualities bring.**

4. **If for any reason a negative thought pops up, shout in your mind (not out loud!) 'STOP' and imagine a red light flashing. Then imagine a peaceful and tranquil scene for a few moments before returning to reflect on your good qualities.**

5. **Spend a little time thanking yourself for these good qualities.**

6. **Wake yourself from the trance.**

Now, with those good qualities at the forefront of your mind, gird your loins and take out the page headed 'Bad Qualities'. First, take hold of your pen and scrub out the heading. Go on, enjoy doing it. Now write in the new heading 'Things About Myself I Am Changing'. Yes, we're back to reframing, which we cover in Chapter 6.

Take a good long look at each item on the 'Things About Myself I Am Changing' list. In your mind, step back and try to think about each item from a different perspective. For example, if you've written 'I'm too blunt with people', you can rewrite that as 'I'm honest and straightforward' – a *good* quality that you can now move to the good qualities list. You may even be able to add a new item to that list that you haven't thought of before: 'People know where they stand with me'. If you have, for example, an item on your 'Things About Myself I Am Changing' list that says 'I'm rude to other people', rethink how you've written that. Perhaps you can write something more positive and empowering, such as 'I'm discovering how to be more tactful with other people'.

Now, take a little time to really whittle things down to those qualities that need addressing and those that have become supportive resources for you:

1. **Spend time going through the 'Things About Myself I Am Changing' list, reframing and perhaps moving items that you now realise are positive to the good qualities list.**

2. **You don't have to do everything in one go. Keep coming back and do a little reframing each time.**

3. **Every so often, reflect on the good qualities list in self-hypnosis.**

What you're left with on your 'Things About Myself I Am Changing' list are the building blocks for change. Your good qualities list is the scaffolding that supports your change and self-hypnosis is the tool that makes the change possible.

Everyone has things about themselves that they want to change, so hoping that your 'Things About Myself I Am Changing' list can ever be empty is unrealistic. In fact, having something you want to change shows that you're a self-aware individual who's continually evolving – as long as you're taking action on the items on the list of changes!

If you feel that you can't find any good qualities and that you can't reframe anything from the 'Things About Myself I Am Changing' list, then you probably need to have a chat with your doctor about the way that you are feeling so that the most appropriate help can be found for you. You care enough about yourself to buy this book, so now's the time to take the next step and ask for help from someone who can give assistance to you.

Enjoying the healthiness of being ordinary

Being ordinary is being yourself. No matter how extraordinary someone may seem to be, to himself he's ordinary. Being ordinary really means enjoying being yourself while enjoying the ordinariness of wanting to change and to improve. That means you're not alone, as the world's full of ordinary people who want to develop themselves and improve the way they enjoy their role in life.

Right now we're focusing on that improvement, as the pieces are in place for you to take another step forward in improving your self-esteem.

Look at the Rosenberg Self-Esteem Scale in the section 'Developing Greater Self-Love'. If you haven't completed the scale yet, have a go now. See how you score each item on that scale. Ask yourself the questions in Table 10-1 and make a note of your answers:

Table 10-1	Analysing the Rosenberg Self-Esteem Scale
1. On the whole, I am satisfied with myself.	
If you scored low ask yourself:	What realistically needs to happen for me to be satisfied with myself?
	How would I like to be feeling?
	How would I like to be thinking?
If you scored high ask yourself:	How can I keep this feeling of satisfaction going?
2. At times, I think I am no good at all.	
If you scored low ask yourself:	How can I improve the way I think about myself?
	What can I be saying to myself that lets me know that I am a good person?
If you scored high ask yourself:	How do I know that I am a good person and how can I keep this feeling going?
3. I feel that I have a number of good qualities.	
Check out your 'Good Qualities' and 'Things About Myself I Am Changing' lists. Reflect on ways in which you can bring about the changes you're working towards that are on the 'Things About Myself I Am Changing' list.	
4. I am able to do things as well as most other people.	
If you scored low ask yourself:	What can I do that other people can't?
	What can I do to help me feel different about this?
If you scored high ask yourself:	How can I keep this feeling going?

Table 10-1 *(continued)*

5. I feel I do not have much to be proud of.

If you scored low or high:	No matter how many items there may be, list those things that you are proud of.
	Make a list of what you want to be proud of that you aren't at the moment. Reflect on how you can change this situation.

6. I certainly feel useless at times.

If you scored low ask yourself:	What needs to happen for me to feel more useful?
If you scored high ask yourself:	How can this feeling help me make changes to my own sense of self-esteem.

7. I feel that I'm a person of worth, at least on an equal plane with others.

If you scored low ask yourself:	How can I improve the way I think about myself?
	What can I be saying to myself that lets me know that I am a person of worth?
	Realistically, what does being worthwhile mean to me and how can I achieve this?
If you scored high ask yourself:	How do I know that I am a worthwhile person and how can I keep this feeling going?

8. I wish I could have more respect for myself.

If you scored low ask yourself:	What does respect for myself mean to me and how can I achieve this?
If you scored low or high:	Reflect on how improving your self-esteem is going to improve your self-respect.

9. All in all, I am inclined to feel that I am a failure.

If you scored low ask yourself:	What does success mean to me?
	What needs to happen for me to realistically achieve that success?
If you scored high ask yourself:	How can I keep this feeling of success going?

10. I take a positive attitude toward myself.

If you scored low or high:	Reflect on how reading this book and taking the time to work through the exercises it contains are helping you to be more positive toward yourself.

Take your time to answer the questions. Don't be surprised if you can't find answers to some of the questions straightaway; these may come with time. In fact, as you develop your self-esteem the answers become clearer to you. You may even be surprised to find that some of the questions answer themselves and that you work through them without being aware of doing so: the power of your unconscious mind unleashed!

What do you do with your answers? Bring everything that you have together in self-hypnosis.

You're only working on the positive and constructive answers to the questions in self-hypnosis. This reinforces your positive aspects and qualities in your mind. As you change the way you feel, you're able to revisit and reframe those unanswered questions and add them to the self-hypnosis melting pot of success.

No need to do all of this in one session. In fact, to maximise the effectiveness you're better to devote a 10–15-minute session of self-hypnosis to each question. Little and often helps keep things fresh and alive in your mind and keeps you motivated to succeed. The following gives you a straightforward protocol that will help you make the most of this process:

1. **Guide yourself into trance and go to your favourite place (for more go to Chapter 5).**

2. **Think about the positive answer to the question you're working on.**

3. **Think about how you're going to apply this to your life.**

4. **Imagine yourself having applied the answer and how this has improved the way you think and feel.**

5. **Thank yourself for what you're doing to improve your daily life.**

6. **Wake yourself from the trance in the way we describe in Chapter 5.**

As you work through this session, remember that time's your friend. Far better to pace yourself and achieve success than to rush things and end up with something far from satisfactory. So take all the time you need and keep out of the clutches of the nefarious law of reversed effect.

The law of reversed effect is very simple and often applies itself when you're rushing to try to do something. The law states that the harder you try to do something, the less likely you are to succeed. What that implies is that in order to succeed, you need to slow down and pace yourself properly.

Coping with Your Worst-Nightmare Situations

Everyone worries from time to time, having concerns over finances, children, work and so on. Worry is a form of anxiety that's a natural human trait, hopefully motivating you to get things sorted out. Things may go wrong when you don't pay attention to your worries, when you let them build and magnify until they end up as nightmare scenarios in your mind that you feel incapable of handling. You start to anticipate a catastrophic outcome, which means that you become too scared to do anything about the problem as you *perceive* the worst. This in turn knocks the stuffing out of your self-esteem and you seemingly lose the ability to be positive, constructive and proactive, letting the situation control you rather than the other way round.

Your *perception* of a situation determines how you respond to it. The worse your perception is, the more you try to hide from the situation. Time to bring in those statistics again. An interesting study carried out by the National Institute of Mental Health in America in 2001 looked at *perception* and *reality* in relation to worry, concluding that:

- 40 per cent of what we worry about never happens and is simply the product of our creative brain that knocks the stuffing out of our self-esteem.

- 30 per cent of what we worry about has already happened and so we can work out how to let it go.

- 12 per cent of what we worry about is needless worry, such as what an unimportant person may think of us.

- 10 per cent of what we worry about is petty and insignificant, such as what to have for dinner that evening.

- 8 per cent of what we worry about actually happens and out of that 8 per cent:

  - For 4 per cent of the total number of worries we have no control over what happens, for example a death in the family or ill health.

  - For 4 per cent of the total number of worries we do have control over what happens, as they are the result of either something we've done or something that we've failed to do.

So in fact, only 4 per cent of our worries are worth the worry!

This section helps you to pare down your concerns so that you can put all your effort into dealing with the niggling 4 per cent of worries that remain. By helping you to feel stronger within yourself you have the foundation upon which you can learn to problem solve more effectively, turning your nightmares into pleasant dreams.

Using self-hypnosis to feel stronger

The power of worry is that you don't confront your concerns and take control over them. This is often because you're afraid to think about the catastrophic outcome you *perceive* and perhaps don't feel that you have the strength to cope with.

Self-hypnosis to the rescue! Everything we talk about in this chapter goes a long way towards helping you turn that nightmare scenario into something you do feel capable of coping with. However, we can add something to the mix in order to help smooth things along while helping you to feel stronger and more able to cope. This is a technique called ego strengthening:

1. **Think about the emotional qualities that you want to have that you feel you don't currently hold.**

2. **Guide yourself into trance and go to your favourite place (for more on this turn to Chapter 5).**

3. **For each quality that you want to have, suggest the following: 'as each day goes by, so I feel . . .' (for example, 'a little stronger' or 'a little calmer' or 'a greater sense of self-control').**

4. **Follow up each suggestion by imagining yourself with that quality as you go through your daily life.**

5. **Wake yourself from the trance (more in Chapter 5 again).**

6. **Repeat this either once or twice daily for a week and see how much better you feel.**

The term 'ego strengthening' comes from Freudian psychology. Your ego's the part of your mind that copes with reality, making sense of your thoughts and of the world around you. The stronger your ego, the better equipped you are to cope.

Problem solving with self-hypnosis

The better you feel about yourself, the more able you are to deal with life's ups and downs. Ego strengthening helps build your self-esteem. As your self-esteem grows, so your sense of being in control grows too and you begin to perceive your problem in a way that means that you take control. The very simple reason for this is that the better you feel about yourself, the more accurate and positive a perspective you gain on anything and everything else.

You can use self-hypnosis to jump-start your problem solving. If you have worked through the previous sections in this chapter, you've seen how you can feel better about yourself. Here's a little tool that helps you solve some of your problems:

1. **Think of the people you most admire and respect. Whether they're alive or dead, real or fictional doesn't matter.**

2. **Think about what defines your problem:**

   a. **Why do you think you have a problem?**

   b. **With whom is the problem happening?**

   c. **How is the problem happening?**

   d. **When is the problem happening?**

   e. **Why do you think you haven't resolved the problem yet?**

3. **Guide yourself into trance and go to your favourite place (for more turn to Chapter 5).**

4. **Even if doing so seems strange, imagine that a large and welcoming conference table is in your favourite place. If you don't like such a corporate image, that's okay. Think of something else that people can sit around to discuss your problem – a set of comfortable beanbags, perhaps.**

5. **Invite into your favourite place all those people you were thinking about in step 1 and then ask them to sit around the table.**

6. **Imagine yourself sitting at the head of the table, calmly describing your problem to the people in front of you.**

7. **Ask this group of people to debate your problem and to come up with a suitable solution.**

8. **Be aware of solutions when they arise. Don't be judgemental about these solutions, just be aware of them.**

9. **When you feel ready, thank your assembled guests and agree to meet them again soon.**

10. **Say goodbye to them as they leave your favourite place.**

11. **Spend a couple of minutes enjoying the feelings you find in your favourite place as you mull over the solution(s) that the group of people presented to you.**

12. **Wake yourself from the trance (turn to Chapter 5 again).**

13. **Write down the solutions, select one that seems most appropriate to you and act on it.**

14. **If you want, you can discuss your progress as often as you like with your panel of the admired to help keep things on track.**

If this technique doesn't bring a solution straightaway, don't worry. As you work through the other exercises in this chapter and your self-esteem rises, things change. If they don't, then perhaps the time's come to visit your friendly neighbourhood hypnotherapist.

 As your self-esteem rises, so does your ability to become aware of a problem before a situation becomes problematic. Try to nip a potential issue in the bud before it becomes a problem. In this way you take control and are able to focus the majority of your attention on the good things in your life, without letting the not so good get out of hand.

 As much as you want a wonderful outcome for all your problems, you can never guarantee that this happens. However, do realise that you can satisfactorily solve many of your problems. For those that you can't solve, you can learn to accept this and live with that fact in a way that allows you to remain empowered and hopefully aware of how to avoid similar problems in the future.

Resolving Conflict with Self-Hypnosis

Everyone experiences arguments and disagreements with other people. This is a natural part of any human relationship. In fact, these conflicts help your relationships to grow and evolve as you understand and accommodate others.

 In this chapter we use the word 'relationship' to refer to any interaction you have with other people, be they friends, lovers, a spouse, children, work colleagues or complete strangers. We cover more intimate relationships in Chapter 17.

The remainder of this chapter helps you explore and discover ways to improve your approach to handling conflict with others. By learning to be self-aware of your own role in keeping a conflict situation going, you will then learn how to reprogram your own behaviour, turning conflict into a victory that is acceptable to both sides of the divide.

Using self-awareness in the fight against conflict

Successful conflict resolution comes from self-awareness. If you've already read several chapters in this book and practised the exercises they contain, you're a long way down the path to self-awareness. This is important, as the keys to successful resolution are the following:

- ✔ **Manage your stress:** Being calm and relaxed helps you to remain in control of your other emotions so that you don't fly off the handle at the slightest provocation. You're also able to gain a more positive perspective on the conflict and see things from another person's perspective.

- ✔ **Control your emotions and behaviours:** This helps to keep the situation calm and allows you to get your point across without threatening or frightening the other party.

- ✔ **Be aware and respectful of the fact that other people have different views:** Recognising that others have opposing views while trying to accommodate those views, helps bring about a positive dialogue.

- ✔ **Be prepared to compromise:** Relationships are about give and take. Where appropriate, compromise – being intransigent for no reason does not help move things along.

Appropriate conflict management not only helps boost your own self-esteem, but that of the other person involved. This helps create a positive environment for your relationship and means that any future disagreement can be handled with a minimum of negative feelings and maximum proactivity.

Using your magic wand to achieve the unbelievable

Time to hand over to Harry Potter as he wafts his magic wand spectacularly over his head and incants: 'Relationship Resolvium!' There! All done. Everyone's happy again.

We wish things were that easy. But ease is in fact the name of the game. By using the magic wand question we talk about in Chapter 3, you can ease the way you respond to conflict and pave the way to more productive interaction with others. You do this in the following way:

1. Guide yourself into trance and go to your favourite place (for more turn to Chapter 5).

2. Become aware of your conflict situation.

3. In your own way, view the conflict as if you're watching a film, seeing yourself and the other person involved. This helps you to gain a more positive perspective.

4. Be aware that the conflict's resolved and notice how differently you're behaving.

5. Notice how positively you're relating to the other person involved.

6. Eavesdrop on your own mind and be aware of how differently and positively you are thinking.

7. Spend time observing yourself as you discover more about your own potential.

8. Make a commitment to apply what you have found out to your interaction with the other person involved in the conflict.

9. Wake yourself from the trance (again, turn to good old Chapter 5).

10. Apply what you have discovered!

Taking the 'win–win' approach to conflict

The word *conflict* implies struggle that demands an out-and-out winner. When resolving relationship issues this is not a desired outcome as one side of the divide will be left hurt, possibly festering away with thoughts of revenge that can lead to further trouble in the future. This part of the chapter explores how you can avoid this by resolving conflict in a way that leaves all parties involved feeling as positive as it is possible to be.

Any conflict has one of the following three outcomes:

✔ 'Lose–lose' whereby neither side progresses and things remain the same, or things get so bad that the conflict damages both sides.

✔ 'Win–lose' whereby one side dominates, with the loser leaving the conflict feeling bad, angry and disempowered.

✔ 'Win–win' whereby both sides come to an amicable agreement. All parties leave the conflict with positive feelings, empowered and ready to progress in the relationship.

And you can probably guess which outcome we encourage you to seek: win–win.

The win–win outcome is based on one word: compromise. This word's an anathema for some, perhaps because they don't fully understand its meaning and implication. And this lack of compromise leads to the maintenance of many relationship conflicts, as both sides stand stoically intransigent while they battle for an all-out win.

Compromise in resolving a problem:

✔ Should *not* leave either party feeling wronged or taken advantage of

✔ Should empower both sides of the conflict

✔ Should mean you accept that you can't get everything you want

✔ Should mean you gain those things you really feel are important in a way that doesn't hurt the other party

As your self-esteem grows, so you find that you're able to feel very comfortable compromising. Here is an exercise to help you on your way. When thinking of compromise:

1. **Practise self-hypnosis for five to ten minutes to create a calm state of mind and then wake yourself from the trance (you can find the 'how to' on this in the ubiquitous Chapter 5).**

2. **List the outcomes that you're personally looking for with regard to the conflict.**

3. **Be honest with yourself and prioritise these outcomes.**

4. **Being honest with yourself again, select the outcomes that are really important to you. The rest are the ones that you can compromise on.**

5. **Practise self-hypnosis and rehearse in your mind a way of calmly putting across your needs, while listening to the needs of the other party.**

6. **Be aware that as you discuss your position with the other person, you may find other areas where you feel you can compromise.**

Always remember that the best way to help another person change is to become more positive in the way you interact with him. Being positive yourself means that others have to change the way they react to you. Old conflict behaviours become replaced with proactive ones that leave a wonderful trail of positivity behind them.

An ability to compromise is something that empowers you as an individual, as it allows you to take control of situations while at the same time being aware of the needs of others.

Chapter 11

Minimising Pain

. . . .

. . . .

*P*ain can be such a pain! If you're in pain, then that has a very nasty habit of pervading all aspects of your life. For many people, pain inhibits both work and leisure activities and can have a very detrimental effect on the way you feel. All in all, pain really stabs at the heart of your quality of life.

The human mind has an amazing capacity to help you cope with challenging situations. You may have heard tales of natural disasters where parents, despite their terrible injuries and seemingly oblivious to the pain, have accomplished great feats as they rescue their child. The astonishing thing is that the parent really doesn't feel the pain – in this chapter we explore how this can be.

How Hypnosis Can Control Pain

Hypnotherapy's one of the many ways you can use to help alleviate your pain, and has a good body of research to back it up. Hypnotherapy has long been associated with pain relief and texts surviving from ancient Egypt, Syria and Greece describe what we now consider hypnotic pain management. Medicine recognises that effective pain management should be *multimodal*, a fact endorsed in early 2010 by the American Society of Anesthiologists. Many health authorities recommend hypnotherapy to complement a patient's pain management. Interestingly, hypnotherapy's often tried when conventional pain-control methods don't work.

Using multimodal approaches means that patient care comes from a variety of disciplines. So, in the case of pain control, a patient may receive drug therapy, massage therapy, acupuncture and good old hypnotherapy, all in the same course of treatment.

Scientists now understand how hypnotic pain control works. By scanning the brain of people experiencing hypnotic pain control, they've found that the area responsible for our perception of suffering (which goes under the somewhat grandiose title of the 'anterior cingulate cortex') isn't active. If a patient's experiencing suffering then this area lights up their scanners like a beacon in the dark.

Safety First!

Before we consider how to manage your pain using self-hypnosis, we need to reach an understanding with you. First and foremost, your pain exists for a reason. The pain means that an area of your body needs looking after. Pain evolved as a safety device to ensure that you don't further damage an area of your body that's been injured or is experiencing a diseased state. In other words, the pain's saying: 'Take care of yourself!' A football player with an injured hamstring doesn't do any good careering about the pitch without a care in the world. This only makes things much worse. So pain makes our football player slow down and limp, taking pressure off the wounded limb.

When working with hypnotherapy for pain control involving an injury or illness, you're minimising your pain, not getting rid of it completely. This ensures that you're still aware of the need to look after that area of your body while improving your quality of life. When working with the pain you experience during surgery, the situation's different. Rather obviously, feeling anything while a surgeon's cutting away at you isn't useful or desirable, therefore all feeling is removed.

Before practising any form of pain management, whether through hypnotherapy or any other therapy, you should consider the following:

- ✔ **Do you have a diagnosis for your pain?** That pain exists for a reason, so make sure that your doctor's checked out the problem and that you know the cause. Even if no apparent cause exists and your pain's psychosomatic, you need to know that too.

- ✔ **Always continue taking any medication that your doctor's prescribed.** Your doctor prescribes drugs for a reason and you should only consider reducing or stopping them with the guidance and permission of your doctor. Many reasons exist for this, the main one being that many pain-control drugs make changes to the biochemistry of your body. In order to ensure that your body copes easily without the drug you may need to come off the medication slowly, reducing the dosage *according to your doctor's guidance.*

✔ **Discuss the use of hypnotherapy with your doctor beforehand.** This helps to keep your doctor in the loop and also means that she can factor hypnotherapy into any changes that may occur to your condition. If your doctor doesn't know very much about hypnotherapy, then you may recommend that she reads the somewhat excellent *Hypnotherapy For Dummies.*

✔ **Inform any professionals you're seeing with regard to managing your pain that you're using hypnotherapy.** As with your doctor, other professionals are then able to factor hypnotherapy into your treatment. You may even find that they encourage you to practise self-hypnosis while they carry out treatment on you to enhance its effect. This may be the case with treatments such as massage or acupuncture.

Understanding Your Pain

To manage your pain you need to understand it. Before you shout at us that you understand your pain well enough because it hurts, remember a recurring theme in this book: understanding your problem begins to give you control over it. To say that something hurts is a very general statement that gives a global description of your pain. In this section we show you how to describe your pain.

Characterising your pain

In order to *understand* your pain you should think about what characterises the pain. So begin to take control by asking yourself these questions:

✔ **When do you experience pain?** Is pain a constant in your life or do you have times when the pain's reduced or you're pain free?

✔ **When don't you experience pain?** If you do have pain-free periods, what's happening or what are you doing that may contribute to the lack of pain?

✔ **What makes your pain worse?** For example, sudden movements, sitting in a particular position, temperature and so on.

✔ **What makes your pain better?** For example, relaxation, temperature, drug therapy and so on.

✔ **How does your pain affect your relationships?** For example, sexual activity, social activity and so on.

- **If your pain were magically removed, what may you be able to do that you can't do now?** After answering this question, immediately look at the next one.

- **When you think of your answer to the previous question, how do you feel?** Be honest with yourself. If you find that you may be able to go back to work and the idea of doing that fills you with dread, have a look at Chapter 3. There you can find out how to set yourself some goals to move towards maybe changing your job.

  Wherever you find a negative when answering this question, you may have a secondary gain that can hinder your path to pain management.

  Wherever you have a positive answer, hold on to this as you can use this factor as motivation.

- **When you experience pain, what emotions do you have?** For example, anger, frustration, anxiety and so on.

- **How do the emotions you experience affect your behaviour?** For example, you may become withdrawn, aggressive, short-tempered and so on.

- **How do you describe how your pain feels?** For example, a crushing pain, a stabbing pain, a dull pain and so on.

- **If you were able to see your pain, what does it look like?** This gives you a metaphorical description. Our patients have given various creative descriptions such as 'It's like a band of steel tightening around my head', 'It looks like a jagged shape covered in spikes' or 'It's a swirling red colour'.

The answers to these questions define your pain and give you plenty of information for you to use in the self-hypnosis exercises in the section 'Strategising Your Pain Management', later in this chapter.

A *secondary gain* represents the benefit you're gaining from having your symptom. The interesting thing is that you don't realise you have that benefit. For example, a patient's doctor referred her to Peter for pain management. When Peter asked her the question 'If you wake up tomorrow morning and your pain's gone, what are you able to do that you can't do now?', after a few moments thought she replied, 'I'm able to do the weekly shopping.' When asked how she may find that, she screwed her face up and replied that she hated shopping. This dislike may have hindered her therapy and so the issue was addressed. Eventually she came to view shopping as a necessity, one that when she felt able to do it was a positive indication that she was on the mend.

Using scales to rate your pain

Pain clinics use scales a lot to help both doctor and patient get an understanding of the level of pain. This is useful as the scale gives a good measure over time of how effective treatment is. Below are the three most common scales. Have a look at them, select the one that means most to you and rate your experience of pain right now. Keep a record of your rating and then rate yourself daily, as this helps you monitor your pain management.

Visual analogue scale

This is a commonly used scale that rates your pain from 0 (no pain) to 10 (the worst you can imagine). Figure 11-1 shows you what it looks like.

Figure 11-1:
The visual analogue scale.

Wong Baker FACES pain-rating scale

Developed by D. Wong and C. Baker as a scale for children to rate their experience of pain, this scale also appeals to adults, especially those creative types who can't relate to visual analogue scales. Figure 11-2 illustrates it.

Figure 11-2:
The Wong Baker FACES pain-rating scale.

0	2	4	6	8	10
NO HURT	HURTS LITTLE BIT	HURTS LITTLE MORE	HURTS EVEN MORE	HURTS WHOLE LOT	HURTS WORST

Verbal scale

Some people can only rate their pain in terms of words. This scale recognises that and dispenses with numbers and pictures, instead focusing on commonly used words to rate pain. Figure 11-3 shows you what it looks like.

Figure 11-3:
A verbal pain scale.

No Pain   Mild   Moderate   Severe Pain

Looking at Different Types of Pain

The much-revered ancient Chinese military general and strategist Sun Tzu wrote in his 6th-century treatise *The Art of War*, 'If you know your enemies and know yourself, you can win a hundred wars'. You can look on this wise pronouncement in the context of pain management as meaning that if you can understand your pain and understand your personal responses to that pain, you can overcome many of the hurdles that pain puts in your way. In this section we look at what pain is, above and beyond the fact that it's a warning to your body that you need to pay attention to something.

Health professionals don't look at pain as one simple experience. In order to help them understand their patients better, they use different classifications:

- ✔ **Acute pain:** Sometimes called short-term pain, this is of short duration, such as the pain you may experience when you have a tension headache.

- ✔ **Chronic pain:** Also called long-term pain, this describes pain that lasts for a prolonged period, such as the pain of arthritis or cancer.

- ✔ **Episodic pain:** Whether acute or chronic, if you experience pain that comes and goes this title applies. You may also hear this referred to as intermittent pain or recurrent pain. Back pain that sitting with a particular posture temporarily relieves can be described as episodic, for example.

- ✔ **Somatic pain:** This is pain that comes from damage to your skin or deep tissues such as muscles, for example cutting yourself or feeling the pain of aching muscles after overdoing exercise in the gym.

- ✔ **Visceral pain:** This is pain that originates from the organs in your body, for example period pains or indigestion.

- ✔ **Neuropathic pain:** Sometimes called neuralgia, this pain's the result of a problem with one or more nerves in your body, such as when you trap a nerve or the pain you experience with multiple sclerosis.

- ✔ **Sympathetic pain:** This has nothing to do with being given sympathy and everything to do with your sympathetic nervous system (have a look at Chapter 2 to sympathise more with your nervous system). This type of pain's the result of over-activity of your sympathetic nervous system and you can experience it as extreme sensitivity to touch or temperature, for example in the skin around an injury.

- ✔ **Psychosomatic pain:** This is pain for which no demonstrable physical cause is present. That doesn't mean that the pain doesn't exist, rather that it's the result of psychological factors. A good example is chest pains caused by stress or panic attacks. However, we must point out that if you do have chest pains of any kind and your doctor hasn't checked you out, please make an appointment as soon as you can. Remember: safety first!

Psychosomatic comes from two Greek words: *psyche* which means mind and *soma* which means body. The term describes physical conditions that are the result of psychological processes or are heavily influenced by emotional factors.

Seeing that Pain's Subjective

Some people seem to be able to handle lots of pain while others express agony over the slightest scratch. Many reasons exist – most of them subjective – for this difference in pain threshold.

 The word 'subjective' has a variety of meanings. In medicine the term means that the way a patient experiences a disease or condition is influenced by her moods and feelings.

- **Fear and anxiety:** The more scared you become, the more active is your fight or flight response. That means that you grow more aware of and pay attention to anything that you think's a threat to your survival, including any pain you're experiencing, inadvertently turning up the feelings. For more on your fight and flight response have a look at Chapter 9.

- **Low mood:** The more depressed you are about your pain, the more you focus on that pain. And the more you focus on it, the worse you perceive the pain to be – because you're depressed about it in the first place.

- **Interpretation:** How you interpret pain can raise or lower your pain threshold. For example, you may perceive the pain you experience after working out at the gym as less than a pain of similar intensity that you experience as a result of being kicked in an attack. This is because going to the gym's a pleasant experience (well, we think so) so the pain makes you feel good. However, the pain of being attacked brings fear and anxiety into the equation, which makes you feel even worse.

- **Prior experience and anticipation:** If you've had a previous bad experience with pain, when faced with that experience again you may begin to anticipate that the pain's going to be bad. That then brings in those annoying friends we prefer not to have: fear and anxiety. Throw those two into the mix and all you get is 'ouch'. You don't even have to have experienced the pain before, as if you think it's going to be bad, it's probably going to be because that's what you're expecting. Think of the dentist (dental phobics better turn to Chapter 9 before doing this). Many people are scared of the dentist and therefore feel more pain than necessary when going through a procedure.

A simple message comes out of all of the above: if you can alter the way you think and feel about your pain, then you can change the way you experience pain.

The point at which a sensation turns into pain is known as your *pain threshold*.

Strategising Your Way to Pain Management

Before reading this section, please keep in mind our safety advice at the start of this chapter.

You are a unique individual. Your response to the pain that you experience will be unique to you as is your response to hypnosis. You may find that certain approaches to inducing trance (see Chapter 5) or helping you manage problems appeal more than others. In this section you will read about several different ways that can help you take control of your pain. As you read through this section you can formulate an effective strategy of pain management based on the following exercises. As you practise these, you can find the approaches that are most effective for you.

You may find that some of the techniques in this section are more applicable to working with pain that results from having an illness or injury, while others are useful for acute pain such as you experience when undergoing a medical procedure. However, practising all of the techniques is worthwhile so that you really do feel you're taking control. Use the exercises in this section in conjunction with Chapter 5, where we show you how to guide yourself into self-hypnosis, and Chapter 6, where we help you record your own dulcet tones if you find being guided by a recording easier.

As soon as you begin to feel you're taking control, you're already stamping on two of the subjective factors that make your pain worse: fear and anxiety.

After practising self-hypnosis for pain relief, always make sure that you get up gently from wherever you've been doing the exercise. This prevents any sudden movement that may undo all the good work you've just done.

Practice makes perfect! The more you practise these techniques, the more likely you are to manage your experience of pain effectively. So make time for yourself on a daily basis if necessary and enjoy the path to relief.

Visualising your relief

You may find it strange that you can see your pain fading away, but that's what this section is all about. By describing your pain as we explain in 'Understanding Your Pain', earlier in this chapter, you have already used your amazingly creative mind to generate meaningful visual interpretations of your pain. When you focus on these images then the chances are you are going to feel the pain they represent. If you can do that, then you can do the same for pain relief. The following exercises teach you how you can begin to manipulate the way you experience pain.

Using colour or shape

You can use this exercise for both chronic and acute pain:

1. Imagine your pain as a colour and/or shape.

2. Imagine the colour and/or shape of the absence of pain.

3. Guide yourself into self-hypnosis and go to your favourite place.

4. Focus your attention on the area of your body that's experiencing pain and imagine that area as the colour and/or shape of pain.

5. Begin to imagine that the colour/shape is beginning to change into that of pain relief.

6. Spend time doing this slowly, and as you do so notice how the feeling in that area of your body is changing.

7. When the colour/shape has changed to that of relief, then suggest to yourself that this feeling's going to remain as you continue with your day.

8. Spend a few moments imagining yourself coping better with your pain as you continue with your day.

9. Imagine yourself having the pain relief while taking care of the injured area of your body.

10. Awaken yourself from trance.

Using your description of pain

You can use this exercise for both chronic and acute pain:

1. Take yourself into self-hypnosis and go to your favourite place.

2. Think of how you describe your pain. For example, you may describe the pain of your headache as if your head's full of pressure.

3. Think of something that represents pain relief for you. For example, you may imagine a pressure valve releasing the pressure as the pain decreases.

4. Fully imagine the experience of pain relief. For example, imagine the pressure pouring out of your head as your pain decreases. Then imagine the valve closing and the relief remaining.

5. Suggest to yourself that the relief's going to last throughout the day.

6. Imagine yourself having the pain relief while taking care of the injured area of your body.

7. **Wake yourself from self-hypnosis**.

Relaxing away your pain

You may be surprised to hear that for some types of pain relaxation's the key to relief. This boils down to the fact that when damage occurs to an area of your body the muscles surrounding that area tend to contract, inadvertently putting extra pressure on the damaged part. That extra pressure increases your experience of pain. Likewise, if the muscle itself is damaged, as may be the case in some types of back pain, then the muscle goes into spasm. Result: worse pain. If you can relax those muscles, you can bring down your levels of pain.

You can use this exercise for back pain, joint pain, muscular pain and so on:

1. **Guide yourself into self-hypnosis using the progressive relaxation technique you can find in Chapter 5 and then imagine yourself in your favourite place.**

2. **Spend a few minutes enjoying the feelings of relaxation.**

3. **Focus on the area of your body where you're experiencing pain and imagine the muscles surrounding that area.**

4. **Focus on imagining these muscles relaxing. Imagine all the tension melting away from them.**

5. **You may want to imagine the colour of relaxation flowing into this area.**

6. **You may want to imagine the fibres of the muscles relaxing.**

7. **As you relax that area of your body, notice how the sensations you experience begin to change.**

8. **Suggest to yourself that you're going to be gentle with your movements (to avoid accidentally causing the muscles to contract).**

9. **Suggest to yourself that the pain relief's going to last throughout the day.**

10. **Imagine yourself having the pain relief while taking care of the injured area of your body.**

11. **Wake yourself from self-hypnosis.**

Setting yourself up for a better experience

You can use this exercise to set yourself up for a more positive experience if you're about to undergo a medical procedure. You should imagine how you want to be before, during and after the procedure. Imagining yourself after the procedure is important, as it tells your mind that before and after do exist and that you're going to get through everything okay!

1. Spend some time thinking about how you want to be thinking and responding during the procedure.

2. Guide yourself into self-hypnosis and visit your favourite place.

3. Suggest to yourself that as you experience the procedure you remain calm and relaxed and that you enjoy a sense of self-control.

4. Suggest to yourself that you're going to be surprised at how well you cope with the experience.

5. Imagine yourself being calm and relaxed as you enter the surgery before the procedure.

6. Imagine being relaxed and calm as you're prepared for the procedure.

7. Imagine yourself going through the experience enjoying a sense of calmness, relaxation and self-control.

8. Imagine yourself having coped well with the experience as you leave the surgery.

9. Imagine what you may be doing after leaving the surgery – for example, going home and relaxing with friends.

10. Once again, suggest to yourself that you're going to be pleasantly surprised at how well you cope and that as the procedure's carried out you remain calm and relaxed with a feeling of self-control.

11. Spend a few minutes enjoying your favourite place.

12. Wake yourself from self-hypnosis.

13. As you go through your daily life, if you find that you start thinking in a negative way about the procedure, then shout a loud 'stop' in your mind (make sure you shout in your mind and not out loud!) and imagine a bright red light flashing on.

14. Then think about being relaxed, calm and feeling in control throughout the procedure. In this way you further set yourself up for success.

 Even though these visualisations are more effective when you do them in self-hypnosis, you can carry out any of them very quickly at any point during your day without the need to go into trance. For example, as you're sitting at your desk if you notice the pain appearing again, you can quickly imagine that sensation turning to the colour of pain relief.

Manipulating your pain

In this section we show you various techniques that use a natural ability all humans possess known as dissociation. Dissociation simply means a splitting of awareness and explains how the injured parent we talked about at the start of this chapter was able to rescue her kids oblivious to her own pain.

Her awareness was focused away from her pain as she carried out the heroic deed. Thankfully you don't need to be put into such extreme situations to be able to benefit from dissociation. Maybe you're experiencing it already as you enjoy reading the words on this page and your awareness of your partner busying away in the background fades . . . and fades . . . and fades . . . until all you're aware of is the content of this book!

Floating away your pain

You can use this exercise for both chronic pain and the pain you experience when undergoing a medical procedure:

1. **Guide yourself into self-hypnosis.**

2. **Imagine the area of your body that's experiencing pain.**

3. **Imagine that all the pain and discomfort in that area's floating up and out of your body.**

4. **Imagine only comfort's left behind.**

5. **If you're undergoing a medical procedure, then you can imagine that you're floating away from the surgery and going to your favourite place. Enjoy the feelings of being in your favourite place.**

6. **When you're ready, suggest that the pain relief lasts throughout the day.**

7. **Imagine yourself having the pain relief while taking care of the injured area of your body.**

8. **If you've been in your favourite place, then imagine yourself back in the present.**

9. **Wake yourself from self-hypnosis.**

Visiting the control room of your mind

You can use this exercise for all types of pain:

1. **Guide yourself into self-hypnosis and imagine that you're in your favourite place.**

2. **Spend a few minutes enjoying the feelings that you experience there.**

3. **Even though its presence may seem odd, imagine a beautiful door in front of you.**

4. **Imagine that you're going through that door and into a most incredible control room.**

5. **Have a look around the control room. As you do, realise that this is the control room of your mind.**

6. Imagine that this control room houses all the controls that govern how your body works.

7. Spend time finding the controls that are responsible for the levels of pain you're experiencing.

8. Notice that the levels are turned up too high.

9. Take time to adjust these controls so that they're set to provide relief.

10. Have a look around your control room to see if any other controls need adjusting to help you with your pain relief, for example those that control muscle tension.

11. When you're ready, leave your control room and find yourself back in your favourite place.

12. Once again, spend a few minutes enjoying the feelings that you find there.

13. Suggest to yourself that the pain relief lasts throughout the day.

14. Imagine yourself having the pain relief while taking care of the injured area of your body.

15. Wake yourself from self-hypnosis.

Numbing your pain

The two techniques in this section are classics that hypnotherapists have used for many years to help relieve all types of pain. Their themes have several variations, but they all end up with the same result: numbness.

Using glove analgesia

Analgesia means that something's taken away pain without having rendered you unconscious. In other words, you're fully aware but have little discomfort.

1. Guide yourself into self-hypnosis.

2. Imagine a bucket full of ice-cold water in front of you.

3. Imagine what the bucket looks like, the condensation dripping down the sides, perhaps a cold mist coming from the water.

4. Imagine testing the water with the tips of the fingers of one of your hands and finding out just how cold that water really is.

5. Imagine dipping your hand in a little further and then taking it out again because the water's so cold.

6. Imagine having the courage to dip your hand in again and keeping it in the water a little longer as it gets colder and colder.

7. Imagine that you can keep your hand in the water as all the sensation begins to leave your hand.

8. Really focus on your hand becoming numb as you feel all the sensations fade away.

9. When you're sure that your hand's numb, perhaps feeling as though you're wearing a glove of numbness (hence the name 'glove analgesia'), then place that hand over the area of your body where you feel pain.

10. Tell yourself that you're going to slowly count from 5 to 1 and that when you reach the number 1 all the numbness transfers from your hand to the affected area. Tell yourself that when the numbness has transferred your hand's going to regain all its sensations.

11. If you find difficulty in putting your hand on the area where you're experiencing pain, for example your back, then you can suggest that as you count from 5 to 1 the numbness travels up your arm and then on to where you need it, arriving there by the count of 1.

12. Suggest to yourself that the numbness lasts throughout the day.

13. Imagine yourself having the pain relief while taking care of the injured area of your body.

14. Wake yourself up from self-hypnosis.

Remembering numbness

As most people have experienced numbness before, perhaps during dental treatment, a very simple way to experience numbness is to remember what having that feeling is like.

1. Guide yourself into self-hypnosis.

2. Remember a time when you experienced a feeling of numbness.

3. Spend time focusing on where that sensation was on your body and on what that sensation feels like.

4. Allow yourself to really feel that numbness.

5. If the numbness has appeared somewhere other than where you need it, tell yourself that you're going to count from 5 to 1.

6. Tell yourself that when you reach the number 1 the numbness has moved to the area of your body that needs pain relief.

7. Tell yourself that all other areas of your body have returned to normal sensation.

8. **Suggest to yourself that the numbness is going to last throughout the day.**

9. **Imagine yourself having the pain relief while taking care of the injured area of your body.**

10. **Wake yourself up from self-hypnosis.**

Did you know that more and more people are electing to go under the surgeon's knife using hypnosis as the only means of pain relief? This is very useful to those who have an allergic reaction to anaesthetics and is something those who don't want to be chemically coshed also ask for. Obviously the use of hypnosis has to be agreed in conjunction with the surgeon and anaesthetist. You also require several sessions with a qualified and experienced hypnotherapist for the pain relief to be successful. So don't try this one on your own! Check out web resources such as YouTube where you can watch people undergoing surgery with hypnosis and then talking about their experience.

Chapter 12

Ironing Out Anger

· ·

In This Chapter

▶ Uncovering your own anger

▶ Knowing to keep an eye on your anger

▶ Understanding when anger's healthy

▶ Changing your angry behaviours and thoughts

· ·

Most of us know someone who has an 'anger management' problem. You may even consider yourself that person!

Anger's probably one of the hardest emotions to control. The word 'anger-holic' describes a person who's addicted to anger and over-expresses anger as his main reaction to life. But from the perspective of achieving good mental health, the goal isn't to get rid of anger, but to *manage* it. You don't want your anger to control you, but vice versa.

Anger's on the increase in our society due to our increasingly stressful and uncertain world. Who even heard of road rage only a generation ago?

Anger's an emotion with associated costs: to your health, relationships and even your job. Although admitting to having problems managing your anger can initially be embarrassing, keep in mind that if you're serious about seeking help, you may be pleasantly surprised at the level of support those around you are willing to offer.

Anger isn't always bad, however. In the right context, anger can be useful and appropriate. For example:

✔ Anger against injustice has led to many great reforms throughout history.

✔ In therapy sessions, accessing long-suppressed anger can help to combat depression and overcome illness that's emotionally based.

When you are having to overcome feelings of frustration, connecting to your suppressed anger, combined with learning to express this constructively and assertively, can also help to liberate you from acting passive-aggressively.

The main thing to keep in mind is that in itself, anger's neither bad nor good. How you express anger, and how anger's triggered within you, denotes whether anger's become a problem for you.

In this chapter we explore how to better understand your anger and what strategies you can employ to manage your feelings of anger when they become problematic. You also discover how to express appropriate anger more constructively.

Calmly Understanding Your Anger

Everyone's experience of anger is different. Research shows that various factors come into play such as culture, gender, age, the availability of emotional support, lifestyle choices and general health. For example, men tend to express anger more in briefer but more intense outbursts, while women tend to feel angry for longer.

Individual perspectives on an angry act vary widely, as one person may view another's righteous or vengeful anger as irrational or vicious.

If you feel that you have extreme anger problems, maybe you don't understand the difference between hostility and aggression. *Hostility* is the expression of a 'bad attitude' and often involves fear or paranoia. *Aggression* is the deliberate intention to hurt others.

These behaviours may have roots based in your past, stemming from, for example, witnessing hostility or aggression from a childhood carer or parent. We describe in the later section 'Stopping before the flashpoint' how to work with anger before it becomes out of control.

Understanding your anger doesn't mean taking away your rage, but is more about being cleverer in expressing upset feelings. By understanding your anger you can improve your communication skills, increase your emotional vocabulary and gain a new perspective on matters so that anger becomes a less frequent response.

Finding out how anger works for you

Different people view anger in a range of different ways. Those who come to therapy often see their anger in negative ways, but from a therapy perspective, anger is simply a human emotion. It is not something that we should try to rid ourselves of, but to understand. Anger can be either healthy or unhealthy, depending on how we express it. This chapter will help you to begin to understand your anger and how best to work with it to make sure your communication is clear and reasonable.

Ask yourself the following questions:

✔ **When's my expression of anger *healthy* and when's it *unhealthy*?**

Is anger negatively affecting your relationships, health or work life? If the answer to any of these is 'yes', then this aspect of your anger is toxic or unhealthy.

✔ **How often do I *feel* angry?**

By monitoring your daily feelings of anger, you increasingly understand your patterns and what you react most angrily towards. Monitoring can also become a way to measure your progress over time as you begin to cope better.

✔ **How often do I *express* angry feelings?**

How do you express angry feelings? Do you suppress them and keep them inside? Do you use 'sideways' communication to express them, such as sarcasm, pointed humour or passive-aggressive behaviour? Or do you express angry feelings directly in a confrontational way?

✔ **How *intensely* do I feel anger?**

Rate yourself on an anger scale between 0 (no anger) to 10 (extreme anger), so 0–4 = no anger to irritation; 5–6 = anger; 7–10 = rage. If your anger rating's 7 or above, consider yourself to have moved beyond anger into the area of **rage.** Rage is extreme, more serious anger. We discuss anger that is inappropriate in the next section titled 'Judging when your anger's inappropriate'.

✔ **How *many times a day* do I express anger?**

Once a day is probably within the normal range. If you *frequently* express anger two or more times daily, then consider yourself as having an anger problem.

Ask yourself whether you consider yourself to be an angry person. What may seem like direct communication or straight talk to you, others may perceive as an angry response.

If you're unsure whether you have an anger problem, ask yourself the following:

✔ Do other people act as if they're afraid or wary of me?

✔ Do other people comment on my aggression?

✔ Do I find most people to be rude or inconsiderate?

✔ Do I feel that most people are incompetent at their jobs in ways that affect me?

✔ Do small problems really upset me?

    ✔ Do I tend to strongly disagree in conversations with other people?

    ✔ Do I have arguments with people regularly?

After reading this list, if you feel a need to answer 'yes, but . . .' to more than one question, stop before you complete the 'but' part of that statement and accept that you probably have a problem controlling your temper.

In a nutshell, anger comes from your thinking about the events you experience and the behaviours that you select to respond to these events. In the next section, we explore how your thinking about events creates appropriate or inappropriate behaviours.

Don't be surprised that even as you read these words, you may begin to feel impatient and angry: 'Okay, I *know* that I have an anger problem, but what do I do about it?' We're moving towards strategies in the final part of this chapter, but in the meantime here's a quick, general tip.

When you feel yourself becoming angry, try to slow your breathing and relax all of the muscles from the top of your head to your fingers and down to your toes.

Judging when anger's inappropriate

It's important that you understand that anger is a neutral emotion. We all place connotations on anger being 'bad' or 'out of control' or 'justifiable' based on our own values. Most people who have done counselling learn to be more accepting and honest about their motivations and emotions, in particular anger. In this session, we want to help you to increase your awareness about how to view the appropriateness of your own feelings of anger.

In the following scenario we demonstrate the link between your thoughts, emotions and behaviours and how you can choose either appropriate or inappropriate behaviours as a result.

Imagine that you've had a bad day at work and are driving home in an already bad mood. You're in heavy traffic and you're rudely overtaken by another driver who cuts suddenly in front of you, causing you to hit your brakes to avoid a collision. Minutes later you both come to a traffic light, the rude driver in the next lane to you. You shout angrily at this driver through your car window; he simply ignores you and rolls his window up to block out the sound of your voice.

Now examine the potential outcomes – here are some possible things you may think:

✔ 'I'm not taking this, I'm going to get out of my car and do some damage.'

✔ 'This driver has children in his car who are probably distracting him, just like mine do when they're with me.'

✔ 'Everyone at work today has insulted me, now this driver's doing it too.'

✔ 'He probably didn't mean anything personal.'

Here are some possible ways you may behave:

✔ You get out of your car and attack the driver.

✔ You tell him through your window to drive more considerately, even though he can't hear you.

✔ You wave your finger at him and then forget about the whole incident.

✔ You do nothing, but sit and fume, making yourself more angry.

✔ You do nothing, but turn on some soothing music to distract yourself.

Which of these thoughts and behaviours are you most likely to think or do? Do you see how some of these are more extreme than others?

Our goal is to have greater control over our anger without suppressing it. In most situations, at some level, we probably know what the most appropriate response to anger is. This can vary in each situation. In some cases the most appropriate response may be to *not* express anger directly – especially if this becomes counter-productive for you. Through self-hypnosis, we can begin to make suggestions to contact the part of us that knows exactly what the correct response is in any given situation.

Defining Your Anger Triggers by Keeping a Diary

To begin to make changes to your behaviour, you need to become more familiar with how your anger's triggered and manifested in your everyday life. Keeping an anger diary helps you see exactly how your anger's triggered and find strategies to manage anger better. The diary's something you should be able to carry with you at all times so that you can write into it whenever you lose your temper.

Imagine writing out an anger scenario like a mathematics equation:

External events + Internal processes = Behaviour reaction

The formula above is the essence of what you want to record in your anger diary. You want a record of how your anger's the result of your mind and your body's reaction to events in your life.

Specifically, what we want you to record in the diary are:

✔ The things that happen in the external world (*Events*)

✔ Your internal processes (*Thoughts*) and (*Feelings*) that lead you to . . .

✔ The sort of angry reaction (*Behaviour*)

The words in italics – Events, Thoughts, Feelings and Behaviour – should become headings on each page of your anger diary.

Creating your anger diary

If you read literature about keeping a journal of your feelings, you may notice that some writers make a distinction between anger diaries (for long-term monitoring) and anger journals (for instant assessments of anger reactions). We needn't enter that debate here. If you keep in mind the dual purposes of diaries and journals, you can even combine both functions – to develop as you go and occasionally review what you've written over time.

What's important is not only to observe your anger by writing about how you experience it each day, but rapidly and accurately to describe your emotional feelings as soon as possible after they occur. This gives you more raw, impressionistic writing and a truer flavour of your anger. Wherever you write, just try to do this in a place that's as quiet and private as possible.

To help you decide what to write in your diary, here are two examples of not-so-useful and more-useful diary writing.

An *insufficient entry's* something like:

'3:35 p.m.: Got angry at a co-worker at work for criticising my paperwork. I rated my angry outburst 6 out of a possible 10 on the anger scale. Felt bad for 30 minutes.'

A *better entry's* something like:

'Jane told me off today about my paperwork. Screamed at her and called her a stupid idiot at the top of my voice. I thought she was trying to humiliate me. Felt embarrassed, because she was right. I don't understand what I'm supposed to be doing with the paperwork. Felt angry at myself. Got a headache and felt hot and sweaty afterwards.'

Notice that the entry's written sketchily, but still gives the information that allows you to understand what happened at that moment.

Make sure that you use emotionally descriptive words to portray your emotions. Words like mad, bad, sad and glad depict emotions.

Don't include thoughts or actions to describe your emotions. Try to use words like 'mad' (angry), 'bad', 'sad' or 'glad'.

The diary increases your awareness and enables you to manage your impulses.

The writing should be honest and direct about your feelings. The point of the diary is not about creative writing, it is much more important that you capture your feelings and your physical reactions to angry incidents you experience in plain and simple language.

Keep in mind that your journal's private, you're not sharing it with anyone. In this way you can keep your writing real – you give yourself licence to be impolite, to be unfair and to have sloppy handwriting and misspelt words. But what's essential is that your entries reflect the annoyance, anger or murderous rage that you felt during the incident you're describing.

Try to maintain your emotional journal for at least three or four weeks. This raises your awareness of the connection between events, thoughts, bodily sensations and behaviours, and helps you to become instinctively more in control.

Increasing feelings of self-control are crucial, as people with anger issues usually feel out of control and powerless in the face of their own emotions of rage and anger. Because of these feelings of powerlessness, their inner critic has a field day and makes them feel increasingly worse about themselves. So the anger problem is compounded by decreasing self-confidence.

But the good news is that after reading this book, you have not only the keys to deal with anger, but also the techniques to increase your self-confidence.

You come to believe that you can have greater self-control. At this point, if you're using a hypnotherapist he can introduce any number of new coping strategies, based on your recently enhanced sense of confidence and control.

Using your diary to change your anger

Imagine you've been very dutiful about writing daily in your diary for about three weeks. You can now use your entries to start to make a change.

To begin with, do some self-hypnosis to decide how you want to feel after you get angry. You can do this without any fancy inductions and this can be a rapid hypnosis session, indistinguishable from daydreaming.

Here's a self-hypnosis plan to begin your change:

1. **Choose a past incident from your journal where you lost your temper and became very angry.**

2. **Close your eyes, slow your breathing and imagine the incident from start to finish, but imagine it like an old-fashioned black-and-white movie.**

Now rerun the situation in your mind **in colour**, but rewrite your reaction in your imagination, with an outcome this time where you're more in control and get what you want without losing your temper and where the other person also feels pleased with the outcome. In other words, imagine a win–win (you–them) outcome where everyone's satisfied.

This self-hypnosis script's more powerful than you may initially realise. By imagining the original incident in black and white, you're taking the humiliating power out of the memory and fading it in your mind. This diminishes the cringe-making loops you may replay incessantly in your mind, which lead you to feelings of powerlessness and, ultimately, low self-esteem.

By rewriting the new desired reaction in colour, with a win–win outcome, you're giving yourself a hypnotic suggestion to do something different in the face of a typical anger-provoking situation.

Resist the conscious pull to have a specific plan, as this isn't the point. You can just skip the 'solution' part of the in-colour self-hypnosis visualisation and go straight to you and the other person smiling and laughing and being relaxed without knowing how you made the change. In fact, your self-hypnosis is more powerful when you don't feed your conscious mind with plans or strategies, but go straight to the feeling of the problem resolved.

Here are some other things that are also important when reviewing your diary entries:

✔ You need to own up to your anger issues as you read the entries. Avoid blaming others for your anger. You've documented the repeating patterns of your loss of temper and these are now there for you to change them.

✔ As you read the entries, try to focus on your anger, not on individuals or specific situations that may repeatedly arise. The aim Is for you to own the problem, not to eliminate situations. (And certainly not to eliminate people!)

✔ Try to understand other people's positions. Imagine you're the other person and arguing passionately against yourself. What points are important to you as the other person? By understanding the other person's viewpoint, you can begin to avoid overly identifying with your position.

✔ Avoid bad behaviour. Don't personalise, don't swear, don't use sarcasm and patronising language, and please don't be violent. These behaviours cause an escalation of aggression that becomes difficult to escape. These behaviours can also cause the other person to say hurtful things or take actions that you may both regret in the long run.

✔ Use self-hypnosis to imagine solutions that are already achieved. Although we're repeating ourselves a bit here, the point's worthwhile. Without having a specific solution in mind, remember that the unconscious is the genius part of you that can easily achieve results that your conscious mind can't think up. Your unconscious can generate new behaviours and modify your unhelpful beliefs so that you can spontaneously work out solutions without having to 'think' them into being.

Being Assertive with Your Anger

Assertiveness training's very popular in the self-help therapy world, as so many people struggle with asserting themselves appropriately.

In terms of communicating our anger. Four basic styles exist:

✔ **Passive:** Passive communication involves not communicating what you feel or communicating in such a weak or ineffective way that your message is not understood by those who need to understand you. Passive communicators often carry a great deal of anger, anxiety and/or depression because they feel stuck or not listened to.

✔ **Aggressive:** This style of communication usually involves using too much force, which can result in violating the rights of others. Aggressive communicators are frequently verbally and/or physically abusive. Blaming others and not taking personal responsibility is part of their communication.

✔ **Passive-aggressive:** This style involves an underlying anger that is concealed by outwardly co-operative or passive behaviour. Sarcasm and sabotage are typical of this sort of communication.

✔ **Assertive:** This form of communication is clear, direct and yet does not violate the rights of others. In fact, in the best situations, assertive communication maintains the rights of both parties involved in a dispute. Consistent assertive behaviour also leads to high self-esteem compared to the previous three forms of communication.

When you feel frustrated and are trying to get your point across, you may either overdo the assertiveness (by being aggressive) or underdo it (by being passive aggressive).

If you keep in mind that anger in and of itself is neutral and that what matters is the way you use it, then you can begin to use anger in a much more constructive way. Like a surgeon's sterile scalpel, you can cut to the quick and do the job you intend to – which is to communicate clearly.

Using your anger constructively

Anger can be either a destructive or useful emotion, depending on how it is expressed. Anger can be a powerful tool to help free you from depression and to help others understand your frustration. If used constructively, at times anger can even help you to get what you want in certain situations. Usually, this involves understanding how you can most appropriately use your anger, which is what we discuss in this section.

Here are some ideas for using your anger in an assertive way:

- ✓ **Use the emotional feedback template statement to convey your feelings.**

  The emotional feedback template statement is: 'When you do (*state the action that has angered you*), I feel (*state your emotional feeling, for example mad (angry), bad, sad or glad*).'

  For example, 'When you interrupt me while I'm talking, I feel angry' or 'I feel angry when you interrupt me'. This lets the other person know the consequences of their actions.

  Avoid saying 'You *make me feel* angry', as feeling angry's your choice. Saying 'you make me feel' any emotion implies that you're under the control of the other person. You're not a puppet! More empowering is realising that you've chosen the emotional reaction all by yourself.

- ✓ **Say what you mean and mean what you say.**

  When expressing anger, less is always more. Don't defend or excuse your anger. Get straight to the point and be very specific about what action or situation's angering you.

- ✓ **You can be both angry and respectful.**

  So no swearing, please. Your message only gets lost or the person you're being rude to just stops listening to your message and focuses on their answer. You want your message and your anger to be clearly understood so the person wants to respond to you. In fact, you can be both angry and empathic at the same time. Express your anger in such a way that the person doesn't feel completely overwhelmed and, because of your consideration, wants to respond positively.

'What do you feel like if you're being interrupted when you try to speak?' is an example that causes the person to understand your feelings.

Stopping before the flashpoint

Most people with anger issues feel out of control. This lack of control feeds their inner critic, which in turn makes them feel increasingly awful about themselves. The antidote to this is to apply self-hypnosis approaches to

✔ Feel more in control

✔ Build up your confidence.

You may want to make an appointment to see a hypnotherapist to help you get started. But as this is a book about self-hypnosis, we can assure you that even the simplest techniques can help. For example, if you regularly apply self-hypnosis suggestions to increase your confidence, you feel that you have greater self-control. (This is known as ego strengthening.)

After a session or two of hypnosis to boost your confidence, you can introduce any number of new coping strategies, based on your recently enhanced sense of confidence and control, including some of the following:

✔ **Articulate anger rather than acting anger out:** By saying that you're angry you don't have to have the loss of control that accompanies an angry eruption. Give yourself suggestions like 'I can more easily say that I'm angry in a controlled manner'.

✔ **Turn down your anger meter a notch or two:** See your range of anger responses numerically from 0 (calm) to 10 (murderous rage). Think of past angry experiences and see the anger meter go up, up, up. Do self-hypnosis by breathing slowly and relaxing your muscles and see your anger meter gradually go down as you relax. Practise this a lot and see the anger meter in various ways: a thermometer, a sound level meter (with a red zone for the upper limits) and other images. In this way, you're training your mind and your body to be under your control when you want to lower your anger level.

✔ **Avoid angry people:** Angry people wind you up with their anger and make you feel more out of control. Make a suggestion such as, 'I look forward to spending more time with people who are happy and people I feel good to be with.'

✔ **Increase your emotional intelligence:** You have a better chance of 'catching' yourself if you can quickly identify your emotions. Think 'mad/bad/sad/glad' if you're confused, and choose one feeling. If you choose anger, then you feel mad. Because many people are out of touch with their emotions, this helps immensely in identifying the need to remove yourself from an anger-provoking situation or to do something different rather than exploding. 'Do something different when I get angry' should be a regular self-hypnosis suggestion to yourself. You can leave the something unspecified and your unconscious understands that you're implying doing something healthier and more constructive.

The something different can include a range of activities such as:

- Breathing more slowly.

- Saying and doing nothing.

- Listening but not responding.

- Thinking of something amusing that makes you smile.

- Reminding yourself to not take the bait, so not exploding in anger.

- Thinking of the cost of acting out your anger.

If you succeed in restraining yourself and doing something more positive, you should in some way reward yourself – savour the incident and make a note that you've done well.

Changing your angry behaviours and thoughts

Previous sections in this book have discussed how better to observe your angry behaviour and how to begin to stop it from getting out of control. Now we want to talk about how to get to the roots of those behaviours by changing your angry thoughts.

You can channel your anger in a way that changes your actions and your thinking. By changing your angry behaviours and thoughts you can communicate your message more clearly to others.

The proof of the effectiveness of your self-hypnosis is that your behaviours and thoughts should change in such a way that people understand you more clearly – without you having to lose your cool.

The challenge is to use your anger in the most positive, constructive way possible. This sentence alone may require you to adjust your attitudes about anger in order to see its therapeutic potential.

Anger does have some constructive aspects, however. Here are a few examples:

- **Anger can be uplifting:** For example, in ending an abusive relationship.

- **Anger can transform your apathy into energy:** When it helps, say, in finding the spirit to work through long-term depression.

> ✔ **Anger can be your bodyguard in times of danger:** It can help when fighting back in self-defence.

> ✔ **Anger lets people know how you feel:** Communicating your anger may stop someone from violating your rights.

When you get angry, you feel frustrated because your needs are blocked or your message is misunderstood. This doesn't call for you to foam at the mouth in rage, but to become a more skilful communicator and tactician.

Here are some examples of the types of things you might say as part of your self-hypnosis. These statements are called 'scripts', which are discussed in detail in Chapter 6: 'Working with Words: Becoming Your Own Recording Star'. As you learn to write your own self-hypnosis scripts, you can develop more tailor-made constructive responses to anger that suit your needs and personality.

'I can rapidly check if my angry feelings are appropriate before I act'.

'I acknowledge my angry feelings but I can also rise above them'.

We've already stated that venting your anger's counter-productive and only makes you angrier, so another self-hypnosis script fragment to develop may be something like:

'I can easily communicate my angry feelings calmly to . . . (the person you're angry with)'. Contrast this statement to venting. This is vastly healthier than uncontrolled venting.

'I may be pleasantly surprised as I find a different way to help make matters better'.

Alternatively, if you decide that your anger's justified, a script like this may be useful:

'I'm directing my focus to the problem, not to the people associated with the problem'.

This helps you to:

✔ Identify the roots of the problem

✔ Not personalise, blame or attack others who may potentially help you to resolve the problem

'The angrier I become, the more calmly and clearly I speak about what's important to me at that moment'.

The thinking behind constructive anger involves asking yourself what you want to achieve and what makes you feel that a 'good enough' outcome's been reached. Ideally, this should be as close as possible to a win–win outcome where both parties feel good enough. We readily acknowledge that in the real world win–win may not always be possible and that you don't always get your way.

For these occasions try scripts with phrases like:

> 'I can more easily cope with the times when my anger can't change things'.

> 'I can more easily put my anger into perspective'.

> 'I'm able to transform my anger into energy that allows me to move into the new situation that I need to adapt to'.

> 'I can easily choose another feeling that helps me to cope better'.

> 'I can choose to focus on ways forward' (that is, instead of hating the person(s) associated with the problem).

> 'I can choose to feel that ultimately this situation can be pleasantly resolved'.

Keep in mind that simply by reading the self-hypnosis script fragments listed above, your unconscious is already generating its own variations on further approaches that you can undertake that may help you to alter your behaviour and thoughts. In this way you become increasingly in control and more effective in communicating calmly with others.

Chapter 13

Overcoming Insomnia

· ·

In This Chapter

▶ Understanding the range of sleep problems

▶ Defining your specific sleeping patterns

▶ Developing new ways of helping yourself sleep better

▶ Using self-hypnosis to help you sleep

· ·

*M*ost people have problems sleeping from time to time, especially when they're stressed, upset or worried. But when sleep disturbance begins to cause problems coping with everyday life, you may need to take action.

Whether you describe yourself as having 'sleep problems' or 'insomnia' doesn't matter – the good news is that you can use self-hypnosis to help you overcome your sleep problems and achieve sleeping habits that are right for you.

In this chapter, we uncover some common sleep problems to show you what you need to change in order to sleep better. We help you understand your own sleep patterns and areas in your life that may affect your sleep. By understanding your specific sleep problems, you can make environmental, emotional or lifestyle changes to help you sleep better.

When you have a good understanding of the practical areas to look at and alter, we introduce self-hypnosis techniques that help you get the sleep that you feel you need.

Throughout this chapter, keep in mind that if your sleep disturbances are due to anxiety, then we suggest that you also read Chapter 9.

We conclude this chapter with an extensive script for insomnia that you are free to use and modify to suit your own needs. The script also appears in audio form on the CD that accompanies this book.

Investigating Insomnia and Sleep Disorders

Sleep problems come in many different flavours. The term insomnia refers to sleep disorder symptoms. Insomnia's neither a disease nor a diagnosis, but rather a way of describing various types of sleep disorders.

Sleep disorder symptoms differ with individuals, but usually they include problems falling asleep or staying asleep or both. Some lucky people you know may be able to get by with little sleep and function okay in the daytime. Others suffer more if they don't get enough sleep – no hard-and-fast rules exist, as individual requirements can vary greatly. But generally, insomnia describes those unlucky people whose daytime functioning is impaired as a result of ongoing sleep disturbance.

If you have problems sleeping this can cause overall tiredness, sleepiness during daytime hours, problems with your physical co-ordination and weight gain. Ongoing sleep problems can affect your health by weakening your immune system, which in turn may make you more susceptible to illness, especially during the winter.

People with sleeping problems tend to be worriers and anxious types. So this may be a big clue – by reducing your anxiety levels, you may improve your sleep patterns. Later in this chapter, in the section called 'Using self-hypnosis to improve your sleep', we offer some specific strategies for doing that. In this section, we deepen your understanding of the different types of sleep problems, which can help you to design a strategy specific to your needs.

Defining different types of sleep disorder

Insomnia's just another way of describing the *symptoms* of sleep disturbance. While these symptoms can vary, we can generally describe them under three categories or types: transient, acute and chronic.

- **Transient insomnia**, probably the mildest form of insomnia, typically lasts for only brief periods ranging from a few days to a few weeks. This type of insomnia usually results from stress, depression or changes in your life.

- **Acute insomnia** is a more enduring form of sleep problem. This can last for periods exceeding one month to half a year.

- **Chronic insomnia** lasts for several years. This is the most serious type of sleep disorder, often resulting from illness or severe emotional problems. Possible symptoms include extreme tiredness and physical problems, especially with vision. Interestingly, some people adapt to their chronic insomnia and can still function in their daytime activities with clarity of mind.

Uncovering the causes of sleep problems

Sleep problems are usually a by-product of another, more fundamental problem. Sometimes the causes in your own case aren't immediately obvious, but the following list gives some clues:

- ✔ Change – moving house/city, starting university.

- ✔ Environment – noise, discomfort, time zone change.

- ✔ Medical conditions – heart, breathing, stomach, digestive, high blood pressure, arthritis, anorexia.

- ✔ Pain – one of the commonest causes.

- ✔ Prescription drugs – including some contraceptives, diuretics, slimming pills, beta-blockers and stimulants.

- ✔ Recreational drugs – including nicotine, caffeine, heroin, cocaine, amphetamines, LSD and cannabis.

- ✔ Sleeping pills and tranquillisers – which can actually cause sleep disturbance.

- ✔ States of mind – anxiety, depression, worry, anger, grief or anticipating a difficult event.

Hypnotherapy is not effective in dealing with insomnia that is due to deeper medical issues, such as mental illness or side effects of medications, but with insomnia that is not influenced by medical conditions, self-hypnosis can be helpful.

Sleep disturbance can result from problems relating to physical health (known as 'organic' disturbances) such as illness or injury, or the problem can stem from emotional issues ('non-organic') such as fear, anger, bereavement or other upset feelings.

Sussing Out Your Somnolent Solution

Most people are vague about defining their sleep problem. As a result, they may exaggerate how little sleep they're getting, not realising that they're actually sleeping for small amounts, even if this sleep's interrupted. One way to begin to assess your sleep patterns and become even clearer is to keep a sleep diary for a week or two.

Keeping a sleep diary

Keeping a sleep diary helps you discover your sleep patterns and how your sleep affects your everyday life. You only need to have the briefest possible entries for each category. Keeping this diary's not about writing well, it's more about getting a running snapshot of patterns, with both your sleeping and your dreaming. Most sleep diaries look only at the physicality of sleep problems (restlessness and so on), but by combining this with comments about any dreams you remember just as you wake, you begin to connect to the emotional issues that may be at the root of your sleeplessness. Also any dreams that may make you feel good and refreshed – no matter how rare – are also worth recording.

Try making notes under the following headings in your sleep diary:

✓ **Dreams:** Start by *briefly* recording any dreams you may recall when you wake. Have a pen and notepad by your bedside so that you don't even have to get up. Be careful to write the minimum possible – a sentence or two's enough – so that you don't lose or add to the dream. Simply write a phrase that describes your dream (for example 'lost in a tunnel' or 'kissing Angelina Jolie') and the main emotion you felt (sad, frightened, angry, happy and so on). Freud called dreams 'the royal road to the unconscious' and by regularly recalling your dreams, you may begin to access any emotional issues that are making your sleep difficult.

✓ **Waking up:** After a brief dream description, make an entry under the heading 'waking up' that describes:

  • Your own patterns about how you wake up.

  • Whether you wake up easily or too early or too late.

  • Whether you wake up naturally or use an alarm clock.

  • How you feel physically and emotionally when you wake (for example, tired or refreshed).

  • Any disruptions you had during the night (noise, nightmares and so on).

✓ **Getting out of bed:** Under this heading in your sleep diary, enter a brief phrase that describes what you do immediately after waking, like:

  • 'Jumped out of bed straightaway. Late for work'.

  • 'Reset alarm four times. Woke up tired'.

  • 'Got up at 3 a.m., 5 a.m. and finally got out of bed at 6:30 a.m. and got dressed'.

  • 'Got up in time for work, but felt drowsy' (or rested and so on – an energy level description).

- 'Got out of bed and felt really sad' (or angry, bad, glad and so on – a mood description).

These phrases, although brief, provide a perfect image of and can help you to understand more about how you get out of bed. Your descriptions need to say something about your energy levels and mood when getting out of bed.

✔ **Description of the day:** How did you feel during the day? Did you feel tired, irritable, up or down? Did you have a busy day, do any exercise, have a nap, have any problems or any highs or lows?

✔ **Evening activities:**

- Times of meals and snacks.

- Alcohol and caffeine intake.

- Whether you smoked anything.

- Activities preceding bedtime.

- Any emotional upsets during the day that are on your mind before bedtime.

✔ **Going to sleep:**

- The time you're ready to go to bed.

- Whether you're actually sleepy just before bedtime.

- Anything you do just before going to bed.

- The time you actually turn the lights off.

Using the entries in your dream diary, you can now begin to have a view of your particular sleep patterns. Patterns vary depending on the individual, but here are some examples:

✔ Sleeplessness after drinking too much alcohol.

✔ Bad arguments causing sleeplessness with headache.

✔ Worry about work or family pressures causing frequent waking.

✔ Drinking late at night causing frequent urination.

Aim to fill in your sleep diary for about two to three weeks, which is enough to enable you to check your sleeping habits. The point of this checklist isn't to become self-obsessive, but rather to reveal patterns and any triggers that may exacerbate poor sleep.

Also please do write about the nights where you may have good sleep (if any) and try to document in your sleep diary why you think you may have slept better on these occasions. By being this observant, you're in a much stronger position to improve your sleep.

Watching what you eat

You don't have to be a nutritionist to exercise a bit of common sense about the types of food and drink to limit (or altogether avoid) if you have sleep problems. You should certainly avoid foods that are stimulants in your evening meals, as well as spicy foods if they're likely to upset your stomach. Similarly, keep alcohol to a minimum. If possible, experiment with abstinence from alcohol while you keep your sleep diary to see if this improves your sleep or makes no difference.

Certain foods contain a chemical called tryptophan, which the body converts into an amino acid that promotes sleep. This happens because the amino acid, called 'L-Tryptophan' helps the body to produce serotonin, a hormone that facilitates the brain to send sleep messages to the body.

The type of foods that contain high amounts of tryptophan include: dairy products such as cheese (especially Cheddar, Gruyere, and Swiss), milk and eggs. Also foods such as nuts, beans and fish.

Additionally, foods that are high in carbohydrates or fats can assist in sleeping if eaten within a couple of hours prior to bedtime. These foods help to release serotonin in the body. High-carbohydrate foods include cereals, milk, sugary foods, such as cake and ice cream, dates, figs and chocolate. Starchy foods such as potatoes and spaghetti are also high in carbohydrates.

If you wake to urinate, avoiding fluids for the final two or three hours before sleep may also be an idea to experiment with during your diary keeping.

Discovering how much sleep you need

How much sleep is normal depends on you as well as factors like age, stressors in your life and whether you live alone or have young children.

You probably don't need as much sleep as you think. Someone's probably told you at some point that you need eight hours sleep to have a good night. But contemporary sleep research indicates that adults vary too much to apply the eight-hour rule across the board to every adult.

Additionally, the amount of sleep you require varies depending on the different stages of your life.

In Table 13-1 we give a rough guide to sleep required within a 24- hour period based on your age. So for infant and toddlers, this would include naps within a 24-hour period. Keep in mind that the amount varies for the individual involved:

Table 13-1	Amount of sleep needed according to age	
Group	*Age Range (Years)*	*Sleep Needed (Hours)*
Infants	0–1	14–15
Toddlers	1–3	12–14
Pre-schoolers	3–6	11–13
Primary school	6–12	10–11
Adolescents	13–19	9
Adults		8
Elderly		Less than adult group

Below we offer a simple way to figure out how much sleep you personally require:

1. **Set aside a week or two in which you can focus on your sleep and not allow disruptions or changes to your sleep schedule.**

2. **Select a typical bedtime and stick with it, night after night.**

3. **Allow yourself to sleep in as long as you want, awakening without an alarm clock in the morning.**

4. **After a few days you pay off your sleep debt, and you begin to approach the average amount of sleep you need.**

5. **Once you determine your need, try to set your bedtime at an hour that allows you the sleep you need, while still waking up in time to start your day.**

Practising Practical Sleep Strategies

Combating your insomnia involves common-sense, practical approaches that are appropriate for your specific sleep problems. In this section we explore various strategies for helping you to overcome your sleep problems.

Becoming knowledgeable about sleep

What's blindingly obvious to one person may be new information to another. Sometimes a very basic starting approach is to gain as much information as you can from knowledgeable sources about your sleep problem.

This can include basic things like understanding how emotional problems that you're suppressing may arise at night, or how diet and change of environment may also affect you. Read as much as you can about the causes of sleep disorder, especially the emotional difficulties that you may be experiencing and avoiding if you're finding them too unbearable to think about.

Some useful resources to learn more about sleep include:

✔ **Books**: check out the following:

- *Sleep disorders For Dummies* by Max Hirshkowitz, Patricia B. Smith and William C. Dement (Wiley).

- *Baby & Toddler Sleep Solutions For Dummies* by Arthur Lavin and Susan Lavin (Wiley).

✔ **Websites**: Try these:

- National Sleep Foundation (www.sleepfoundation.org). A USA-based, non-profit organisation supporting public education, sleep-related research and advocacy related to sleep deprivation and sleep disorders.

- Sleep Matters Helpline (www.medicaladvisoryservice.org.uk/page10.html). A UK-based non-profit organisation, part of the Medical Advisory Service.

- Sleep Council UK (www.sleepcouncil.com/HelpfulLinks/). Various organisations with specific interests in sleep disorders. Some involve payment for services.

Increasing your social support

Many reasons can exist for insomnia. Two people may experience similar levels of stress, but the person with little support and few or no effective coping skills may experience more sleep disturbance compared to someone who has friends to talk to about their problems and some practical strategies to help with their sleep.

Tips on how to increase your social supports

Some ways that you can begin to improve your social skills:

✔ Develop your social skills:

- Practise self-hypnosis to gain confidence.

- Practise self-hypnosis to have higher self-esteem.

- Share more personal information about yourself and ask others about their thoughts and feelings

✔ Get to know your neighbours and community:

- Smile and say hello to those who live near you and introduce yourself.

- Make small talk with people in local shops.

- Become a 'regular' at a local park, coffee shop or similar neighbourhood location.

✔ Do volunteer work at any place you feel you can contribute to.

✔ Find a person who can be supportive to share your living space.

These are just a few ideas. Perhaps you can begin to find others that will help you to reach out to others and find people who can be friendly to you.

Using medication for sleep problems

In some cases – however, certainly not all – taking medication to help with sleep may be useful for short periods, but not as a long-term solution. Although sleeping tablets and other sedatives may be helpful in the short term, their use involves a well-known risk of causing dependence, including:

✔ **Psychological dependence:** Where the person taking the medication feels that she can't sleep without drugs.

✔ **Physical dependence:** Where the person experiences withdrawal symptoms and/or emotional disturbance when she stops taking the medication.

If your sleep problem's fairly recent or infrequent with no obvious reasons, we suggest that you simply aim to change your sleep disturbance pattern. Doing this with hypnotism's one way of dealing with the problem. Taking a mild sedative or hypnotic at bedtime for a week or two often suffices – but only after talking with your doctor first.

Sometimes insomnia may be the result of illness or a side effect of prescription drugs. If either of these is the case and you have sleep problems, see your doctor.

Using self-hypnosis to improve your sleep

Hypnotherapy can be helpful with sleep problems when:

✔ Your doctor's ruled out a medical cause

✔ You're resistant to pharmacological approaches

✔ Emotional issues are contributing to your sleep problem

A self-hypnosis script for insomnias

Below is a script for insomnia that you can read. This script is also in audio file on the CD that accompanies this book. This script can also be a springboard for you to use to modify if you want to rewrite it and record it for yourself.

'And as you are relaxing more and more . . . becoming deeper and deeper relaxed . . . deeper and deeper relaxed . . . I want you to know that . . . it is only natural for you to find that each and every night . . . you sleep well . . . sleep better

Each and every night . . . you go to bed at the same time . . . in that way . . . you establish . . . and create . . . a healthy and regular sleeping pattern

And as it comes time for you to go to bed . . . you find that you feel so wonderfully tired

You relax . . . become so relaxed as it gets closer to the time for you to go to bed . . . to sleep

You relax in the knowledge that you are so wonderfully tired

Each and every night . . . calm relaxed and so wonderfully tired that it is only natural for you to . . . look forward . . . look forward to having a wonderful night's sleep

Look forward to enjoying falling asleep . . . and sleeping well throughout the night

And as your bedtime approaches . . . all unwanted thoughts . . . ideas . . . images . . . and feelings fade away . . . fade away . . . fade away

And you enjoy the wonderful sensation of peace . . . calmness . . . and relaxation just before it is time for you to go to bed

As your bedtime approaches . . . all unwanted thoughts . . . ideas . . . images . . . and feelings fade away . . . fade away . . . fade away

And you are left with the wonderful sensation of peace . . . calmness . . . and relaxation just before it is time for you to go to bed

And as you get ready to go to bed . . . your eyelids begin to feel heavy . . . wanting to close

You feel so wonderfully tired . . . and relaxed . . . as you get ready to go to bed

As you get into bed . . . to sleep . . . so the very touch of your bed . . . and the very touch of your sheets . . . becomes a cue . . . a trigger . . . a cue and trigger for you to feel so sleepy and drowsy

Sleepy and drowsy as you get into bed each and every night

And as you lay on your bed . . . gently covered by your bed sheets . . . these are a cue . . . a trigger for you to feel even more sleepy . . . sleepy and tired

The very touch of your bed . . . and the very touch of your sheets . . . becomes a cue . . . a trigger . . . a cue and trigger for you to feel so sleepy and drowsy

And in a strange and curious way . . . as you lay there in bed . . . tired . . . drowsy . . . your eyes wanting to close . . . you try to stay awake

You try to stay awake

And I want you to know that the harder you try to stay awake . . . the sleepier . . . and drowsier you become

Sleepier and drowsier until you drift off to a deep . . . refreshing sleep

The harder you try to stay awake . . . the sleepier . . . and drowsier you become

Sleepier and drowsier until you drift off to a deep . . . refreshing sleep

Being in bed . . . for you . . . means sleep . . . sleep

And you enjoy your sleep

Enjoy your sleep when you are in bed

And you sleep well

Sleep deeply

Sleep throughout the night

Waking at the appropriate time for you . . . each and every morning

And as you sleep . . . sleep throughout the night . . . any thought . . . idea . . . feeling . . . or image . . . can be processed . . . can be worked through . . . at a very safe . . . and deep level . . . so that you really do sleep throughout the night

And the only sign that your mind is working deeply . . . safely . . . processing the thoughts . . . ideas . . . images . . . and feelings of the day . . . will be in the form of lovely . . . beautiful . . . wonderful dreams

No matter what your mind processes whilst you sleep . . . the only sign will be in the form of lovely . . . beautiful . . . wonderful dreams

And should you awaken in the night for any reason . . . perhaps to use the bathroom . . . or to have a drink . . . maybe for no reason whatsoever

Immediately you have done what you need to do and are back in your bed . . . you instantly . . . and immediately fall back into a deep . . . deep . . . refreshing sleep

And if you have awoken just because you have awoken . . . you turn over . . . relax . . . and before you know it . . . you fall asleep again . . . deeply . . . deeply asleep

Sleeping throughout the night

Sleeping well

Whatever thoughts . . . ideas . . . feelings or images from the day . . . or even the week . . .

no matter how old they may be . . . they are processed at a very safe . . . and deep level

As you sleep well . . . sleep deeply . . . sleep throughout the night . . . waking at the most appropriate time for you in the morning

And when you awaken at the right time in the morning . . . you wake up feeling so refreshed

Each morning . . . you wake up revitalised . . . refreshed . . . energised . . . and ready for the day to come

You sleep well throughout the night

Waking each morning . . . revitalised . . . refreshed . . . energised . . . and ready for the day to come

Your mind crystal clear and alert as you awaken each morning

And you go through each day . . . calmer . . . more relaxed . . . more in control than you have felt in a long . . . long while

You find that you handle each and every challenge the day brings you . . . in a way that is so much more calmer . . . efficient . . . and appropriate for you . . . and the needs of that situation

So that when it is time for you to go to bed each and every night . . . you relax . . . relax deeply . . . and enjoy the sense of tiredness . . . and fatigue that grows . . . and grows and grows as it gets to the time for you to go to bed . . . to sleep

Each and every night . . . sleep well . . . sleep deeply and sleep throughout the night . . . and awaken refreshed . . . and alert each and every morning

Every night . . . sleeping well . . . sleeping deeply . . . sleeping throughout the night . . . awaking refreshed . . . and alert each and every morning'

With regular counselling, you can spend much longer talking about the causes of the sleeplessness and still not necessarily solve your sleep problem. Hypnotherapy can be useful in this situation by both addressing unconscious issues and changing behaviours.

Before thinking of medication to help you sleep, consider whether you can take practical measures first, such as:

✔ Changing the room conditions where you're trying to sleep

✔ Dealing with areas of personal stress more effectively

✔ Getting help with financial problems

✔ Undertaking counselling or hypnotherapy sessions

✔ Practising forms of relaxation therapy, such as meditation, yoga or self-hypnosis

If you've read some of the other chapters in this book, you may understand that self-hypnosis helps you in several ways, such as:

✔ Increasing your ability to relax

✔ Allowing you to change unhelpful behaviours

✔ Enabling you to challenge unhelpful beliefs, replacing them with more constructive beliefs

✔ Allowing suppressed, difficult emotions to become conscious when you're ready to work on these issues

The above areas are key to working on emotional and behavioural issues that are often fundamental to sleep disturbances *where no underlying medical problem exists.*

Before applying any of the following hypnotherapy approaches, seek help from your doctor if you suspect that medical conditions may be contributing to your sleep problems. This is important because some type of insomnias that have a medical basis (called *organic insomnias*) will be unlikely to be amenable to hypnotic interventions and require medical attention. But the good news is that most insomnias are not biologically related, but rather more connected to anxiety. Hypnotherapy can certainly help with anxiety-based sleep disorder.

When you think of how to apply self-hypnosis, keep in mind that people with sleep problems often go to bed anticipating a bad night. If you have a sleep problem, think how you experience any anxiety about sleeping. For example, you may become upset at bedtime or just before bedtime. You may become fearful, anxious or experience thoughts about something seemingly unrelated that prevents you from relaxing and being able to sleep.

This anticipation and upset feelings directly lead you into the problems around sleeping and then, of course, the vicious circle develops that you're probably already familiar with – the particular frustrations that you experience that prevent you from sleeping.

Here are three main self-hypnosis approaches for working with sleep problems:

- **Suggestions for relaxing:** A good place to start is giving yourself suggestions to go to sleep when you take your favourite sleep position. Here's an example script you can use after an induction:

  . . . and as soon as I take my favourite position for sleeping . . . this is the signal for my unconscious to enter a hypnotic sleep. This sleep then quickly turns into a restful, undisturbed night's sleep from which I awaken at the appropriate time.

- **Suggestions to return to sleep after awakening:** Some people can sleep but then awake and find returning to sleep difficult, especially if they wake up with a need to urinate. If you find that you frequently wake yourself by needing to use the toilet in the middle of your sleep, you may give yourself suggestions to limit your fluid intake in the hours preceding your bedtime. Here are some possible phrases for your self-hypnosis applications:

  I have no desire to drink fluids in the hour preceding my bedtime.

  I don't have to be wide awake in order to use the toilet and I can do this while remaining partly asleep and then return to bed, where I can go into an even deeper sleep than before.

  I become very involved with boring tasks that I don't enjoy until sleep becomes a more attractive idea . . .

- **Suggestions that you can eventually sleep:** Many people with sleep problems over-estimate the amount of time they're awake. Often people with sleep problems *do* actually sleep during some part of the night *but don't realise that they do*. If you suspect that this is happening for you, then try giving yourself reassuring messages that you can gradually fall asleep. You can also reassure yourself that:

  . . . my physical health isn't suffering and I can become even healthier and better able to cope in the daytime with anything, anybody or any situation that I have to handle in my daily life.

This is important so that you don't worry about your health or ability to cope while you're working with self-hypnosis to improve the quality of your sleep.

✔ **Using suggestions that work with the natural rhythm of sleep cycles:** Human sleep cycles include rotating through phases of lighter and deeper sleep states. If you understand that this variation in sleep states is natural, then experiencing the various states of sleep becomes okay. A sample self-hypnosis script for this may be something like:

. . . and I'm very relaxed in my lighter states of sleep and accept that these are completely natural and lead to even deeper sleep states.

The more you understand yourself, the more you're able to adapt some of the example self-hypnosis scripts. Avoid saying things that are unconstructive and especially avoid direct commands to 'go to sleep now'. Think more seductively, educationally and reassuringly. Also, be patient and don't expect an overnight cure. You do eventually get the sleep you want.

Part IV

Overcoming Problems with Self-Hypnosis

The 5th Wave   By Rich Tennant

"Here's a tip – if you hear yourself snoring, you're hypnotised too deeply."

In this part . . .

In this Part we lift the lid on dealing with those behaviours which can cause you health problems. If you're concerned that you may eat or drink too much, or if you want a leg up to help you quit smoking, you can find what you need right here.

We show you how to recognise the emotional and behavioural factors that push you towards making unhealthy choices in the way you live, and how to use self-hypnosis to gain control over them.

Chapter 14

Quitting Smoking

Smoking's a pleasant pastime for many people. We're not trying to be controversial, nor are we trying to negate what this chapter's about – we're simply explaining why an estimated 1.3 billion people in the world spend huge amounts of their hard-earned cash on doing something that's probably, in the end, going to kill them. The good news is that once the realisation kicks in that the health benefits of quitting far outweigh the pleasure you gain from puffing away like a steam engine, then everything's over for the coffin nails (or should we say coughing nails?).

The most potent factor involved in keeping you attached to your fiery pacifier is nicotine. Nicotine's the drug in cigarettes that keeps you hooked. With each puff of cigarette smoke you take, you inhale nicotine into your bloodstream, which then carries the nicotine to your brain. Over time, your body and brain get so used to having nicotine floating around that when you try to stop smoking your body throws a major hissy fit, *et voilà*: you go into withdrawal. In order to feel normal, you have to inhale more cigarette smoke and you're addicted.

Addiction and *withdrawal* are terms to describe how your body handles certain drugs. If you and your body can only function properly with the drug in your system, then you're addicted to that drug. The nasty physical and psychological feelings you get when you don't take that drug mean that you're in withdrawal. In order to get rid of those nasty feelings you take more of the drug and then you can function normally again.

Nicotine isn't the only drug in cigarettes. Up to 600 other chemicals are legally added to tobacco in order to make smoking more palatable.

Unfortunately, when you burn many of these they create toxic substances that can do all sorts of nasty things to your body. In case you aren't aware, cigarette smoking can result in:

- Cancer
- Lung disease
- Heart disease
- Sexual performance and fertility problems
- Premature aging
- Making illnesses such as asthma or diabetes worse

Even though the above may seem very depressing for a smoker, the UK organisation Action on Smoking and Health (ASH) brings you some very good news. Its statistics show that when you quit smoking you immediately begin to reduce all the health risks and start to maximise your chances of good health:

- After 20 minutes your blood pressure and pulse rate begin to drop.
- After 8 hours the nicotine and carbon monoxide levels in your blood have reduced. Carbon monoxide's a gas that the burning cigarette creates that bullies oxygen out of the way in your bloodstream, making breathing more difficult.
- After 24 hours carbon monoxide and nicotine have disappeared from your body. Your senses of smell and taste improve too.
- After 1 month you begin to look younger as you rehydrate and your wrinkles begin to fade.
- During the first nine months coughing and wheezing reduce.
- After a year your risk of having a heart attack lessens by a half.
- After ten years your risk of developing lung cancer halves.
- After 15 years your risk of having a heart attack's no different to someone who's never smoked.

You can quit smoking in many ways, the most common of which include:

- **Nicotine replacement therapy:** Sometimes called NRT, this is a means of getting nicotine into your body without you having to inhale all of the other hazardous chemicals that cigarettes contain. Once you've swapped the cigarettes for the NRT, you start to decrease the amount of nicotine you're taking until you no longer need the drug.

✔ **Other drug treatments:** These help by altering the way your body responds to nicotine. However, some controversy exists about the side effects that some of these drugs may have.

✔ **Going cold turkey:** In other words, stopping smoking without any form of drug intervention to help you on your way.

Whichever route to living a smoke-free life you choose, you need to understand that each of these routes relies on your willpower and your desire to quit. Self-hypnosis can help you build up both your willpower and your desire to quit.

Understanding Your Smoking Habits

Smoking's an addiction and a habit. Both of these combine to seemingly conspire against the smoker trying to quit. However, this is all part and parcel of the cycle of addiction, which we discuss in Chapter 4 – have a look at that chapter, where we show that part of breaking the cycle's being aware of what keeps it going round . . . and round . . . and round. In effect, by being aware of what keeps the cycle spinning you're poking a metaphorical stick into the spokes of the cycle and stopping it dead in its path.

The word *habit* has many definitions. When used in psychology habit typically refers to behaviour patterns that a person develops over time that eventually become automatic.

The cycle of addiction isn't alone. It has a partner that, when you properly understand it, can be a useful ally in helping you become a non-smoker. So let's welcome the *quit cycle* to the cycle race!

Getting to grips with the quit cycle

If you're thinking about quitting smoking then you're already pedalling away on the quit cycle. In fact, you may have been on it for quite a while already without even realising it. The quit cycle's a recognised set of thoughts and behaviours that accompany every attempt to give something up. That means smoking too. Have a look at Figure 14-1 and see if you recognise where you are on the quit cycle.

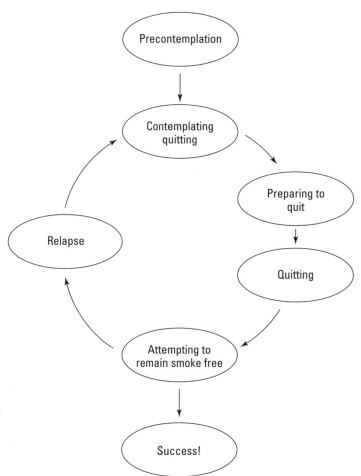

Figure 14-1:
The quit
cycle.

The stages of the quit cycle

Let's look at what each stage of the quit cycle means and how each can apply
to you:

- ✔ **Pre-contemplation:** At this stage quitting hasn't entered your mind.
  You're perhaps unaware of or denying the risks to your health that
  smoking brings. You may not even believe that you can quit successfully
  (oh, but you can) or are even afraid of living without cigarettes as an
  integral part of your life.

- ✔ **Contemplating quitting:** Here, discontent with your smoking's beginning
  to set in. Perhaps you're more aware of the health risks. Maybe that smoker's cough in the morningis getting you down. At the same time you may
  be feeling that you're too attached to those little white sticks to let them
  go. This is a period of toing-and-froing over your attitudes to smoking.

✔ **Preparing to quit:** The benefits of becoming a non-smoker are becoming more and more apparent to you. You haven't quit yet, but you're making serious plans to quit and are exploring the perceived obstacles and possibilities that living a smoke-free life throws your way.

✔ **Quitting:** This is exactly what it says on the tin. You've put your plans into action and have stopped smoking. You're in the early days of the process and you're working hard to succeed.

✔ **Attempting to remain smoke free:** Your new smoke-free life's becoming easier to cope with. Your non-smoking behaviours are becoming more and more natural and you're feeling the benefit of a healthier lifestyle, with thoughts about smoking become fewer and fewer.

✔ **Relapse:** Oops! You thought you had enough self-control to have just one cigarette at that party. The one turned into two, two turned into four and before you knew you were back to being a fully fledged smoker. Or maybe you experienced some emotional crisis that sent you seeking that smoky old aid to calming down. Whatever the cause, relapse is a natural (though not essential) part of quitting and, as many ex-smokers can attest, is simply another stepping stone to success. Relapse is *never* a case of failing, simply that you haven't quite succeeded yet.

If you do relapse don't worry, just step back on to the cycle and continue pedalling. Success really is just around the corner.

✔ **Success:** A smoke-free life's now the norm and you're reaping the benefits of being a non-smoker. Thoughts of smoking are few and far between and any chance of relapse is fading into the past (though don't ever become complacent about that). Be rightfully proud of your achievement!

Factors affecting the quit cycle

You may wonder why some people seem to go from contemplation to success very rapidly, while others spend more time pedalling round via the relapse route before succeeding. Several factors are involved:

✔ **Determination to quit:** The more determined you are, the more likely you are to succeed.

✔ **Willingness to persevere:** Quitting anything has its challenges. If you're determined to succeed then you find the strength to overcome the challenges.

✔ **Reasons for quitting:** If your reason for quitting's motivational then that keeps you determined and fuels your perseverance.

✔ **Life events:** You're far better to quit when you can foresee as far as possible that life's going to run smoothly. In other words, quitting at times of stress such as examinations isn't a good idea, as your feelings on occasions such as this challenge your determination and perseverance.

Wherever you are on the quit cycle, self-hypnosis can help you achieve your smoke-free success.

Working out when you smoke

Every smoker has a pattern to his smoking. Understanding that pattern helps you plan your strategy for quitting. The first thing to think about is how many cigarettes you smoke. Our experience is that many people have an estimate that's quite a few cigarettes short of how many they actually smoke a day. So be honest with yourself. A good way to do this is to keep a smoking diary so that you can note your daily tally.

You can also use the diary to highlight all your smoking habits and give you an understanding of their pattern. You should note the four 'Ws': what, when, why and where:

✔ **What?** Keep a note of the following:

- What type of tobacco you're smoking – for example, is it low tar or high tar?

- Are your cigarettes normal size or king size?

- Are your cigarettes roll-ups or pre-rolled?

✔ **When?** Keep a note of the following:

- The times each day that you smoke

- The number of cigarettes you smoke at these times

- Who you're smoking with

- What you're doing when you smoke

✔ **Why?** Keep a note of why you're smoking each cigarette. For example:

- Are you smoking because that's what you do at that time?

- Are you smoking for emotional reasons such as stress?

- Are you smoking because others are smoking around you?

- Are you smoking because someone's offered you a cigarette?

✔ **What?** For each of the times you note in your diary, think about how you want to be at these times as a non-smoker. Think:

- What do you want to be thinking?

- What do you want to be feeling?

- In what way do you want to be behaving?

- What do you want to be saying to yourself and others?

Keep a note of how much money you spend each day on smoking. Begin to think about how you can treat yourself with all the cash that you save after you give up smoking.

Spend a week working through your diary each day. Remember to include the weekend as this is often when you really will let rip with your smoking. The answers to the preceding questions form the basis for suggestions that you can use during your self-hypnosis.

People often make the mistake of thinking that smoking's a great stress buster. They may use this as an excuse not to stop, claiming that smoking keeps them calm. How wrong they are! If you look at how nicotine and the other chemicals in cigarettes affect your body, you can see that they cause the physical effects of stress: increase in blood pressure, increase in heart rate, increase in adrenaline and so on. What people perceive as being stress release is the distraction that smoking provides. In this day and age legislation dictates that you have to go outside in order to smoke, which removes you from the stressful environment. The ritual of lighting up distracts your mind. In effect, you take a break. As a non-smoker you can still benefit by taking a break and getting out of the stressful environment. As a non-smoker you get the added benefit that you aren't pumping your body full of chemicals that mimic stress, and so you find that you cope with stress in a much better way.

Understanding the difference between need and habit

No matter what brand of cigarettes you smoke, everything boils down to the fact that for most smokers really only two types of cigarette exist: those that they need because of their addiction and those that they smoke out of habit.

- ✔ **Need:** As we say at the start of this chapter, need's a physical feeling that's the result of your body looking for the nicotine that it's missing when you don't smoke. An intense craving for a cigarette often characterises the need. Once you cave in and have a cigarette, the craving and any other unpleasant feelings go away.

- ✔ **Habit:** This is the conscious or unconscious psychological drive to have a cigarette that comes from behaviours you develop as you go further in your smoking career. The conscious drive comes from missing the ritualistic behaviour of smoking. The feelings aren't intense, however the psychological compulsion to smoke triggers the behaviour. You often notice the unconscious drive at those times when you've lit up without even realising that you're doing so. The behaviour's sunk into your mind so deeply that you light up on autopilot.

Being aware of the difference between habit and need is very useful as you can create strategies to deal with each. You can often deal with your habits by finding alternative healthy behaviours that overcome the compulsion to smoke. For example, instead of nipping out for a fag break at work you can nip out for a quick walk and a drink of water or fruit juice. A much healthier alternative!

You can deal with the need by building up your willpower to get through those nicotine cravings. The cravings generally last between three to five minutes and then they're gone. During this time you can distract your mind by focusing on why you're quitting smoking.

Most smokers risk dehydration because they exhale more water vapour from their lungs than non-smokers. By drinking more water regularly throughout the day you help rehydrate your body. A very similar thing also happens to vitamin C and other vitamins. Smokers can have 40 per cent less vitamin C in their body than non-smokers as the various toxic substances in cigarette smoke help destroy the vitamin. By enjoying natural and healthy sources of vitamin C, such as fruit and fruit juice, you can help rebalance the vitamin C depletion while at the same time finding a healthy distraction from smoking.

With this in mind, note in your diary those cigarettes that are purely habit and those that you feel you need. Be honest with yourself and you may be surprised to find how few cigarettes you actually need compared with the number you smoke. Consider ways of helping yourself overcome these habitual behaviours and needs and note them in your diary too.

Preparing to Quit

Now's the time to prepare as you say goodbye to cigarettes. First, as you plan your way forward to a smoke-free life, have a look at Chapter 3, where we talk about goal setting. Planning things gives you a structure around which to work while incorporating your self-hypnosis.

The first thing to decide is your quit date. Choose a date in the near future. Make sure that it's a time when you're reasonably sure that you're not going to be experiencing any major life events to reduce the temptation to relapse. You can look on your quit date as the date on which you're going to give yourself the gift of health.

Make a list of all the reasons for wanting to quit. Make copies of the list and keep one with you as a motivator.

Look over your smoking diary that we discuss in 'Working out when you smoke', earlier in this chapter, and really understand your smoking pattern. Then look at all the notes you've made about how you want to be a non-smoker at those times when you normally smoke. We show an example in Table 14-1.

Table 14-1	Smoker vs. Non-smoker
Times When I Smoke	*How I Want to Be as a Non-smoker*
First thing in the morning with a cup of coffee.	To avoid thinking about smoking as I enjoy a healthy orange juice.
As I walk to the train on my way to work.	To focus on planning my day and forgetting about smoking.
Enjoying a beer with friends in a bar.	To enjoy the company of my friends, focusing on the conversation and forgetting about the fact that other people are smoking. To feel comfortable just holding the glass in my hand and nothing else.
	To feel proud of myself that I'm smoke free.

Have a look at Chapter 6 where you will learn how to create some suggestions for yourself based on the 'How I Want to Be as a Non-smoker' column and your list of reasons for quitting.

Don't forget the money side of things either. Look at how much you can save as a non-smoker. Plan what you're going to do with that extra cash and create suggestions for this too. After all, thinking about this treat for yourself helps motivate you to stay free of tobacco.

Some people find a useful idea is to half fill a large jar with water and after smoking each cigarette to put the stub into the water and shake the jar up. As the jar fills up you can open the lid and have a sniff of the foul-smelling concoction it contains. This acts as a reminder to yourself that this is what you're putting into your body.

Advertising you're a smoke-free zone

Don't hide your light under a bushel. Let the world know what you're doing. Tell your family, friends and work colleagues. Share with them your quit date and keep them informed of your progress.

By letting others in on what you're doing, you create a network of support that helps keep you on the right track. Choose a few people who you can trust to talk to if you feel that you have a risk of relapse. This, combined with your self-hypnosis, creates a formidable ally on your route to a new and healthier lifestyle. Who knows, you may even be the good influence that others need in order to join you in quitting smoking.

Positively dumping the paraphernalia

Smoking's a ritual: taking the packet of cigarettes out of your pocket, selecting one and placing the cigarette in your mouth, finding the lighter, lighting up, arranging the ashtray and so on. Like every smoker, you have the tools of your ritual littered around your house and workplace. These tools and accoutrements provide subtle yet powerful cues that worm their way into your mind, whispering away at you to smoke: 'Go on. You know you want one.' They become part of maintaining your smoking habit.

When your day comes to quit smoking, search your drawers and cupboards and root out all those old lighters, boxes of matches, empty and half-empty packets of cigarettes and all the ashtrays you can find . . . and bin them. Get rid of them. Trash them.

The importance of removing these items from your environment is that they're no longer there in the background tempting you to step off the straight and narrow. In fact, you may want to counter the old smoking ritual that these represent with a ritual removal and destruction of these trappings of your ex-smoking life.

Using Self-Hypnosis to Stop Smoking

Hypnosis isn't magic and can't help you stop smoking if you don't want to. If you don't want to quit then that means you're still in the pre-contemplation part of the quit cycle. As hypnotherapy can't make you do anything you don't want to, self-hypnosis is of little value to you at this time. But keep reading. You never know, you may change your mind.

However, you're probably reading this part of the book because you do want to make a change and stop smoking. Self-hypnosisis a powerful aid that helps build on your own willpower and desire to stop. The four exercises in this section address different aspects of quitting that relate to the quit cycle that we outline in 'Getting to grips with the quit cycle', earlier in this chapter. However, no matter where you are in the quit cycle, each exercise is of value to you as they all reinforce what you're doing.

As you prepare for each exercise, refer to the suggestions you prepared earlier in this chapter under 'Preparing to Quit'. Chapter 5 gives guidance on going into and out of trance.

Preparing to become a non-smoker

This exercise relates to the 'contemplating quitting' and 'preparing to quit' parts of the quit cycle:

1. Spend time reviewing why you want to stop smoking.

2. Set your quit date and commit to keeping that date.

3. Plan and then commit to practising self-hypnosis at least once a day between now and the day you've committed to quit.

4. Each time you practise:

   a. Guide yourself into trance and go to your favourite place.

   b. Spend a minute or two being aware of how good you feel in your favourite place.

   c. Think of your quit date and suggest to yourself that you're keeping this date and that you're looking forward to enjoying becoming a non-smoker.

   d. Begin to review all your reasons for wanting to become a non-smoker.

   e. Imagine yourself enjoying all the benefits that being a non-smoker brings you. This should include the social, financial and health benefits.

   f. Affirm to yourself that you're becoming a non-smoker because you want to.

   g. Think of all those people who are pleased and delighted that you're stopping.

   h. Think of how pleased you are that you're stopping.

   i. Once again, review your reasons for stopping and congratulate yourself for doing this.

   j. Create an image that you're able to think of each day that helps keep your motivation going.

   k. Imagine yourself back in your favourite place.

   l. Once again, think of your quit date and reaffirm that you're keeping to it.

   m. Wake yourself up from trance.

Becoming and remaining a non-smoker

This exercise relates to the 'quitting' and 'attempting to remain smoke-free' stages of the quit cycle. Practise this sequence as soon as you can on your quit date. Make sure that you've got rid of all your smoking paraphernalia from your home and office. Commit to practising this exercise and the two that follow as often as you feel necessary.

Review your daily smoking habits. Review how you want to be as a non-smoker at the times you used to smoke.

1. Guide yourself into trance and go to your favourite place.

2. Enjoy spending a minute or two in your favourite place.

3. Imagine that you can feel the confidence to stop smoking and remain a non-smoker flowing through your mind and body.

4. Review your reasons for becoming a non-smoker.

5. Tell yourself how happy you are that you're now a non-smoker.

6. Tell your body that you're now looking after it and have made cigarettes a thing of the past.

7. Tell your body that it can be pleased that you're now a non-smoker.

8. Begin to imagine a typical smoking day. As you imagine each time you used to smoke, tell yourself that you're now a non-smoker and then imagine how you want to be at that time as a non-smoker.

9. Imagine being around other smokers and enjoying yourself as a non-smoker.

10. Imagine feeling proud as you say 'no thank you, I don't smoke' to those who offer you a cigarette.

11. Imagine all the money that you're now saving as a non-smoker and what you're going to use the cash for as a reward for yourself.

12. Imagine all the health benefits you're now receiving as a non-smoker.

13. Imagine that you're back in your favourite place and enjoy the feelings you find there.

14. Imagine that you're absorbing all the psychological strength you need to help you cope with any challenging feelings or situations.

15. Wake yourself from trance.

Many people quit cigarettes with minimal withdrawal. However, if you find withdrawal symptoms challenging you, remember that the feelings only last a few minutes. Have a drink of water or fresh fruit juice as this helps distract you. Then remind yourself of all the reasons why you're becoming a non-smoker. Perhaps give one of your trusted friends a call and talk to them. Any withdrawal symptoms you may experience lose their power as they fade over a couple of weeks. Keep using self-hypnosis and before you know where you are you're feeling fine and any unpleasant feelings are a fading memory.

Handling temptation

This exercise relates to 'attempting to remain smoke free' while helping to avoid the 'relapse' point on the quit cycle. You should practise this as soon after quitting as possible and then reinforce the exercise several times a week as necessary. If you know that you're going into a situation where you're likely to be tempted to smoke, then plan for successful coping by practising this exercise while focusing specifically on that situation. Forewarned is forearmed!

Make a note of all the times you think temptation may rear its ugly head and think of how you want to be at these times:

1. **Guide yourself into trance and go to your favourite place.**

2. **Spend a minute or two enjoying the feelings you find there.**

3. **Thank yourself for becoming a non-smoker.**

4. **Review the reasons why you stopped smoking and again thank yourself for becoming a non-smoker.**

5. **Repeat to yourself three or four times that you are now, and are going to remain, a non-smoker.**

6. **Tell yourself that no matter the temptation, you have the strength to remain a non-smoker.**

7. **Begin to imagine those times when temptation to smoke may come your way.**

8. **At each of these times, imagine how you want to be thinking, feeling and behaving in order to remain a non-smoker.**

9. **Imagine yourself remaining a non-smoker after the temptation has passed.**

10. **Congratulate yourself for all the times you've already resisted temptation and then congratulate yourself once more for all the times you have yet to resist temptation.**

11. Once again, imagine that you're back in your favourite place and enjoy the feelings you find there.

12. Feel a sense of pride in yourself for becoming a non-smoker.

13. Again, remind yourself of all the reasons why you've become a non-smoker and congratulate yourself for doing so.

14. Wake yourself from trance.

If you relapse, don't worry. Congratulate yourself for having done so well already, affirm that you're now going to do better and then start again on the quit trail.

Inhaling healthier habits

This exercise relates to 'attempting to remain smoke free' and reinforces 'success' on the quit cycle. The exercise offers healthy habits that help reinforce your reasons for remaining a non-smoker. It also addresses a concern that some people who are quitting feel that they may put on weight as a result.

1. Guide yourself into trance and go to your favourite place.

2. Spend a minute or two enjoying the feelings you find there.

3. Spend some time focusing on the health benefits that becoming a non-smoker brings you.

4. Imagine how much extra energy you have that makes you more productive during the day.

5. Imagine how much more attractive you are now that you're no longer deliberately aging yourself prematurely through dehydration.

6. Again, imagine how much more attractive you are now that you no longer smell like a stale ashtray.

7. Congratulate yourself for having become a non-smoker and commit to remaining a non-smoker.

8. Suggest to yourself that you're not replacing cigarettes with anything other than good health and healthy habits.

9. Suggest to yourself that you're also controlling your eating as you're not replacing cigarettes with food.

10. Imagine being in control of your eating habits as you enjoy a much healthier lifestyle.

11. **Imagine yourself as a smoke-free, healthy person who's more in control of your lifestyle than ever before.**

12. **Imagine yourself back in your favourite place and enjoy the healthy feelings you find there.**

13. **Congratulate yourself for being a non-smoker and for being in control of your healthy new lifestyle.**

14. **Wake yourself from trance.**

If you find that you do need some extra help controlling your weight, then have a look at Chapter 16, where we talk about controlling your eating habits.

Use all of the exercises in this section as often as you need. Remember that you were born a non-smoker and therefore you already know how to be a non-smoker, so why not be reborn into a healthy new lifestyle?

Chapter 15

Keeping a Handle on Your Drinking

Drinking's a huge part of western society but alcohol consumption's a slippery subject. When does 'a little drink' become a drink too many? The control of drinking's also a matter of perception.

Often one of us (Mike) has met new clients who've come to receive hypnotherapy to be able to 'drink less'. After speaking further to clarify their goals, what these clients often mean is that they want to be able to be more in control of their drinking habits. So, for example, if you are urged to go out after work for a 'quick drink', you do just that and don't end up closing down the bar, and having a bad hangover the next day. So typically, people with drink problems have fuzzy goals. They typically want to drink less, but less is a moveable target. Compare 'less' on a Tuesday night when you have to get up for work on Wednesday morning with 'less' on a Friday evening after work to celebrate someone's birthday. Of course, less on a week night compared to less at a bar on a Spanish beach while on holiday is also a vastly different proposition.

Keep in mind that hypnotherapy works with people who want more control over their problems. In this chapter we discuss how you can assess your drinking. However, the chapter can't address working with untreated alcoholism.

Alcoholism's a medical condition that only a doctor can diagnose. You can't self-diagnose for alcoholism.

Alcoholism's a different matter to wanting to drink less, and alcoholism requires medical attention as a priority before any other treatments. In fact, *any* addiction with a biochemical basis is the domain of the physician first. Hypnotism isn't effective for treating alcoholism if medical treatment hasn't occurred first.

With that caveat out of the way, hypnotherapy and self-hypnosis in particular can be very effective ways of maintaining good control over drinking. So this chapter's most relevant to those who don't have a severe problem in terms of drink addiction (alcoholism), but who do want to have greater control over their drinking.

This chapter helps you reach a greater understanding of how your thoughts and emotions can influence your drinking patterns. This helps you to identify your drinking habits and thereby have greater control over them.

And yes . . . drinking less is possible – especially if the 'less' is a *consistent, quantifiable* less throughout the week.

Understanding Your Emotional Need to Drink

Drinking can often be used as a way of helping you to cope with personal problems. Initially a drink may help you to feel better, but dependence on it as a way of coping soon develops into an additional problem. By understanding and dealing with the emotional pain that you are trying to numb with alcohol, you can begin to overcome your problems with drink.

It should also be noted that for serious alcohol addiction problems, you should always seek medical help first.

A helpful therapeutic concept is that thoughts give birth to emotions. Therefore, by directing your thoughts, you have greater control over your emotions.

Which best describes how you handle difficult emotions (for example anger, sadness, stress, fear, self-loathing, anxiety)? Do you:

- Allow yourself to feel your feelings
- Distract yourself through keeping busy with activities
- Get upset and take your feelings out on the furniture
- Have a few drinks and numb your feelings

Understanding the problems of alcohol

Because alcohol's a depressant, when you drink in small amounts you can feel more confident, happy and relaxed. But drinking too much alcohol can rapidly lead to impaired judgement, anger and low feelings.

Alcohol also plays a large part in suicides, particularly among young people. One study by Shafii et al. of suicide victims aged 12–19, reported in the *American Journal of Psychiatry*

in 1985, found that almost three-quarters (70 per cent) had a history of alcohol or drug abuse.

Alcohol dependency can also wreck relationships, particularly if both members of a couple develop a dependency on drink. Because alcohol can amplify your existing mood, drinking when angry can often lead to feelings of being out of control, with rage that you don't normally express when you're sober.

Two things may be blatantly clear in the above list: 1) We prefer that you choose the first choice; and 2) The choices get progressively worse in descending order!

Difficult feelings are what humans tend to be frightened of, yet when you face them they provide the key to overcoming your problems.

Thinking about how you feel about drinking

Let's assume that you're drinking too much and that an emotional basis exists for this. Most therapists assume that this is the case.

tMany people feel that their dependence on alcohol may have begun for some of the following reasons:

- ✔ **A habit that got out of control:** For example, weekend drinking as a youth with friends.

- ✔ **Dutch courage drinking:** Being in an environment where drinking's encouraged to perform a difficult task, such as the entertainment industry or some forms of public speaking.

- ✔ **Occupational drinking:** Certain jobs or pastimes may lead to drink, for example working late-night shifts in a restaurant, or having to wine and dine clients, being involved in work that's based around drink and food, being involved in bar-based environments such as with a rock or country music band, a work environment where going to the pub or bar's a regular activity and so on.

✔ **Loneliness:** Feeling sorry for yourself can lead to increased alcohol dependency, which in turn can compound the problem of not being able to form a lasting relationship. Research by Dr D Cornah for the Mental Health Foundation in 2006 shows that almost one-third of people in the UK drink to forget their problems.

At the end of this chapter we include a self-hypnosis script (see 'Script for challenging low self-esteem issues related to drinking'), which will help you to feel better about yourself and begin to help you address alcohol issues.

The strength of any drink is described as the proportion of the drink's volume that's pure alcohol, using *alcohol by volume* or ABV.

One *unit* consists of 10 millilitres or 8 grams of pure alcohol. That's the amount in a 25-millilitre single measure of spirits (ABV 40 per cent), a third of a pint of beer (ABV 5–6 per cent) or half a 175-millilitre glass of red wine (ABV 12 per cent).

Facing up to your feelings

Feelings create the spice in your life and without them we would be robots. Part of being human is having an emotional life. While people have opinions about emotions, few people understand – let alone can manage – their feelings when they feel emotionally wounded or hurt. At times like these, we can avoid facing the pain, via many possible escape routes, such as alcohol, or we can learn to face up to our feelings.

So how do you confront your difficult feelings that may lead you to drink? Chances are your closest friends have been dropping useful hints as they observe the increase in your drinking. That is, if you haven't lost all of your friends already.

Here are some practical tips on managing your emotions:

✔ **Become more physically active::**Regular exercise can help to lift your moods.

✔ **Eat healthily:** Ensure that you have not let your eating habits deteriorate into fast foods or junk foods. Eat well, but also avoid overeating.

✔ **Cultivate friends you can trust:** Spend time with someone supportive you can confide in who will keep your conversation confidential.

✔ **Sleep well:** Try to sleep regular hours. Don't go to bed too late.

✔ **Practise self-hypnosis:** Through regular practice you can calm yourself, boost your confidence and develop new coping skills.

We want to manage our feelings rather than have them manage us. We want to be clever about understanding why we feel hurt and what thoughts we have that give birth to these feelings. It is difficult to be objective about your feelings when you are upset, but the ability to stand back and observe how your thoughts influence your feelings is what helps you to develop emotional intelligence.

If you are going through a difficult period in your life, stopping drinking during that time is advisable until you find a way to resolve your problem. You're then able to better understand what feelings are dominating you and causing you to drink. Certainly, if you find it impossible to stop drinking, then this is a clear sign that you need to seek professional help. Start with your doctor as drink problems can have potential medical implications. You could also at the same time seek help with your emotional issues from a counsellor or hypnotherapist.

Keep in mind that a medical professional's probably not able to help you with the emotional side of things, but can give you guidance on any biochemical and/or physical conditions that you need to attend to. You should do the 'facing your feelings' part in conjunction with a clinical professional, such as a counsellor or psychotherapist, or a hypnotherapist who has a good background in working with emotional difficulties. We strongly recommend against doing this on your own. If you've developed a problem with drink, the chances aren't good that you can sort the problem out alone, and you should overcome any feelings of shame or humiliation at not being able to do so. Simply feel the fear and do it (contact help) anyway.

You may feel that you have little motivation to seek help and that you can weather the storm and your drinking problem's going to go away. And the problem may go away – temporarily. But do you discover how to avoid the problem in the future by taking this approach? Probably not. Willpower and determination can be helpful, but working with a counsellor or hypnotherapist can provide you with both insights and new understandings that can lead to lasting changes in your behaviour and your thinking – and hence your feelings.

Discovering Your Drinking Patterns

This chapter's about reaching a greater understanding of the best way for you to use alcohol. Unless you're a medically diagnosed alcoholic, you don't necessarily have to stop drinking altogether. But you do need to be consistent in keeping to your limits. If you can't stick to a limit, then you probably should consider abstinence from alcohol.

However, through the use of hypnosis, you can be both relaxed and vigilant about keeping to your limits. The first step's understanding your alcohol drinking patterns.

If you feel that you have a serious problem with any of the drinking issues this section lists, you can reassure yourself that people, professionals and organisations exist that can help you. You can also use self-hypnosis techniques to help you to maximise the help that you receive.

In 'Establishing your drinking goals', later in this chapter, we look at specific self-hypnosis approaches that you can use to ensure that you decrease your drinking and establish safe drinking goals.

Working out how much you drink

Before we tell you about hypnotherapy techniques, your first practical step is to focus on how much alcohol you drink.

If you note your alcohol consumption pattern over a typical week, for example, you can begin to understand your drinking pattern. This understanding can help you to have greater control over the way you drink and hence greater pleasure.

Keeping an alcohol diary

Try keeping a written record of how much you drink and under what circumstances. This should be something that you can do quickly. A sample alcohol diary might look like Table 15-1:

Table 15-1	A Sample Alcohol Diary
Monday	No alcohol
Tuesday	Evening meal with Antonia = 2 units
Wednesday	Went to Jim's and watched football on TV = 10 units
Thursday	No alcohol
Friday	Mark's going away party after work – 20 units
Saturday	Dinner at my father-in-law's = 6 units
Sunday	Two glasses of wine at Mary and Tom's house = 2 units

Each week you could try totalling the units of alcohol that you have consumed. To calculate units of wine, here are some guidelines:

✔ A glass of wine rated at 13 per cent in a 175-millilitre glass = 2.3 units

✔ A glass of wine rated at 13 per cent in a 250-millilitre glass = 3.25 units

You can measure other units of alcohol by searching on the internet under phrases such as 'units of alcohol calculator' or 'alcohol by volume calculator'.

Focusing on factors that affect your drinking patterns

Have you ever had a drinking buddy who could outdrink you? I (Mike) had a seven-foot tall, extremely fit basketball-playing friend in college who used to mischievously challenge me to try to keep up with the amount of beer he could drink. Needless to say, I could never keep up with my giant drinking buddy and paid the price more than once for trying.

One of the important considerations is to understand how alcohol impacts on you directly – as opposed to a friend who is a seven-foot tall athlete – and why you may be more likely to feel the effect of booze before someone else does. Hint: physical characteristics have a LOT to do with it!

Three factors to consider to help understand your drinking patterns include:

✔ **Your specific physical characteristics:** Physical characteristics to keep in mind regarding drinking include the following:

- Age

- Physical size

- Gender

- Whether you drink with food or on an empty stomach

- General health and fitness levels

Because everyone's different, the above factors are all relevant in terms of how alcohol affects you. For example, a single glass of wine has more effect on a petite, elderly woman in frail health than a 20-something male who's fit and healthy.

Official health departments provide information on the recommended maximum alcohol consumption levels for men and women. You should consider your physical characteristics as a crucial part of your drinking patterns. For the US, you can find information at the National Institute of Alcohol Abuse and Alcoholism: www.niaaa.nih.gov/. For the UK, you can find information at the Department of Health: www.dh.gov.uk/en/Publichealth/ Healthimprovement/Alcoholmisuse/DH_072581 and at the NHS: www. drinking.nhs.uk/.

Working out what type of drinker you are

Self-hypnosis works most effectively when you have some understanding of your problem. With drinking problems, this means understanding the why and how of your own issues. Once this is understood, you can more accurately tailor your own approach to resolving your problems by dealing with how you have understood your specific issues. In this section, we explore the 'why' of drinking in terms of describing the *motives* people have for drinking. We explore the 'how' in a following discussion about drinking *styles*.

Your drinking motives

To get to grips with why you drink, it might be useful to understand your *motives*. In 2006 researchers Emmanuel Kuntsche, Ronald Knibbe and Gerhard Gmel wrote a paper called 'Who drinks and why?': A review of socio-demographic, personality, and contextual issues behind the drinking motives in young people. *Addictive Behaviors*, 31(10), 1844–57.

Their paper outlined four different personality-based motives for drinking:

- ✔ **Social motives:** People with social motives drink in order to feel part of a group, be it the after-work drinking crowd, or being at a party. We have all heard the expression, 'social drinker', and this implies someone who drinks moderately and only in social contexts. People with a social motive tend to drink less at home, in bars and more at gatherings with members of the opposite gender.

- ✔ **Conformity motives:** This group includes those who drink due to pressure from others, in order to be accepted by them. The research for this group could not generalise on a specific personality type nor on the context in which conformity drinking occurred.

- ✔ **Enhancement motives:** These people drink to feel good, to get drunk, or just for its own sake. They are looking for excitement in the form of intense and new experiences. In terms of personality, they tend to be outgoing, impulsive and can also be aggressive. They tend to drink in bars, or at the homes of friends, and usually with friends of the same sex.

- ✔ **Coping motives:** This group describes people who drink in order to cope with stress or difficult emotions. These people tend to have much lower self-esteem than the other groups. Drinking tends to occur in the home, and less so in social settings.

Of the above four drinking motive groups, those that tend to have problems with alcoholism are the enhancement and coping types. These two groups tend to be the heavier drinkers. If you feel that you fit into one of these two groups, you should seek help from your doctor.

Your drinking style

✔ Above we looked at the 'why' do you drink by discussing motives. The second part of working out what type of drinker you are involves looking at the 'how' you drink part of the equation – your drinking style.

✔ People use alcohol differently. Look at the drinking styles in this list and consider which one(s) best describe how and when you drink:

- **Habitual:** this style involves associating specific locations and situations with alcohol.

- **Bingeing:** drinking huge amounts in a single drinking session, but with periods of moderate or no drinking in between. Friday or Saturday night binges are common.

- **Periodic:** similar to bingeing except the periods of drinking large amounts last longer and then are interspersed with periods of moderate or no drinking. An example is a style of heavy drinking lasting for several days followed by a slowing-down period.

- **Addictive:** Not being able to cope or relax without alcohol and experiencing withdrawal symptoms from a lack of alcohol. An example is the increasing use of alcohol for 'Dutch courage' or to get through regular routines at work or at home.

✔ **Your emotional state before drinking:** Some people drink because they're happy and want to celebrate, while others drink to forget or because they're alone. The mood you're in prior to beginning to consume alcohol can directly influence how you drink.

This is important because alcohol is a mood enhancer. Booze can amplify any emotions you're experiencing before drinking. A common example of this is the link between alcohol and violence.

Additionally, because alcohol's a depressant, it also impairs your thinking and reflexes, lowers inhibitions and, most importantly, affects your judgement. So the combination of distorted emotions and impaired judgement can have unwanted effects. For this reason, if you're upset or angry, you should probably avoid drinking altogether – particularly if you're likely to vent these feelings on anyone else. The therapeutic approach is to discuss these feelings with someone you trust who's sober and constructive. Best of all's to speak to a counsellor or hypnotherapist if your problems with alcohol and violence are serious and ongoing.

Social drinking

Social drinkers think of themselves as people who drink to feel better. Simple as that. No medical issues here with social drinkers. However, the term itself seems to minimise the effects of regularly drinking. Social drinking means different things to different people:

- A beer after a hard day's work – every day.
- An increased intake of booze during the Christmas holiday season, beginning with the office party.
- 'Middle-class' drinking, implying a classier sort of social drinking, for example a glass of wine with each meal.

You can easily blur the lines between social drinking and dependency on alcohol. Here are some clues to whether you're becoming dependent on alcohol:

- Your tolerance increases and you need to drink more to feel the effects of the booze.
- Others start to comment on your drinking habits and this causes you to avoid those people or feel anger towards them.
- Alcohol becomes a way of coping and avoiding difficult emotions.
- You experience blackouts, when you forget what happens when you've been drinking.
- You drink more and more by yourself.
- You avoid the company of non-drinkers.
- You have accidents due to being drunk.

If you recognise these problems in yourself or someone else, time to be honest and admit that a problem with alcohol exists. Time to stop blaming others and start taking responsibility to reclaim your health.

Lone drinking

People who drink alone begin to relate to alcohol as a companion, a friend who can see them through their darkest hours. The canon of country and western music's full of songs about people's relationship with alcohol.

Alcohol's a friend whom the dependent drinker defends to the hilt, at the cost of relationships, family and even employment. The loneliness that usually leads to people drinking alone deepens as the drinker begins to isolate those who may have previously offered support, but who have now been hurt or pushed away.

The hazards of binge drinking

Binge drinking's disastrous not only on an individual level, but also on a national level. According to BBC News, in the UK alone binge drinking represents a huge cost to the national economy of around £20 billion a year, comprising:

✔ 17 million working days lost to hangovers and drink-related illness

✔ A cost to UK employers estimated to be £6.4 billion

✔ A cost to the UK National Health Service in the region of £1.7 billion

✔ Billions more spent dealing with alcohol-related crime and social problems

✔ in addition, 22,000 premature deaths each year attributable to alcohol-related problems

No reason exists to believe that the UK's unique among other countries with a large-scale alcohol problem. If the statistics coming from the UK even remotely reflect binge-drinking patterns in other countries, then we're witnessing a self-harm issue that's become normalised on a nationwide scale.

Ironically, the first step in altering the behaviour of drinking alone is to make a public statement. By telling your family and friends that you want to stop drinking alone, you're letting them know that you recognise the problem.

If you feel embarrassed or unable to stop drinking, that doesn't matter. This public declaration means that other people can more easily accept your problem and your need for help. This may begin to help heal the hurt you've caused them as well.

Your declaration may lead the bravest of your supporters to help you to find a counsellor or an organisation that can offer you objective, professional support.

Binge drinking

Binge drinking's about getting drunk as fast as possible. We all know what alcoholic bingeing looks like, either directly or indirectly:

✔ The person who's ready to party

✔ The person who's angry and wants to let rip.

✔ The person who's drinking to forget their pain.

Alternatively, bingeing can also be about drinking consistently high amounts over a long period.

Social drinking can easily blur into binge drinking, especially if friends support excessive drinking, organisationally or culturally. Celebrations such as

Christmas and New Year are culturally endorsed periods of excessive drinking. Television adverts for alcohol are usually more prevalent just before and during these times, to reinforce the need to stock up on alcohol for the holidays.

So how many drinks constitute binge drinking? Actually, you can't quantify this easily, as the amount depends on individual physical characteristics, as we discuss in 'Focusing on Factors that Affect Your Drinking Pattern', earlier in this chapter. However, common sense may prevail.

If you continue to drink when you know that you're already inebriated, consider yourself to be binge drinking. At this point, you really aren't justified in continuing and you must ask yourself why you now want to harm yourself.

From a therapy point of view, bingeing's a form of self-harm. For that matter, you can consider any unhealthy, unnecessary activity as self-harm, but we're focusing at the moment on using this term as a wake-up call. You may associate self-harm with cutting or suicidal behaviours that lead to immediate mutilation or a fatal outcome. This is too narrow a viewpoint, since binge drinking and also smoking are prime examples of (decreasingly) socially acceptable behaviours that result in thousands of deaths annually.

Using Self-Hypnosis to Reduce Your Drinking

If you've worked out why and how you drink based on the descriptions in the previous section, you now have a greater understanding of your drinking pattern.

Establishing your drinking goals

To begin to make changes to your drinking pattern, you need a clear goal. So what's your goal for your new drinking habits? Ask yourself whether you want to:

- ✔ Reduce your drinking
- ✔ Drink in a way where you don't lose control
- ✔ Quit drinking altogether

Script 1: Enjoying the feeling of being alcohol free

...now...as I go deeper and deeper relaxed... deeper and deeper relaxed....

'I can more easily enjoy the feeling of being alcohol free. With each outbreath I am becoming more relaxed in my body... and more relaxed in my mind.... with each day it becomes increasingly easier to.... enjoy the feeling of being alcohol free...

...and as I continue to breathe slowly and deeply... I feel more in control of my health and happiness.'

...with each outbreath, I can go deeper and deeper relaxed ...

'And as I go deeper relaxed.... I begin to enjoy even further the physical feelings of a clearer head as I wake up each morning, full of greater energy and optimism.'

'Because I'm enjoying the feeling of not drinking alcohol, I find that I feel more in control of the way I think... feel... and behave.'

Self-hypnosis can be very effective when you use the hypnosis to go directly to the feeling of a problem gone. To devise a self-hypnosis approach for establishing drinking goals, ask yourself the following questions:

✔ 'What may I feel like if I go for several days without alcohol?'

✔ 'What may I feel like if I drink more safely?'

✔ 'What may I feel like to enjoy life without alcohol?'

These questions all form the seeds of potential self-hypnosis scripts, which we describe in the next section. In fact, by using as many of your imaginative physical senses as possible, you deepen the self-hypnosis by *feeling, seeing, hearing, smelling* or *tasting* your way into life with the alcohol problem solved. In a sense, through this type of 3D hypnotic imagination you're providing the sensory impressions that stimulate your unconscious to develop new, more helpful beliefs and behaviours that achieve your goals.

Thinking through self-hypnosis scripts for your drinking

Below are the brief seeds of self-hypnosis scripts using the three questions in 'Establishing your drinking goals' above. If you understand what type of drinker you are (see previous section) and can answer why you drink and how you drink, then you can add your own visions and goals to these core script ideas. (For more information about scripts, see Chapter 6: 'Working with Words: Becoming Your Own Recording Star'. Your scripts will enable you to create a more personalised approach to self-hypnosis. Below are some ideas to begin to help you develop your own scripts for greater control over your drinking:

What follows are brief examples of three potential scripts to address different drink problem issues. We developed these by taking the questions from the 'Establishing your drinking goals' section above and converting them into hypnotic suggestions. These suggestions become action statements, which will affirm your intentions about overcoming your drinking issues. We would also invite you to further develop these to tailor scripts to your needs.

Please note that these statements are to begin *after* you have already induced a light trance state. If you need to review how to do this, see Chapter 5.

Remember, as you develop your own self-hypnosis scripts, you don't have to write more than a page or two, because you can repeat phrases to yourself and the statement's certainly impressed on your unconscious mind.

Recite your statements to yourself frequently throughout the day. Even better, record yourself slowly speaking your personalised self-hypnosis script – a brief recording of three to five minutes is fine. (Skip to Chapter 6 for more on becoming your own recording star.)

Decreasing your drinking

In the earlier section of this chapter, 'Discovering Your Drinking Patterns', we help you assess your use of alcohol, including the events and conditions that lead you to drink too much. Once you've established this self-awareness, you can tailor your self-hypnosis scripts to develop new responses to the situations that influence you to drink or drink too much.

When we are upset, we have various ways of coping – healthy and unhealthy – to compartmentalise our suffering in order to cope with daily life. Drinking is often used to avoid dealing with difficult emotions. When we regularly use alcohol as an unhealthy substitute for dealing with pain, we have a problem. The healthy part of us seeks to decrease our drinking.

Below is an example of the use of alcohol as an unhealthy means for coping with emotional difficulties. Let's say that Mary drinks in the following situations:

- ✔ After conflicts with her mother
- ✔ Tinking about her ex-boyfriend and feeling sad about him leaving her three months ago
- ✔ Feeling incompetent at work

Script 2: Feeling as if I can drink more safely?

...now...as I go deeper and deeper relaxed.... deeper and deeper relaxed...

'Each day I'm feeling increasingly able to drink safely. I find it easier to drink safely and enjoy the feeling of being more in control of my drinking.'

'I can hear myself as I sit with my friends refusing their offers of alcoholic drinks after I've already had my limit. I increasingly enjoy the feeling of being able to say no to alcohol.'

'...and as I go even more comfortable...wonderful feelings of deepening relaxation.......I feel emotionally satisfied, and perhaps even a little smug...as we leave the bar/restaurant/party and I'm the most sober person...

And as I hear the slurred speech and watch their slightly embarrassing behaviour...I feel proud to be sober...I feel happy that I have learned to be in control of my drinking...I am pleased that I can drink more safely than I ever dreamed possible....'

Mary's pattern is that when any of the above happen or she dwells on these matters, she feels upset and drinks alone, or arranges to meet with two of her drinking buddies to talk in a victim-like way about her feelings. She doesn't talk to them about solutions or ways forward, but about how others have treated her badly. This leads to her feeling worse and drinking more.

With self-hypnosis Mary can use some of the following approaches:

- ✔ Imagining having a positive discussion with her mother.

- ✔ Imagining a future relationship feeling happier and/or being with a better partner.

- ✔ Imagining receiving the support she needs to do her job better and achieving a new level of competence.

You need some thought to be able to sit down and write a script that doesn't restate the problem, but instead focuses on solutions and the desired outcomes.

Example phrases for Mary are:

- ✔ 'I can more easily talk to my mother.'

- ✔ 'I'm becoming more optimistic about the future.'

- ✔ 'I'm able to find new ways to do my job better.'

Script 3: Enjoying life without alcohol

....now.... as I go deeper and deeper relaxed... deeper and deeper relaxed...

'my unconscious mind already understands how wonderful it can feel to be relaxed and fresh... and as I go even deeper relaxed I can begin to smell that my breath is cleaner at the end of the evening... and I am proud that my breath is cleaner at the end of the evening...

because I've had no alcohol to drink.'

'... and as I go even more relaxed... I increasingly begin to enjoy life feeling more in control of my thoughts, feelings and behaviour.'

'... And I increasingly enjoy life without alcohol. ..."I can feel that I'm able to walk in a co-ordinated way because I'm sober.'

'I can think and speak coherently and I've really had a good time being sober.'

'... and as the days and weeks go by... I increasingly enjoy life without alcohol. ...'

In your own self-hypnosis script to include specific suggestions regarding your alcohol plans the phrases might be:

✔ 'I'm coping better and drinking far less alcohol.'

✔ 'I have no desire to drink alcohol when I'm upset and can more easily do self-hypnosis to feel better.'

This is a two-fold approach to writing succinct, elegant self-hypnosis scripts:

✔ Think like a lawyer: use scripts that are not too vague.

✔ Don't be too tightly-worded: don't create something that's overly pre-scriptive (for example, 'and I want the changes to occur in the following manner...') or too literal (for example, don't say 'and this happens by Tuesday at noon').

So from the two suggestions above, you can see that a certain amount of artful vagueness allows your unconscious to achieve things in ways that your conscious mind may never have conceived.

So try to avoid telling your unconscious how to do its job – don't tell your unconscious how to help you to achieve your goals with self-hypnosis. Trust it to generate changes naturally. In fact, most of what we suggest is about trusting your unconscious to deliver its own method of problem solving that it may not communicate to your conscious mind.

You can do a lot with a single page in self-hypnosis. In fewer than 300 words you can create a skilfully worded self-hypnosis script that:

- Addresses self-esteem problems – central to feeling motivated to tackle alcohol issues.
- Demonstrates an 'Ego-strengthening' technique – a core concept for working with many self-destructive habits, as with drinking.
- Demonstrates the hypnosis approach of being 'artfully vague' referred to above.
- Enables you to change your unhelpful beliefs about yourself so that you can decrease your drinking and feel more in control of how you use alcohol.

As before, these statements are to begin *after* you have already induced a light trance state. If you need to review how to do this, see Chapter 5: 'Entering a hypnotic trance with traditional self- hypnosis'.

Going for total abstinence

Some people are simply better than others at limiting their drinking. If you're honest with yourself and have a history of serious drink problems, then you probably need to consider abstaining.

Abstinence technically means refraining from drinking for any period ranging from just one day to a lifetime. Here we're addressing longer-term abstinence. One of the most important factors to remember is that when attempting to abstain, you're not unusual if you occasionally fail and return to drinking. When this occurs, what's crucial is not to beat yourself up, but to gain from the experience and resume your abstinence routine. In this way, you gradually discover how to be successful.

Finding ongoing support's also vital in maintaining an alcohol-free lifestyle. Avoiding your old drinking buddies is probably important here, instead finding people and activities more suitable to a booze-free lifestyle. Also having ongoing involvement with a good counsellor or support group helps you immensely. Going for abstinence alone is probably not advisable if you've struggled and failed with limiting your drinking in the past.

Given the above principles, you now have the tools to be able to tailor your own self-hypnosis scripts to reinforce these suggestions to remain alcohol free.

Script for challenging low self-esteem issues related to drinking:

Now. . . as I go deeper and deeper relaxed . . . deeper and deeper relaxed . . .

'By going deeply relaxed, I am also relaxing my inner critic . . . the critical grip that it once had is now loosening. . . . relaxing . . . with each out-breath . . .

With each outbreath my critical thoughts are slowly softening . . . slowly changing into more helpful, supportive thoughts . . . and as I go deeper relaxed those thoughts shift to helpful words ... and these words will circulate in my deepest thoughts . . . replacing critical thoughts. . .

Helpful words like . . .

'Health'

Helpful words like . . .

'Success'

Helpful words like . . .

'Motivation'

And as I go deeper relaxed. . . . I begin to think what these words mean to me on deeper. . . and deeper levels. . .

'What does health feel like to me . . . ? What does it feel like to be in 'good health'?

'What does success feel like to me . . . ? What does it feel like to be 'successful'?

And what does 'motivation' feel like to me? What does it feel like to be motivated?

And as I go deeper relaxed these words begin to go deeper into my mind. . . helping me to generate new behaviours. . . helping me to feel differently. . .

Feeling more healthy

Feeling more successful

Feeling more motivated.

And as the days go by, I become healthier, more successful and more motivated. . . .'

Chapter 16

Controlling Your Eating Habits

*1*f you're chewing away at that weighty problem of slimming down or you've been escaping into the comfort of food to avoid your emotions, then this is the chapter for you. The simple and essential pleasure of eating's a source of angst for many people and can have a serious impact on your quality of life. We're surrounded by food wherever we go: food's in our homes, on our high streets, even in the media we watch, read and listen to. This means that we're continually being bombarded with the message to eat. Unfortunately, we're often encouraged to consume the least healthy of foods.

At the same time, we're increasingly leading more and more sedentary lifestyles as technology advances to help us do less. Even our social life is being beamed into our living rooms via satellite and the internet, which means that we don't go out as much as we used to. This may sound very nice, but if you're having weight problems this can be a recipe for disaster as you aren't taking enough exercise.

Let's stop with the doom and gloom as help's at hand: say hello to your unconscious mind. The part of your psyche that makes you *you* is a very powerful ally in helping you to achieve your healthy eating and weight goals. True, this help may have been a little lacking if you've been having problems, but that can change. Read on and discover how to take control.

Chewing Away at Why You Eat

Food is fuel that keeps you healthy and gives you the energy to carry out your day-to-day tasks. Whenever you eat, food passes into your body where many complex processes occur to break the food down into energy. For the squeamish, look away now as Figure 16-1 shows you your digestive system.

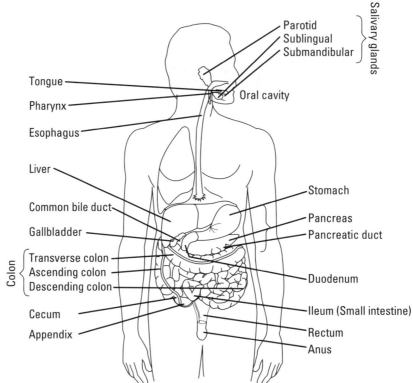

Figure 16-1:
The human
digestive
system.

Each part of your digestive system has a very specific function in helping extract the right nutrients from every mouthful you consume:

- **Mouth:** The entrance. Here you prepare food for digestion by chewing, which effectively breaks the food down into small pieces ready for swallowing.

- **Salivary glands:** These produce saliva that's the lubricant to help the broken-down food pass into your stomach. Saliva also contains enzymes that start the digestion process.

- **Oesophagus:** This is the flexible tube down which food passes into your stomach.

- **Stomach:** This is a muscular sac that holds your swallowed food while churning it up, mixing the food with stomach acids that break it down further, preparing the food for absorption.

- **Small intestine:** This is where the majority of digesting and absorption occurs.

✔ **Large intestine:** This is where you absorb water into your body.

✔ **Rectum:** This is the waiting room where everything that's left after you've digested your food is stored before passing out of your body.

✔ **Anus:** Here you follow the exit signs as what's left of your food passes out of your body.

Digestion's the process by which your body mechanically and chemically breaks down food, then absorbs the appropriate nutrients in order to keep you healthy and fit.

Your digestive system's very much in touch with your brain. The digestive system lets the brain know when you're full and when you need to eat. These messages can sometimes become scrambled, and that leads to many of the problems people experience with regard to food.

Understanding emotional hunger

Usually, when your body needs refuelling it sends messages to your brain saying that it's hungry. Your brain then triggers behaviours that send you off in search of food to eat. However, for some people this 'I'm hungry' message gets triggered by emotions. Emotional hunger occurs whether you're physically hungry or not. Instead of addressing the physical need to refuel, emotional hunger addresses the need to handle your emotions. Unfortunately this kind of hunger does this by making you eat. In other words, you begin to eat in response to the emotional state you're in.

Here are some things that may trigger emotional eating:

✔ Sadness

✔ Confusion

✔ Feeling down

✔ Stress or anxiety

✔ Boredom

✔ Anger

✔ To avoid thinking about something

✔ To avoid doing something

Emotional hunger leads to emotional eating as a means of gaining comfort.

Things aren't too bad if the only thing you eat when emotional hunger kicks in is a healthy salad. Unfortunately this isn't always the case and you may tend to go for high-calorie, sweet foods that pile on the weight. This is because this kind of food gives you pleasure. The pleasure doesn't just occur in eating the food, but in how your body handles these types of food, because they can make your brain release a substance called serotonin. Among its many complex functions, serotonin's responsible for making you feel good. Not surprisingly, you get to know to eat these unhealthy foods when you're feeling down or stressed, as doing so helps pick you up and makes you feel a bit better about things.

Two problems occur with this:

✔ Emotional eating only satisfies the emotional need for a very short time and so you tend to eat more and more.

✔ You don't develop healthy strategies to cope with your emotions.

Discovering the emotional eater in you

To determine whether you're an emotional eater, try answering the following questions:

✔ Do you eat because you're bored?

✔ Do you eat without realising you're eating?

✔ Do you eat as a result of something unpleasant happening to you?

✔ Do you crave certain foods when you're emotional?

✔ Do you feel guilty or ashamed after eating?

✔ Do you eat in response to seeing advertisements for food?

If you answer 'yes' to any of these questions, you may be an emotional eater. However, bear in mind that many of us respond to emotional situations by eating *on occasion*. When that eating becomes the norm is when you need to take yourself in hand and address the issue.

If you have very strong emotions triggering your eating, we recommend you chat with your doctor or hypnotherapist in order to find the most appropriate and effective way of overcoming that emotional hunger.

Changing your emotions

Your first port of call is to begin to keep an emotional diary. This diary allows you to track your emotions while at the same time maintaining track of what you're eating. In your diary, consider the following each day:

✔ When you eat

✔ What triggers your eating (hunger or emotion)

> ✔ What you eat
>
> ✔ How much you eat
>
> ✔ What you think about before, during and after you eat

If you find that you're regularly eating until you're so full that you feel nauseous, you make yourself sick after eating large amounts of food or you regularly starve yourself, then please discuss this with your doctor so that you get the appropriate help.

At the end of each day, reflect on your day's eating and write down how you want to respond at times when emotional hunger takes over.

An eating diary helps to identify the triggers to your eating. Your daily reflection identifies the strategies you can use to replace food as a coping strategy. From this you can take the next step into creating a plan of action, which may include the following stages:

1. Use self-hypnosis to help deal with your emotions. Check out the chapters relevant to you in this book: Chapters 9, 10, 12 and 17.

2. Start to eat more healthily. Chuck in the bin any unhealthy food, especially the food that you eat emotionally. Have a look at 'Changing Your Mind to Change How You Eat', later in this chapter, to help yourself install healthy eating using self-hypnosis.

3. Develop a regular pattern of healthy eating – and don't skip meals, as this can lead you back onto the unhealthy food path.

4. Find new ways to relax and keep yourself occupied at times of stress or boredom. Imagine that you're successfully doing these relaxation methods when you practise self-hypnosis.

Practice makes perfect! Don't be surprised if you don't get your eating right all the time and you fall back into bad habits occasionally. The more you make the effort, the more you create new, healthy and durable behaviour that satiates your emotional hunger.

Understanding physical hunger

Physical hunger's your body's clarion call to eat because you need fuel. As we explain in the previous section, the emotional hunger that calls for you to address your emotions can usurp your physical hunger. Table 16-1 helps you tell the difference between physical and emotional hunger.

Table 16-1:	The Two Types of Hunger.
Physical Hunger	*Emotional Hunger*
Builds up over time	Hits suddenly
Doesn't require urgent attention	Compels you to eat urgently
Goes away after eating	Is there even when you're full
Is determined by the time since you last ate	Is there irrespective of when you last ate
You feel satisfied once you've met the hunger	You feel guilty or shameful after eating
Focuses you on eating a variety of foods	Often focuses you on eating one type of sweet, highly calorific food

Physical hunger often appears up to five hours after you've last eaten and physical signs such as a rumbling stomach frequently accompany it.

When you eat, food passes from your mouth into your stomach. You can think of your stomach as a holding and processing room that food passes into before the real job of absorbing nutrients begins. As you continue to eat, so your stomach begins to fill up. If you look at Figure 16-1 you may notice that we refer to your stomach as a muscular sac. Your stomach's designed to stretch as you put more into it and then to hold the bulk of your food as it churns the food up ready for digestion. As the walls of your stomach stretch, so your nervous system recognises this and begins to send signals to your brain telling you that you're getting full. Once your stomach reaches a capacity of about a litre of food, your nervous system sends out the signal 'Full!' and you stop eating – or at least you're supposed to stop eating . . .

Even though your mind says that you don't need to eat any more, you may continue to eat after the 'Full!' message has reached your brain. You may be emotionally eating or you may simply be eating through social pressure, so as not to offend the host at a dinner party, for example. Whatever the reason, your stomach begins to adapt and expands even further beyond its original one-litre capacity. If this is just a one-off experience then no harm's done except that you may feel uncomfortably full and bloated. Problems start to manifest when this type of overeating becomes a normal behavioural pattern. Being wonderfully adaptive, the human body allows your stomach to stretch far beyond its original capacity to accommodate the consistent extra volume of food you're eating. Your nervous system resets its default setting of being full at one litre to a much higher one – anything up to four litres!

This is why those who enter eating competitions as well as many overweight people seem to have an amazing capacity for consuming large volumes of food before they satisfy their hunger and have to stop. The good news is that if they consistently reduce the volume of food they eat, their stomach and nervous system does, over a relatively short period, return to its original one-litre default setting.

Your stomach tells your brain that it's full about 20 minutes after you reach capacity. If you rapidly gulp down your food, then even if you've reached the one-litre mark the message that you're full hasn't got through to your brain and you continue eating. So eat slowly and when you're full you have a lot less food in your gut, meaning that you don't put on unnecessary weight.

Knowing whether to drink or to eat

Those pangs of hunger you feel may actually be pangs of thirst. This is because you're misinterpreting messages that the area of your brain responsible for letting you know you're hungry or thirsty – the hypothalamus – is sending out.

Your hypothalamus is pretty impressive. It's a relatively small structure towards the bottom of your brain that has a huge role in controlling many systems in your body. The hypothalamus is responsible for:

- Helping regulate your body temperature
- Helping regulate your moods
- Producing your sex drive
- Controlling the release of hormones from your glands
- Helping you sleep
- Controlling thirst
- Controlling hunger

As your body and nervous system detect the need for more fuel or water, your hypothalamus sends out a message that triggers the feeling of hunger or thirst and that in turn triggers food- or drink-seeking behaviours. Once you've eaten or drunk your fill, your hypothalamus sends out the signal that you've had enough and the drinking or eating behaviour stops. Quite why you erroneously read the message to drink as a message to eat is a matter of debate with scientists. Whatever the reason, you need to bear in mind that your hunger may be thirst. Therefore if you're eating when you should be drinking, this may lead to you putting on extra weight. So what can you do about this?

✔ Drink at least 2 litres of water spread throughout the day. This is the recommended minimum limit to keep yourself hydrated. If you're exercising, or if the weather's hot and you're sweating, then you should increase the volume you drink throughout the day.

✔ When you notice that you're hungry, have a glass of water. Wait half an hour and if you're still hungry, then that message really was your hypothalamus telling you to go and eat.

Keep hydrated by drinking water. Other drinks such as coffee, cordials and fizzy drinks can trigger your body to remove more fluid than you put in. And if you're trying to lose weight, these drinks may be high in calories too, contributing to you piling on the pounds.

Damage to your hypothalamus as a result of head trauma, surgery, cancer or other disease can result in a condition known as acquired Prader-Willi syndrome. This is a condition whereby your hunger has no off switch and no matter how much you eat you're never satisfied. Unfortunately this means that people who have this condition are often profoundly obese. True Prader-Willi syndrome is a genetic condition that on top of the appetite problems is accompanied by physical and behavioural issues.

Digesting Diets

The word 'diet' has two meanings. Diet can refer to the type of food you're eating on a daily basis, as in 'he has a healthy diet'. Or diet can refer to the restriction of food in order to lose weight, as in 'I'm on a diet so I can lose 10 pounds'. However you look at the word, you need to remember that 'diet' is the crux of the matter in healthy eating and losing weight.

Your body's a finely honed piece of machinery that you need to look after in order for it to work at its optimal efficiency. The body works within a set of parameters that allow you to get the best out of it as long as you don't exceed them. One of those parameters is the fuel that you put into your body in the form of your diet. To put the message bluntly: the better the quality of fuel, the better the performance!

Today we live in a culture where we believe that speed is of the essence. Many people feel that they don't have the time to sit back and prepare a decent meal for themselves or their family. Unfortunately, this has led to the rise of a fast food culture, in which speed of preparation or delivery has superseded nutritional quality. Many of the fast foods that are available via restaurants and supermarkets are promoting a diet that's high in taste while at the same time being poor-quality fuel for your body.

The problem with fast food is that it tends to be high in fat, salt and sugar. Fat, salt and sugar all improve the taste of your food, but at a price, because in the quantities you find them in some fast foods they're positively danger- ous to your health if you consume them for long periods. That means that over-reliance on eating these types of food can lead to weight gain and its associated health risks, such as heart disease or diabetes.

Fast foods, sweets, cakes and so on are crammed full of calories. One of the parameters to which your body runs efficiently relates to the number of calories you consume each day. If you're not overweight and don't carry out much exercise, then the recommendations are:

- ✔ A man should consume 2,500 calories.
- ✔ A woman should consume 2,000 calories.

Women need fewer calories than men because of differences in the amount of muscle and body fat. Muscles use up energy and fat stores energy. In general, women have less lean muscle and a higher body-fat percentage, which means that they need to consume fewer calories to keep healthy.

A *calorie* is a unit of energy. The more calories food has, the more energy that food contains. If you consume more calories (energy) than you're using up in your daily activity, then that energy gets stored in your body in the form of fat.

Irrespective of your gender, if you exercise and are of normal weight then you should consume more calories as your body demands more fuel to keep going. If you're overweight then you should consume fewer calories so that you burn up the excess fat.

Seeing how diets can help – or not

An entire industry has been created around the second of our definitions for the word diet, a regime for weight loss.

In our opinion and in the opinion of many psychologists and eating disorder experts, weight-loss diets don't work in the long-run. There, we've said it, much to the horror of an industry that makes millions from us as consumers. We've had them all: food combination diets, diets that severely restrict food groups such as carbohydrates, diets that focus on the consumption of one specific food claiming miraculous fat-busting properties and so on. Despite the allure that these weight-loss diets have, especially if a celebrity's promoting them, they all have one thing in common: they offer a short-lasting quick fix. Research has shown that up to 95 per cent of people who lose weight through dieting alone subsequently put the pounds back on again. Fad diets promise the world and generally deliver very little except frustration and disappointment.

An old adage goes that the faster your fat comes off, the faster it returns. To some extent this is true. Much of the weight that you lose through fad dieting's in the form of reducing bulk waste passing through your body (you can have anything up to 11kg of faecal matter in your body at any one time depending on how much you eat) and loss of water through dehydration. The moment you break the diet and start eating again: whammo! The weight piles back on and you're back where you started – or worse.

Fad diets that seriously restrict your calorific intake can be counter-productive as they push your body into starvation mode. That means that your metabolism slows down and you burn up less fat as your body wants to preserve its available resources. After all, your body doesn't know when the next decent meal's coming its way. In some cases you may even put on weight as your body shoves all the available energy you consume into storage to help it through the lean times.

You may still want to consider dieting – but as long as you remember that effective weight management can only come through lifestyle change. And the following formula promotes that change: eating less + eating healthily + exercising more = weight loss.

✔ **Eat less:** Aim to lose about half–1 kilo of weight a week. Most experts consider this healthy as this amount encourages an achievable change in your dietary habits. In order to lose half a kilo of fat per week, you need to reduce your daily calorie intake by 500 calories.

✔ **Eat healthily:** We cover this in the next section 'Cooking up a healthy diet'. Remember that losing weight's not just about how much you eat, but what you eat too, as this gives you the energy to exercise more efficiently.

✔ **Exercise more:** When you exercise you use up energy. With the reduction of energy going into you in the form of calories and the increase in calories you're using, your body soon pays a visit to its storehouse of energy and starts to work its way through the fat that it finds there.

The word 'exercise' is anathema to some people as the term possibly encourages thoughts of having to go to the gym or of playing some kind of sport. When we refer to exercise in this book, we mean any increase in your physical activity. This can be walking more or climbing the stairs rather than taking the lift, for example.

Always talk to your doctor before starting any exercise programme or making any radical change to your diet, as he's able to give you the most appropriate advice to ensure that what you're doing's healthy for you.

Even though we talk about calories, this doesn't mean that you have to become a calorie watcher. By eating a healthy diet and reducing the amount you eat at each meal, you automatically reduce the calories you consume.

You can figure another factor into the equation to help smooth things along – enjoyment. If you enjoy managing your weight in a healthy way, you're more than likely to stick to your new lifestyle and keep that weight off. Flip to 'Changing Your Mind to Change How You Eat', later in this chapter, to find out how self-hypnosis can help you add this component to the weight control formula.

Cooking up a healthy diet

In this section we look at what a healthy diet comprises. By following the tips in this section, you can set your body up for optimal health and maximise your chances of losing weight.

Perhaps the first place to start's with what constitutes a healthy, balanced diet. Of the many approaches to this, the most popular's the food pyramid. Have a look at Figure 16-2 and its explanation, as this is your guide to a healthy diet.

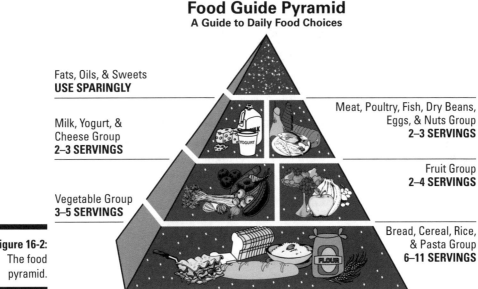

Food Guide Pyramid
A Guide to Daily Food Choices

Fats, Oils, & Sweets
USE SPARINGLY

Milk, Yogurt, & Cheese Group
2–3 SERVINGS

Meat, Poultry, Fish, Dry Beans, Eggs, & Nuts Group
2–3 SERVINGS

Fruit Group
2–4 SERVINGS

Vegetable Group
3–5 SERVINGS

Bread, Cereal, Rice, & Pasta Group
6–11 SERVINGS

Figure 16-2: The food pyramid.

The food pyramid gives you an indication of the maximum number of servings daily you should have from each particular food group. To help put things into perspective, the following indicates one serving size for each example of food:

- ✔ **Fats, oils and sweets (eat sparingly):** These include salad dressings, cooking oils, cream, butter, margarine, sugar, soft drinks, sweets and sweet desserts.

- ✔ **Dairy products and meat, poultry, fish, dry beans, eggs and nuts (2–3 servings):**

  - 0.25 litres of milk or yogurt

  - 45 grams of natural cheese (for example Cheddar or Edam)

  - 60 grams of processed cheese (for example pre-sliced cheese with additives)

  - 1 egg

  - 60–85 grams of cooked lean meat, poultry or fish

  - 2 tablespoons of peanut butter

  - 115 grams of cooked dry beans

  - 140 grams of unsalted nuts

Choose lean meat as this contains the lowest levels of fat. Try cooking with vegetable oil or virgin olive oil instead of lard, butter or margarine.

- ✔ **Vegetables, including potatoes, and fruit (2–5 servings):**

  - 230 grams of raw leafy vegetables

  - 115 grams of other vegetables, cooked or raw

  - 0.2 litres of vegetable juice

  - 0.2 litres of fruit juice

  - 1 medium apple, orange or banana

  - 115 grams of chopped, cooked or unsweetened canned fruit

Try dressing salads with virgin olive oil or nut oil instead of mayonnaise. Only 100 per cent fruit or vegetable juice counts, so avoid any juices that contain added sugar. Fizzy drinks and cordials do not count as fruit juice.

✔ **Bread, grain, cereal, rice and pasta (6–11 servings)**

- 1 slice of bread

- 115 grams of rice, cooked cereal or pasta

- 230 grams of ready-to-eat cereal

Try to eat wholegrain bread, cereal and pasta. Wholegrain foods have more valuable vitamins, minerals and fibre than those made with white flour.

Don't forget to cut down on your alcohol intake too. Two or three glasses of alcohol could easily take up a third of your daily calorie allowance! If you need help controlling the amount you are drinking, then have a look at Chapter 15.

If you eat a healthy diet, then you may not need to take vitamin or mineral supplements, as what you're eating may meet all your nutritional needs. If you want to know more about nutrition, have a look at the excellent *Nutrition For Dummies* by Sue Baic and Nigel Denby (Wiley).

Changing Your Mind to Change How You Eat

Taking control of your eating habits or taking control of your weight means changing your lifestyle. This may sound daunting to begin with, but with perseverance and the aid of self-hypnosis you can make those changes a welcome part of your day-to-day life. In order to do this you need to change the way you think about and relate to food. If you focus on the fact that you can enjoy food (important for eating to be fun), that you eat in order to keep yourself healthy (with an emphasis on healthy) and that you're now prac-tising controlling your eating, then you're setting yourself up for success. We suggest that you also have a look at Chapter 3, about setting goals, and include the following in your goal setting.

Homing in on helpful healthy eating strategies

The first step of any change to lifestyle is awareness. That means that you need to become aware of what you eat and drink and how much exercise you take on a daily basis by keeping a diary. Your diary shows you which areas of your diet and exercise habits you need to focus on. Try to record the following information each day:

- ✔ Every time you eat or drink, including snacking and alcohol.
- ✔ What you eat and drink.
- ✔ When you eat and drink.
- ✔ How much you eat and drink each time you do.
- ✔ How much exercise you take, including walking, walking up stairs, housework, gardening and so on.

As you keep your diary, be honest with yourself. No point 'forgetting' food that you've eaten or downsizing the volume you've consumed, as this gets you nowhere. Being honest with yourself keeps you on your path to success.

Use the food pyramid in the previous section to help change your diet and continue making entries in your diary. In this way you continually reinforce your healthy eating choices. You don't have to keep making diary entries for the rest of your life. After you develop new and healthy lifestyle habits and achieve your goal, you can archive that diary while basking in the continued glow of your success.

You can use self-hypnosis to encourage keeping your diary up to date. While in trance, imagine writing your entries regularly and then imagine having reached your weight control or healthy eating goal. In this way you reinforce the importance of the diary for yourself.

You may want to use some technological gadgets to help you with your diary keeping. Many computer programs and mobile phone applications can help you keep track of your eating, drinking and exercise. Some are even free to download, so have a bit of fun searching the net and see what you can find.

Here are some other healthy-eating tips to help you:

- ✔ **Don't ban anything:** Prohibition leads to desire. We've seen too many people completely cut something from their diet, such as chocolate, only to cave in after a couple of weeks, resulting in a binge. Instead, use self-hypnosis to teach self-control. In trance, imagine having one bar of chocolate a week, as opposed to several, and then imagine yourself having achieved your weight and eating goals to reinforce your reason for doing this.

- ✔ **Make sure you eat at regular intervals – and never skip breakfast:** Eating regular healthy meals reduces your need to snack. Eating a healthy breakfast breaks the overnight fast you experience when you sleep. By doing this you stimulate your metabolism to start working and breaking down fat, while at the same time ensuring that you avoid unhealthy snacking to keep your energy levels up. In self-hypnosis imagine eating healthy meals at regular intervals. Develop suggestions to encourage this by having a peek at Chapter 6.

✔ **If you need to snack, snack on fruit or sugar-free oatmeal bars:** These are healthy, nutritious and tasty too. The energy they give is long-lasting and prevents further snacking. Again, in self-hypnosis develop suggestions for healthy snacks and imagine yourself avoiding unhealthy snacking.

✔ **Eat slowly and eat less:** This helps to reduce your stomach capacity, meaning that less food's there when your brain registers that you're full.

Changing how you feel about your body

You may want to control your eating habits and lose weight because you want to feel good about the way you look. As you progress and begin to lose weight (and if you're exercising, tone up), your body image changes. Here's an exercise that encourages you to think more positively about how you look:

1. **Take yourself into self-hypnosis, as we explain in Chapter 5, and go to your favourite place.**

2. **Spend a minute or two enjoying the sights, sounds and feelings you find in your favourite place.**

3. **Imagine a beautiful full-length mirror near to you and go to stand in front of it.**

4. **Notice how the mirror looks, what it's made of and how touching it feels.**

5. **Imagine good, positive feelings coming from this mirror.**

6. **Imagine looking at your reflection in the mirror and that the mirror shows you at a time in the future when you've achieved your weight control goal and have kept to that weight.**

7. **Notice how good you look, how happy you are, how positive you feel.**

8. **Invite the reflection to step out of the mirror and stand next to you.**

9. **Spend a minute or so noticing how those positive feelings coming from the mirror increase and enjoy those feelings.**

10. **Invite your reflection to step inside you and become one with you. Notice how the reflection brings all those positive feelings with it. Listen to your reflection as it tells you how you've achieved this wonderful goal.**

11. **Spend a few more moments in your favourite place.**

12. **Wake yourself from trance, just as we explain in Chapter 5.**

13. **Three or four times a day, think about the reflection of yourself having achieved your goal and say: 'I'm now achieving this!'**

14. **If at any point you have negative thoughts about your self-image, shout 'Stop!' loudly in your mind. Then think about the reflection of yourself having achieved your goal and say: 'But I'm now achieving this!'**

Skinny isn't necessarily healthy. Make sure that you work towards an achievable and healthy body image. Spend time looking at positive body images, perhaps with a friend or family member you trust, and select one that's achievable for you.

Enjoying your menu of success

Your lifestyle is an important factor in managing your weight. If it's a healthy one then your weight will fall off and stay off. The following exercise helps you reinforce your healthy lifestyle changes and should be practised at least three times a week.

Don't forget to refer to other chapters in this book as necessary, especially Chapter 3. Keep practising all the exercises in this chapter on a regular basis as they too will help you shed the pounds and then maintain that weight loss.

1. **Guide yourself into self-hypnosis, as we describe in Chapter 5, and take yourself to your favourite place.**

2. **In your mind, review the healthy lifestyle choices that you're making.**

3. **Say to yourself 'I'm enjoying eating healthily each time I eat' and then imagine doing so.**

4. **Say to yourself 'I'm enjoying eating smaller amounts each time I eat' and then imagine doing so.**

5. **Say to yourself 'I'm enjoying exercising more each day' and then imagine doing so.**

6. **Say to yourself 'Each day I'm a little more calm, relaxed and enjoying more self-control' and then imagine yourself being so.**

7. **Spend time imagining yourself having achieved your weight control or healthy-eating goals and having kept them. Focus on how good that feels and tell yourself that you're achieving this.**

8. **Repeat steps 2 to 7 two more times.**

9. **Spend a minute or so enjoying being in your favourite place.**

10. **Wake yourself from trance, as we explain in Chapter 5.**

If you experience a regular pattern of attempting to lose weight without success, while having made the effort to eat healthily and exercise more, then you should go and have a check-up with your doctor to make sure that everything's okay with your hormones. In this way you receive the most appropriate help to get you to shed those pounds.

Chapter 17

Fostering Good Relationships

- -

- -

*Y*ou may have done a double take at this chapter's title, thinking 'How can self-hypnosis help me with the problems with my mother-in-law/ partner/annoying neighbour/bad boss?'

In this chapter we describe a category of hypnotherapy interventions called *ego-strengthening techniques*. The aim of these techniques is to help you feel more confident, optimistic and better about yourself. The *Hypnotherapist's Bible*, a.k.a. *The Handbook of Hypnotic Metaphors and Suggestions* by Corydon Hammond, says that to experience a full ego-strengthening hypnotherapy session is indescribable. The session can significantly boost your mood and make you a more effective person. Doing so's almost like rediscovering yourself with a new-found sense of appreciation.

Your new sense of self-appreciation directly helps you to foster good relationships as you begin to view life differently. As a result of effective ego strengthening, you feel better about yourself and you relate better to others. This means that you solve problems more creatively and handle challenging situations with greater self-control and influence. This is something that you can easily do through self-hypnosis, as we show in this chapter.

In this chapter we look at a range of issues that you need to be aware of to increase your ability to relate to others. By working with the techniques, you find out more about yourself and others and discover how to be more effective, making more real contacts with people while increasing your own sense of personal power and happiness.

Turning 'Me-Me-Me' Into 'Us-Us-Us'

No man's an island. Phew! Now that we've got that cliché out of the way, we can explore what the sentiment means in terms of helping you to cope better with your relationships.

Loving, supportive relationships can bring out the best in us. But conflict is also an inevitable part of relationships. What is important is how you handle this conflict. If you feel generally okay about yourself, chances are that you will be able to negotiate through problems. However, if you have low self-esteem, and are full of self-loathing, this will make your relationships more strained when conflicts occur. This section is about how you can transform yourself in order to enjoy better relationships.

Practising communicating and listening skills

One of the key problems in relationships is the inability to see the other person's point of view. Sometimes we're so focused on making sure that people understand us that we entirely miss or misunderstand what they're saying to us.

When one of us (Mike) works with couples in therapy, he asks them to practise a communication and listening skills exercise. This is interesting to try with your partner, particularly if you can have a third person who acts as a neutral participant present. The exercise involves the first person speaking to the second, describing an issue that they feel that the second person is either not understanding or responding to adequately, as follows:

1. **The first person makes the statement without using blaming or victim ('poor me') language. The statement must be simple and clear.**

2. **The second person must do two things:**

   a. **Listen to the statement and sit in silence for 60 seconds.**

   b. **Then repeat back what they heard the person say without adding to it and without offering any critical or editorial comment. They should begin with a sentence such as 'What I heard you say was . . .'**

3. **The third person acts as a neutral person who keeps the participant to their task and doesn't allow interruptions or rudeness**

This exercise may sound simple, but for most people it can be difficult to just listen. Especially when you are receiving a critical statement. The successful participants will listen and simply repeat back what they have heard the other person say – without inserting a defensive statement like 'but that's not the way I see it' or 'I disagree'.

If that happens, then the first person must repeat the statement again and the second person must again sit in silence for one second and try again to feed back with a sentence such as 'What I heard you say was . . .'

When Mike uses this exercise with couples, doing so instantly demonstrates how difficult having a true dialogue is and how often when in conflict we only focus on our own perspective and feelings.

Looking outwards to pull your relationships together

Using a 'helicopter view' is another way of saying, 'Let's step back from the small, detailed view of this relationship and take a look at the bigger picture'. Imagine two people in a relationship arguing bitterly over what appears to you to be a relatively trivial matter. The argument over this very small thing becomes more intense – the couple are swearing and threatening to end the relationship.

If you're the sort of person who makes threats that you later regret, consider the big picture: hurtful, damaging things can happen or be said in an instant, especially if alcohol or recreational drugs are involved. You absolutely must consider how to value your relationship in a way where you do not 'throw the baby out with the bath water' when in conflict or when under the influence of drugs or alcohol and feeling sorry for yourself.

If you decide that you want to improve your relationship with someone – be this a romantic relationship, work relationship or friendship – you need to think in terms of the future and whether you can express your point of view *and hear and empathise with theirs* as well. If you feel that you want the relationship to have a future, looking at the bigger picture helps you pull together and look towards that future.

Developing emotional intelligence

Emotional intelligence, or EI, is the ability to understand and control your own strong emotions. The term additionally implies the ability to understand and influence the emotions and behaviours of others. An emotionally intelligent person's more likely to be successful, popular and influential.

The degree of emotional intelligence you possess has clear implications for your capacity to develop good relationships. Good communication and the ability to handle yourself well under pressure are important.

Needless to say, many people who come for hypnotherapy or read self-help books like this one don't feel that they have emotional intelligence or consider that they need to develop their emotional intelligence further.

People with emotional intelligence tend to have some of the following traits:

- ✔ Successfully manage difficult situations
- ✔ Express themselves clearly
- ✔ Gain respect from others
- ✔ Influence other people
- ✔ Entice other people to help them out
- ✔ Keep cool under pressure
- ✔ Recognise their emotional reactions to people or situations
- ✔ Know how to say the 'right' thing to get the right result
- ✔ Manage themselves effectively when negotiating
- ✔ Manage other people effectively when negotiating
- ✔ Motivate themselves to get things done

Why are we going into so much detail about Emotional Intelligence? Because we would like one of the goals for your self-hypnosis for you to be able to achieve some of these points, especially if you can choose one or two that you feel you are in need of improving. It is possible for you to raise your emotional intelligence, especially by using self-hypnosis.

Imagine, for example, that you have problems keeping cool under pressure. Especially when your partner criticises your cooking. Using self-hypnosis, you could, for example, replay a past argument and imagine doing something different that resolves the argument, with both of you having a laugh. In this way you begin to train your mind to not rerun old argument patterns.

Practising self-monitoring

Self-monitoring involves being aware of your thoughts and emotions and also operating from a basis of sensitivity towards the feelings and motivations of others. The benefits of being able to self-monitor include having deeper and more real relationships with yourself and others. The ability to self-monitor is a by-product of emotional intelligence.

Safe Place script

Imagine being in a wonderful, safe, protective place. In this place no problems can be present . . . and no one else is there but you.

As you breathe slowly and deeply . . . try to make your safe place as real and as vivid as possible . . . by using as many of your physical senses as possible.

For example, seeing the objects in this place . . . their shapes . . . their colours . . . their sizes . . .

Perhaps touching the objects in your safe, protective place . . . feeling the textures of things there. Perhaps smelling pleasant smells . . . hearing pleasant sounds that are present in your protective, comfortable, safe place . . .

But most of all imagine the emotional feeling that you have . . . being in this wonderful, comfortable and protective safe place . . . as you continue to breathe deeply and slowly.

If you feel totally unclear about how to begin to develop self-monitoring skills, then often a short course of counselling can accelerate this process. We all have our personal emotional blind spots and a good counsellor can be both supportive and challenging in helping you to face these. In this way you can bring many of your unconscious motivations into self-awareness.

Self-monitoring's a skill that you can deepen if you can generate feelings of inner safety. The 'safe place' self-hypnosis script, which we describe in the nearby sidebar the 'Safe Place script'.

Don't overdo self-monitoring. Constant self-monitoring can be annoying and actually detrimental to relationships, as doing so leads you to be guarded and always trying to 'second guess' other people. Self-monitoring is most useful when not overdone – too little self-monitoring can lead to a loss of spontaneity in relationships while too much can lead to nit-picking and pedantry. In other words, 'all good things in good measure'.

Discover the rules of self-monitoring – and then forget them. In fact, research has shown that when self-monitoring's too high, important emotional characteristics such as openness and emotional stability are lessened. People with high self-monitoring alter their own personality to fit a situation or adapt to someone else's needs even when they clash with their own will. This isn't being real, nor is being like this conducive to being honest in relationships. So don't alter your own personality to be considerate of others and keep self-monitoring to a non-neurotic level.

Focusing on others

Have you ever met someone who made you feel like you could? Chances are one of the things they may have done was to show an interest in you and made you feel like you were being understood. Focusing on others in a genuine way is a way to make real contact with people. It is one of the corner-stones of building rapport in relationships.

Focusing on others is like oxygen. Not enough focus can be fatal (metaphori-cally speaking!) and too much can be toxic (again, metaphorically speaking).

Couples' counselling often involves imparting listening and communication skills, which are essential to developing good relations. What may be more helpful to consider may be the times in the past when others have accused you of not taking their feelings into consideration. When you look back on such memories, what can you discover? More importantly, how do you feel if you've ever been accused of not paying enough attention to the needs of others? Do you feel defensive? Reflective? Guilty? Your initial feeling can be helpful in understanding *how* you focus on others.

This brings us to the safe place self-hypnosis script, which we described in the previous section. If you can generate feelings of safety, and then focus on someone whom you struggle in your relationships with, you find that you're more easily able to put yourself into their shoes. In other words, how do you think they feel about things? How does their perspective differ from or con-verge with yours?

Additionally, by doing ego-strengthening self-hypnosis, you feel more flexible, benign and more willing to focus on others, their needs and their motivations.

Changing Yourself to Change Others

Self-hypnosis is a profound means for personal change and being able to obtain better relationships. While book reading's helpful for intellectual infor-mation, emotional growth occurs for those who can examine their thoughts and feelings, particularly in terms of how they relate to other people.

By examining how you can relate better to others, you get the added benefit of having people begin to respond more positively to you.

You are the centre of your universe. But as you make positive changes, others who are orbiting your personal solar system are also influenced by your vibrations. That's probably enough of the cosmic metaphors for now. What we mean is that if you have, for example, low self-esteem and unresolved anger management issues, others respond accordingly. When you begin to understand what triggers your anger, you can change your responses and begin to improve your communications with others.

Stimulating the stimulus/response

Imagine that you're travelling on a bus at lunchtime and you're very hungry. You're desperate to eat a cheese sandwich. You look across from you and someone's eating – guess what? – a cheese sandwich. The passenger enjoys her sandwich, unaware that you can't stop looking at her. You can even smell her sandwich as you enviously watch her being lost in culinary delight. You feel your stomach rumble. You may even begin to salivate. These physical responses are a type of conditioning to experiences you've had in the past with your favourite food: in the anticipation before eating, your mind and body do certain things. This is normal behaviour.

In a similar fashion, imagine you've had a scary experience with a dog. You may then experience a range of heightened physical responses around certain types of dogs that you view as a potential threat. These responses may include sweating and breathing irregularly.

Your responses to the sandwich and the dog are examples of responses to prior conditioning. The conditions are, respectively, hunger and fear. These sort of responses also apply to relationships. For example, if as a child you grew up with two parents who were both chaotic, violent alcoholics, the chances are high that you choose partners who have tendencies in this direction. Alternatively, you may have difficulty in finding partners who are sober, supportive and live orderly lives.

Tips on breaking relationship patterns based on past conditioning:

1. **Identify your destructive patterns from past relationships**

2. **Identify why you've rejected people in the past who would have been positive influences. (for example, people often describe good influences as 'boring', 'predictable', 'too nice', etc.) Avoidance of good influences can indicate your feelings of low self-esteem in terms of not feeling that you deserve good relationships.**

3. **Don't blame others for past relationship problems. Learn to understand how you have contributed to the problem in order to avoid repeating the past.**

4. **Go outside of your comfort zone and try to meet new people who are different from those you normally come across.**

5. **Do constant self-hypnosis to help you to feel confident and better about yourself.**

Looking in the mirror

One of the most difficult things to do is to see yourself as others see you. Self-hypnosis can be very helpful in allowing you to appreciate and accept yourself for who you really are. This includes being able to honestly assess your own weaknesses in relating to those people who are closest to you – family, friends and work colleagues. As you begin to feel good about yourself you may notice that you relate in a way that is more natural and communicate more clearly what you are feeling.

Self-hypnosis is all about shining a light on both of these aspects, so that you feel confident about your abilities and are willing to change those aspects of yourself that need changing.

Some areas that you could begin to use self-hypnosis to work on include the following. If you answer 'yes' to any of the questions, that's an indicator that you may need to do some work on yourself:

- Do you have arguments with anyone about any aspect of your behaviour?
- Do you get repeatedly nagged by loved ones about something you do?
- Do your friends take you to task repeatedly about some personal trait?
- Do you secretly suspect that any of the above criticisms are valid, but can't admit it?

We're not talking about differences of opinion about politics or whose turn it is to do the housework, but the more important things that can lead to relationship breakdowns. Being able to own up to areas that may be causing you relationship difficulties is important.

So what do you do if you have answered 'yes' to any of the above questions?

You could begin to develop a simple self-hypnosis routine to see yourself improving your responses to the above situations. (See Chapter 6 for how to write self-hypnosis scripts.)

Remember, with self-hypnosis, you don't have to work out *how* you would change your behaviour, but you need to imagine how it would feel if you could have a better outcome and what that would look like. Think in terms of imagining past bad situations in relationships, then re-imagine those same situations with better outcomes where both parties feel satisfied. This is what we refer to as a 'win–win' outcome. By doing this you unconsciously generate new behaviours.

Listening to yourself

How do you describe yourself to others? Do you give yourself good PR? Or do you do yourself down, coming off all apologetic and highlighting your short-comings and latest blunders? If you do put yourself down like this, we want to know why.

If you do overdo the humble and self-deprecating tendencies, cease and desist immediately! You gain no mileage from talking yourself down and this is indicative of low self-esteem.

Self-talk is therapy jargon for the way you describe yourself. The way you describe yourself directly reflects the state of your self-regard, self-awareness and emotional mental health. Put simply, good emotional mental health is equivalent to realistic and positive self-regard. You can express self-talk in a critical or supportive manner. But consider this: the quality of your self-talk over time becomes a form of self-hypnosis. We tend to repeat our self-talk in a way that becomes our 'truth'. As a result, if you describe yourself repeatedly as clumsy, then you begin to act like a clumsy person.

You're better advised to talk yourself up and describe yourself in ways that you want to become like, such as 'I'm getting better at . . .' (whatever you're not good at yet).

Being bravely in control

Few of us feel in control of all areas of our lives all the time. Fewer of us feel in control of our emotions. However, you can take quite a few practical steps that increase your feelings of being in control of your emotions.

Many ways exist to be more in control of your emotions, and thereby your life:

- ✔ Understanding that your thoughts control your feelings.
- ✔ Looking at the evidence that supports your thoughts.
- ✔ Looking at the evidence that contradicts your thoughts.
- ✔ Challenging your assumptions and perspective.

If you can follow these approaches, you're gradually beginning to understand that you're working on your thoughts, not your emotions or feelings.

Thinking gives birth to emotions. If you can challenge or modify your thoughts, you have control over your emotions.

Confidently Attracting a New Partner

This section talks about how self-hypnosis can help you to begin to behave in a different way that will allow you to find it easier to attract a partner who is right for you. As you reinforce positive feelings about yourself, you can begin to be more relaxed in your body and more relaxed in your mind – which are both attractive qualities to others.

Many people search for a partner to make themselves feel more 'complete'. Yet we all know on some level that this feeling of wholeness must come from within and that we can only generate this feeling for ourselves.

When looking for a partner, we recommend you follow a few guidelines:

✔ Be natural – don't pretend to be someone you're not.

✔ Know beforehand the qualities that you want and don't want, but don't be rigid about this either.

✔ Avoid meeting partners in less than salubrious places.

✔ Avoid jumping into bed and having sex before you really know the other person.

Sounds like the sort of stuff your mother says, doesn't it? But this is really about protecting yourself in order to maintain high self-esteem when the right person comes along.

Ego-strengthening self-hypnosis techniques can be very useful for generating feelings of self-acceptance. The nearby sidebar called 'Script for self-acceptance' is a brief script that you could use to boost your feelings of self-acceptance.

Use the above script any way you wish. Think of the script as a springboard for ways to personalise what you need to say to yourself to feel more complete. In that way, you can meet your future soulmate without having to burden them with the responsibility for making you feel better as a person.

Looking at people you admire

Who are your heroes? Who do you look up to? Even if you feel that you have no heroes or no one comes to mind, what human qualities do you admire or aspire to?

Script for self-acceptance

Imagine how you feel to be complete within yourself . . . How does that feel to you? . . . Where do you feel this in your body?

As you continue to breathe deeply and slowly . . . Imagine the difference in the way you think . . . feel . . . behave . . . Imagine how others respond differently and more positively towards you.

Imagine how you become like a magnet, attracting good opportunities towards you. Imagine how you begin to attract good situations into your life . . . Imagine how you begin to attract love into your life . . . Imagine how you begin to attract into your life the right person for you to love and receive love from . . .

When we're young, we all have heroes that we look up to. They may be relatives or people you've never met – historical figures, modern celebrities, world leaders, people from your place of worship, and even people who are just plain nice, such as the postie who always stops for a chat and makes you feel good.

If you can think of any people you admire, think of the specific traits that you like about them. Chances are that these are traits you want to have within yourself, but either can't admit to or don't know how to obtain.

 Shadow traits are those parts that 'others' display shamelessly that you feel negatively about. They are useful to understand as they may point to suppressed aspects of your own personality. You may even aspire to traits that you may feel guilty about, such as power, aggression, sexuality, showing off, wealth generation or being domineering.

Another way to understand your own shadow traits are to think of traits in people who bring up a strong sense of repulsion or irritation. The things that come to your mind may say more about you than about those people you despise. The psychologist Carl Jung was a student of Freud's who wrote eloquently about the *shadow* aspect of our personality, the repressed part of our unconscious that's made up of all our repressed instincts, including our perceived shortcomings. Jung stated that we frequently project our own deficiencies onto perceived moral weaknesses in other people, organisations or even nations.

Once you have even the faintest idea of a trait that you suspect may qualify as your own shadow, you can use self-hypnosis to play with this concept. If for example, you are a shy and retiring type who finds 'show-offs' vulgar, then do some self-hypnosis to imagine being a show-off – with the intention of enjoying the role you are in. Really relish being a show-off and try to understand one good thing that can come from this. In this way you are unconsciously giving yourself permission to embrace your shadow.

Developing a sense of humour

If you read the way people describe themselves in any 'Lonely Hearts' classifieds' columns where people wish to meet others for romance, you will often see the phrase 'GSOH'. This stands for Good Sense of Humour. Humour is one of the most frequent selling points for trying to present as an attractive personality. Why? Because we all like to laugh. Laughing makes us feel good and alive.

While self-hypnosis won't make you a stand-up comedian, there are tips in this section on how we can develop a sense of humour using self-hypnosis.

Think of someone you describe as humourless or overly serious. What feelings arise when you think of this person? Do you feel predominantly mad (angry), bad, sad or glad? Chances are that the emotion 'glad' is last on your list.

Now for a more challenging question: do you think that if someone you know had to name a humourless person, they may choose you? Or, even more to the point, have you ever been accused of being humourless? (If someone was being cruel when she accused you of being too serious, this doesn't count, nor does any form of aggression masked as humour.)

Humour's subjective. People of different backgrounds and ages laugh at different things.

One word of caution: as you develop your sense of humour by using self-hypnosis to feel more relaxed about joking, we need to be careful that our humour is kind and not based on excessive sarcasm or harshness towards others. True humour is simply funny. Stand up comedians may get away with a more harsh kind of humour that individuals in one-to-one relationships.

In fact, the word 'humour' shares its roots with the words 'humility' and 'human'. So the best humour may be humane and have some humility in it. However, all too commonly humour in interpersonal relations may be expressed in the opposite manner – with the intention of showing off or expressing anger. Keep in mind that one person's humour may cause another person offence or shame. Keep this in mind when you're teasing someone, as words can heal or hurt.

However, if you genuinely feel that you can benefit from a better sense of humour, then you should feel no shame nor allow your inner critic to chastise you. You simply need to relax and fine-tune your ego-strengthening self-hypnosis technique.

Becoming charismatic

Charisma's essentially the ability to project attractiveness outwards to others. The word comes from the Greek word 'charis' or 'kharisma', which means grace, gift, authority and/or favoured by God.

The last meaning is particularly interesting, as charismatic people tend to project glamour in the archaic sense of that word meaning a magical spell. And when you think of people like Barack Obama or Marilyn Monroe or the Dalai Lama, they certainly have or had the ability of spell-binding the masses with their magnetic personalities.

Charismatic people can often be confused with manipulative opportunists, but we're not talking about little Machiavellis here, we're talking about people who are real and *genuinely likeable*.

The BBC website states that the three attributes of a charismatic person include:

- Feeling your emotions strongly
- Evoking strong emotions in others
- Not being easily influenced by other charismatic people

The implications for self-hypnosis are clear. Scripts to increase personal charisma should focus on the above abilities and how you feel when you have these traits naturally within yourself.

In this book we focus on helping you to develop yourself so that you're more congruent or true to your own personality. This in itself increases your attractiveness to others and thereby boosts your own charisma.

But what is charisma? The following aspects combine to make another definition of a charismatic person:

- Relaxed
- Confident
- Happy

- Emotionally intelligent

- Sincerely interested in and focused on others

- Passionate, which comes as a by-product of emotional intelligence

- Aware of the needs and motivations of others, again as a result of emotional intelligence

- Clear about what you want

- Influential and persuasive

Practising certain self-hypnosis skills can increase your charisma. For example, you can develop a self-hypnosis script to focus more clearly on what life would be like once your hypnosis begins to work for you. This may involve, in trance, seeing the goal you want as already achieved. Feel the pleasure of success by using different physical senses to imagine how your world has changed by making your dream come true.

By developing an increasing sense of your own unambiguous will, you are also increasing your self-belief and persuasion abilities. These are both core traits of a charismatic personality.

The nearby sidebar features a self-hypnosis script to help you become charismatic. Begin by using similar techniques to those we used in the previous section on developing a sense of humour (also an essential trait for charisma). In order to start to raise the feelings of charisma within yourself, think of a charismatic person, someone *genuinely likeable* who has loads of charm and magnetism. Below is a script that may help you generate feelings of charisma within yourself.

Another way to increase your charisma is to study the subject. Read biographies and interviews of people who you admire, and imitate them in any way you can. You eventually incorporate these traits in a natural way into your own personality and increase your own understanding of overcoming struggles and personal shortcomings.

Also, by regularly doing self-hypnosis to feel more charismatic, you can begin to behave like a charismatic person. Keep in mind that self-hypnosis helps you to feel more relaxed and self-accepting. This usually involves an increasing lifting of your spirit. And with these changes, you're on your way to developing a truly magnetic personality.

Self-hypnosis for charisma

I wonder how I feel . . . being able to be more real . . . admired . . . and popular? What do I feel like being loved by many . . . envied by some . . .?

Imagine looking at your diary . . . you have to enter yet another exciting invitation . . . imagine your pleasant surprise as you struggle to find an available date . . . as you already have a full and exciting diary . . . filled with exciting social engagements . . . and wonderful business opportunities.

Imagine feelings of excitement about each day . . . becoming more optimistic . . . genuinely interested in hearing from the people you meet . . . absorbed in their stories . . . problems . . . and concerns . . .

As you open up more . . . to your own inner emotional life . . . your own feelings become more known to you . . . be they . . . mad . . . bad . . . sad . . . glad . . . feelings.

You're able to express yourself with levels of passion . . . commitment . . . self-belief . . . that you've never before experienced . . . your self-belief becomes contagious . . . helping others to feel excited when they're around you . . .

Others begin to look forward to hearing you passionately express what you feel . . . and the kindness and empathy . . . that you increasingly have for their feelings . . . when excited by you . . . they begin to open up more . . . to their own inner emotional life . . .

Imagine feeling the powers of persuasion that are growing within you . . .

The nods and smiles on people's faces as your ideas become increasingly attractive to them . . .

Imagine other intimidating and forceful people having no influence over you . . . but rather they begin to be influenced by your charisma, charm and personal authority . . .

Part V
The Part of Tens

The 5th Wave   By Rich Tennant

I told you not to stare at yourself in that thing while you're cutting the grass!

In this part . . .

In this part we offer three chapters of hints and tips to help you get the most from you adventures in self-hypnosis. Here you can discover ten creative ways in which you can enter trance. Unsure whether you are in trance? This Part has a chapter to help with that, too. Finally, and with your safety and well-being very much in mind, we offer some advice on why it might be sensible to seek professional advice *before* starting self-hypnosis.

Chapter 18

Ten Creative Ways to Enter Trance

In This Chapter

▶ Practising the techniques of professional hypnotherapists

▶ Transforming yourself and your relationships

▶ Creating new directions for self-hypnosis approaches

As you meet different approaches to self-hypnosis, you gain more confidence in creating new approaches to take yourself into trance and achieve your goals. This can give you an amazing sense of freedom and the ability to make hypnosis work more rapidly and with less effort. You can really have fun as you increase your sense of what you can do with your unconscious mind.

We've described different ways of constructing self-hypnosis scripts throughout this book. Most people discover hypnosis by reading scripts that others have written and then as you gain more confidence, modifying them to work better for you. Eventually, however, you become more creative with the different ways of entering trance and begin to improvise your own methods.

In this chapter we help you develop a variety of ways to enter trance in order to help yourself access the rich inner resources of your unconscious mind.

Boring Yourself into Trance

Have you ever been stuck in a boring meeting or lecture where one person was monopolising the conversation? What happens? You go into trance. Life's full of boring moments and you don't want to waste them. You can be doing hypnotherapy instead of being bored. If it is an opportune moment, you can focus the relaxed feeling that comes from being bored and make it work for you. You can be re-imagining your life or the problems and struggles you face.

When you are bored, you are in a trance state. Your focus is inward and you are muscularly relaxed. Boredom's cheap and in good supply, so feel free to use those many boring moments to see yourself making your dreams come true – and may they all be interesting ones!

Confusing Yourself

Milton Erickson (1901–80), an American psychiatrist, pioneered a range of clinical hypnosis techniques that profoundly influenced subsequent generations of hypnotherapists.

Erickson developed a variety of trance-induction methods called 'confusion inductions', which hypnotherapists worldwide still routinely use. Confusion techniques involve overwhelming your unconscious mind in order to decrease the mental chatter of your conscious, rational mind. In this way your unconscious can more easily receive hypnotic suggestions and act on them. Erickson noticed how few things capture the attention more deeply than being confused and he used this technique to great effect. You can also use confusion inductions effectively for self-hypnosis.

A variety of techniques can interrupt routine rational thinking, such as the following:

✔ Deliberate *ambiguity* and long-winded sentences.

✔ *Word play* ('your conscious mind can forget to remember or your conscious mind can remember to forget').

✔ The rapid use of *opposites* ('think of something in the sky, now think of something under the ground' or 'you can silently listen to your speech') can confuse the mind enough to distract the conscious.

✔ When conducted by a hypnotherapist, unexpected behaviours. (Handshake inductions are a good example of a rapid induction using a confusion technique. This involves the therapist not shaking someone's hand in the normal way.)

You can use most of these approaches for your own self-hypnosis techniques. The one exception may be the use of unexpected behaviours, which requires a hypnotherapist. But maybe some creative readers can devise a way to incorporate even unexpected behaviours into their self-hypnosis regime.

Reading a Novel About Your Life

If you're a literary type, a *dissociative self-hypnosis technique* (one in which you step aside from your problems and view them objectively) involves the use of reading about your life when the problem you were experiencing has gone.

Imagine you're reading a story about a character with similar concerns to you. As the author of this story, you have poetic licence to enable this fictional character (who shares uncannily similar personality traits to you) to resolve their problem easily or achieve their goals effortlessly.

This may sound simply like pointless self-indulgence, but by envisioning a solution, you give an indirect hypnotic suggestion to your unconscious mind that says: 'Make it happen.'

The only thing your conscious mind needs to know is that your unconscious is a law unto itself and doesn't necessarily generate a solution or a change that's even remotely similar to the one conceived in your trance-induced novel. In fact, your unconscious wants to keep your conscious mind clear of its work and leaves it guessing to avoid the conscious mind's critical interference.

Therefore, a certain amount of patience and trust is required as well as avoiding literal thinking.

With dissociative metaphors of any type – which is what this sort of story creation essentially is – you need to avoid taking your own metaphors literally in order to stop limiting your own creative unconscious process.

Staring into Space

If you've ever watched television for too long and begun to space out, you're doing a form of trance induction. Creating eye fixation, which leads to eye fatigue, is one of the easiest ways to induce a trance. Pick a spot on a blank wall and keep staring as you breathe slowly and deeply. You soon notice a shift in consciousness that allows you to give yourself a hypnotic suggestion.

A big hint: you don't have to feel sleepy or significantly 'trippy' to use this state of mind. In fact, you can be very alert, just more relaxed. If you're relaxed and breathing progressively slower, then you should be able to induce a suitable trance state by staring in less than one minute.

Using Your Own Resistance

Resistance is normal for most of us when presented with change. You can think of therapy as change at the deepest level. Our default position is to resist change as a means of feeling safe and protected. Erickson advocated working *with* resistance as a therapeutic tool and developed various induction approaches using resistance.

You can use resistance self-hypnosis in a variety of ways, including:

- ✔ **Talking to the problem part** by speaking directly to the part of you that's creating the problem, reassuring it and giving it something that it needs to change. You can suggest to the part of you that's creating the problem that you don't want to upset it or fight it, but that you simply want to *'understand why it is creating the problem and what it needs to help in a more constructive way'*.
- ✔ **Shifting your position** (quite literally, 'What would it feel like to stand here . . . now . . . over there . . . now a bit further next to the lamp? . . . now moving closer to the door?') By physically moving about, you're creating a metaphor for flexibility and change.

Time Machine Part One: Imagining the Future You Stopping By for a Chat

Hypnosis is a wonderful way to time travel. 'Time distortion' is a range of hypnotherapy techniques that allow you to go backwards or forwards in time to obtain help – from yourself.

Imagine an emotionally related problem that you've had all your life that you need help with. You've no idea how to deal with this. But assume that in the future you solve this problem or achieve a goal. All you need to do is time travel and speak to the future you who no longer has the issue. You can do this with self-hypnosis.

Time Machine Part Two: Imagining the You-Before-You-Had-the-Problem

Sometimes you may want to use self-hypnosis to re-establish your state of mind before you had the problem – for example, how you felt about spiders before you developed a spider phobia.

This form of time distortion involves going *backwards* in time. This enables you to access the mindset and perspective that you had prior to having the problem.

Your conscious mind initially struggles with the concept of working with a past memory of yourself, but your unconscious has no such hang-ups and begins to help you become unstuck.

In fact, you can even *combine* forces by going to the past to seek assistance from the you before the problem and then travelling to the *future* in order to contact the you who's resolved the problem (or achieved the goal).

Tuning into Your Favourite Television Channel

Similar to staring into space, but now you get to be a director of an actual television programme – *The You Show*!

Dissociating from your own problems and manipulating and directing a better outcome is a powerful form of self-hypnosis. By taking the problem that's in your mind and projecting it outwards visually, you enable a powerful means of suggesting to your unconscious mind a way to develop new behaviours that spontaneously lead you towards your goals.

These types of techniques are called dissociative techniques.

Using Your Senses to Deepen Self-Hypnosis

Your physical senses continually provide you with a rich array of data input every second of your waking life. You can also use them to form powerful trance inductions by enriching your creativity, thus making your imagined world increasingly vivid and real. This is the essence of hypnotic inductions. Here are some ways to use your senses to deepen your inductions:

- ✔ **Visual:** View yourself with the problem solved, by seeing a story unfold with a desired outcome.
- ✔ **Auditory**: Use hearing by relating metaphors, telling stories and singing.

✔ **Kinaesthetic:** By using your sense of touch, you can deepen trance by imagining feeling the texture of things. For example, if you have a spider phobia, you can imagine doing self-hypnosis to lower anxiety as you stroke the back of your friend's pet spider.

✔ **Olfactory:** You can also use your sense of smell to deepen the effect. For example, in aversive conditioning for stopping smoking, you can imagine that cigarettes begin to smell like dog excrement whenever you think of smoking one yourself. (Gross, but effective.) You can apply only to bringing a cigarette close to your mouth, leaving other people's cigarettes smelling normally, like tobacco. In this way other people's smoking doesn't bother you, but you yourself find cigarettes foul. You can also use smells in pleasant ways, such as creating a safe place in your mind with the lovely smell of your favourite fragrant flowers or herb plants.

Levitating Yourself into Trance

If you check out any books that teach hypnotherapy techniques, you see that they're filled with a range of levitation inductions. Some are called floating hand inductions, others arm levitation inductions; sorry, legs and feet don't come into it.

Levitation inductions typically involve being hypnotised to unconsciously raise either your hand or your arm and at the point of highest elevation (or dropping to the lap) receiving a hypnotic suggestion. The hypnotherapist typically repeats a phrase like:

✔ 'Your arm/hand is lifting higher . . . higher . . . hold it there' (at this point the hypnotherapist gives the client a hypnotic suggestion).

✔ 'As soon as your arm/hand drops to your lap, you go even more deeply relaxed and . . .' (hypnotic suggestion follows).

Often hypnotherapy techniques function as powerful *ratifiers* – they prove beyond a doubt that you've been hypnotised. You can witness this even while you're in trance. However, if you're past the stage of needing proof (you've already been hypnotised or worked through this book), you already understand what being hypnotised is like and that you can do effective self-hypnosis even in very light trance states.

Chapter 19

Ten Ways to Know You're in Trance

A question that almost everyone asks when they first experience hypnosis is 'How do I know if I'm in trance?' This is rather poignant, as people gain many misconceptions and confusions by watching media depictions of hypnosis that cloud the reality of the experience. Rather than looking at what trance isn't, you're perhaps better to look at the common factors that just about everyone experiences in order to point you in the right direction.

Don't be surprised if you only experience some of these factors in any one particular session. That's quite normal. Likewise, trance is a variable experience that has many factors unique to you, and that includes what you potentially can experience from the following list. Also worth remembering is that the more you practise the easier recognising these tell-tale signs of trance becomes.

Of course, if you really are struggling, then pay a visit to a hypnotherapist who can help you understand your experience.

Your Breathing Slows

Slower breathing tends to be one of the first signs you experience. As your mind and body let go of your day-to-day tensions, your parasympathetic nervous system (which we describe in Chapter 2) begins to slow your breathing down. As you relax into trance you take longer and deeper breaths in a similar way to when you're drifting off to sleep. You aren't going to sleep, but you're drifting into a state that's somewhere between being asleep and being awake.

Your Experience of Passing Time Changes

Time to climb aboard the hypnosis time machine and experience the expansion and contraction of time! Actually time itself doesn't change, rather as you drift in and out of the various levels of trance the way you perceive passing time alters. You may feel that one minute lasts ten, or that after half an hour only five minutes have passed. This is a very natural ability your mind possesses, one that's even entered our daily vocabulary. How often have you said 'I really enjoyed myself. Time just flew by' or 'That was so boring. Time just dragged'?

Your Eyes Move Beneath Your Eyelids

To some people REM is a jolly good rock band, but REM's short for *rapid eye movement* – a natural phenomenon of trance that you also experience when you dream. You typically experience REM when you process something in your mind. So if you imagine doing something, or mull over the solution to a problem while you're in trance, then you may find that your eyes are darting around all over the place. Scientists believe that you experience REM in both trance and dreaming because your nervous system connects your eye movements to the information-processing centres of your brain. Quite why this is so is a question that those scientists are still pondering. Suffice to say that for hypnotherapists and patients REM's a great indicator that someone's in trance and merrily processing.

You Feel Pleasantly Lethargic

As you're drifting off to sleep at night, or when you've just awoken in the morning, you may experience a pleasant tiredness and lethargy. This is because you aren't fully awake and are on the cusp of sleep. The same thing happens when you enter into trance, as you're neither awake nor asleep; you're somewhere in between. Your muscles relax and you can't be bothered to move, so just let yourself enjoy this wonderful feeling of lethargy.

Your Heart Rate Slows Down

As you enter trance, you relax. When you relax your body doesn't need as much access to oxygen and nutrients as when you're up and about being active. Therefore your heart doesn't need to pump as fast in order to meet the needs of activity. If you're aware of your heart as you enter trance, don't be surprised to find that as you lie down, or as you begin to relax, your heart rate goes up and down a little as your body adjusts to a different position. This is perfectly normal. After a short while your heart rate levels out to a slow and regular rhythm.

Your Mind Drifts and Wanders

Many people mistakenly think that when you're in trance you should be listening exclusively to the therapist or that you should be focusing intently on what you're working on in self-hypnosis. This certainly can be the case. However, many people find that as the trance progresses and they physically relax, their mind relaxes too. Thoughts can begin to drift in and out and at times seemingly wander completely off the subject. Don't worry, this is just your conscious mind drifting away. If you go into trance with a specific intention to work on something, that intention registers with your unconscious mind. Even though you may drift off thinking about your upcoming holiday, your unconscious mind beavers away in the background making the changes you want to make.

Your Mind Goes Blank

Just as your mind can drift and wander, so your mind can also go blank, thinking of nothing. This is quite natural as you go deeper into trance and let your unconscious mind get on with its job.

Your Muscles Feel Heavy

Gravity's doing its job! As you relax into trance, your muscles physically relax too. This means your muscles lose the tension that keeps you upright and erect and prevents gravity pulling you to the ground. The feeling of muscular heaviness that people often report as they drift into trance is simply the result of noticing gravitational pull on your body.

Your Muscles Twitch

Myoclonus! No, it wasn't in Jurassic Park: it's a medical term that means involuntary twitching of muscles. We've all experienced little jerks and contractions of muscles as we fall asleep, perhaps to the amusement of our partners.

Exactly the same thing happens as you drift into trance. As your body relaxes so your nervous system settles down. When doing so the nervous system occasionally lets out a nerve impulse that causes a muscle to twitch. Some people twitch more than others, with the degree of twitching varying from the very minor to something that jerks your entire leg into the air.

You Think You've Fallen Asleep

Thinking you've fallen asleep is a typical sign of a deep level of trance. The good news is that you aren't asleep, as is evident when you find yourself coming out of trance at the appropriate time. Even though consciously you may not think you're working on your problem, your unconscious mind is. Alternatively you may at times think that you're drifting in and out of sleep. Again, this isn't the case, you're simply dipping into and out of a deep trance state. And if you do fall asleep that's fine too. Doing so may not be self-hypnosis, but your mind's getting you to do what's uppermost on its priority list for your well-being: sleeping!

Chapter 20

Ten (Or So) Reasons to Seek Professional Help before Trying Self-Hypnosis

In This Chapter

▶ Understanding the overlap between mind and body problems

▶ Knowing when to seek medical attention

▶ Understanding when to ask for help for emotional issues

S ome problems don't clearly fall into the category of a physical health issue requiring medical treatment or an emotionally based problem requiring help from a therapist.

Always go to see your doctor before trying any other approach to treatment. This especially applies if you have any pain or physical discomfort. A reputable hypnotherapist should ask immediately if you've seen a doctor and what his medical diagnosis or opinion is regarding the condition that you've brought for hypnosis treatment. If your hypnotherapist doesn't ask about medical opinions at the first meeting, consider yourself in the hands of someone who isn't operating professionally.

However, if you've seen a doctor whose expertise you trust, who's told you that the problem can't be treated further and may be stress related or due to emotional issues, then seeing a hypnotherapist (or a counsellor) may be a good idea.

In this chapter we help you to understand how to be even clearer about who's in the best position to help you. Please keep in mind that you can always ask your doctor and reputable hypnotherapy accrediting organisations to get advice about whether hypnotherapy can be helpful with certain problems.

Anxiety and Panic Attacks

Anxiety's a side effect of some medications, so if you suspect that medications you're taking may be increasing your feelings of anxiety or panic attacks, you should seek medical help first.

Hypnosis can be a powerful tool in managing anxiety and panic attacks. The key to combating that excess of anxiety, stress or fear is to relax. How your body responds when you relax is much the same as when you enter hypnosis. Throughout this book we offer a wealth of information and practical approaches on how to lessen anxiety and panic attacks (see Chapter 9).

Confidence Problems

Self-hypnosis is one of the most common areas that hypnotherapists help people with. Maintaining confidence through your own self-hypnosis skills can be rewarding and if you're the creative type, overcoming your confidence issues can be an enjoyable area to develop. The potential rewards to developing your confidence via self-hypnosis can open doors to a better life in many respects. This book includes several examples of how you can do this, especially through the 'ego-strengthening' self-hypnosis exercises found in chapter 10.

Depression

Different types of depression occur, which vary in severity of symptoms.

Depression symptoms can range from weight and appetite loss, pessimism, anxiety or lack of enjoyment in life, hobbies and sex, to severe psychotic depression similar to schizophrenia, which includes experiencing visual and auditory hallucinations.

A psychiatrist should treat psychotic depression as a matter of urgency.

Regarding more common, non-psychotic forms of depression, we can all feel sad at times, but if this feeling becomes chronic and you start to suffer daily from depression, you should seek medical help first and then counselling or hypnotherapy.

Self-hypnosis can help in terms of reinforcing positive messages (see Chapter 10) that you've gleaned from counselling. In fact, research has shown improved responses with certain forms of therapy that involve exploring how thinking affects emotions. So if you've explored how to challenge unhelpful thoughts and beliefs, ego-strengthening self-hypnosis found in chapter 10 can be invaluable at continuing and reinforcing thoughts that improve self-esteem and mood.

Eating Problems and Weight Loss

Eating problems and weight loss all require medical attention first. However, issues of low self-esteem, depression, anger management and anxiety are often associated with eating problems.

Hypnotherapy can help with all these conditions, although they're very individual and may require a combination of medical and professional emotional support from others. For more on controlling your eating habits see Chapter 16.

Infertility

You should clearly seek medical attention first for fertility problems. However, if a medical solution to being unable to conceive isn't found, then hypnosis can be useful for a range of issues around conception, pregnancy and even childbirth.

In fact, hypnotherapists are regularly involved with helping couples conceive and get through childbirth with minimum difficulties. (More on this in *Hypnotherapy For Dummies*, Chapter 6.)

Insomnia

Insomnia can range in cause, severity and symptoms. You should speak to a medical professional first, but keep an open mind as to what approach best suits you. A range of approaches exist, including taking medication to help you sleep *initially*. A pharmaceutical approach probably isn't a good long-term strategy, and you may be pleasantly surprised at how effective hypnosis can be in helping you get a good night's sleep.

Phobias

Phobias are exaggerated fears of things or situations. They're expressed immediately when you're confronted with that thing or situation either directly or indirectly. This can include exposure to the feared object or situation through books, television or even in conversation. Phobias can be debilitating and often involve shame and some degree of feeling unable to cope compared to other people.

The fear you experience with a phobic response is an *irrational fear,* and is typically a fear of an outcome that statistically doesn't happen.

Hypnotherapy can enable you to confront the thing that frightens you and give you a sense of self-control and calmness. You're better to work through severe phobias with a hypnotherapist rather than on your own, as a professional can help you to examine your own unconscious fears so that you can overcome the problem. For more on phobias have a look at Chapter 9.

Physical Pain or Discomfort

A doctor should always check out pain *first,* as the pain may be an indicator of a deeper problem that may worsen if unchecked.

If, after a course of thorough examinations, X-rays and lab tests, no medical condition's detected that can explain your pain and your doctor infers that your pain is stress related and doesn't feel that further medical tests are necessary, then an initial session of hypnotherapy may be useful.

Hypnosis provides a range of pain-management approaches. For example, hypnosis can totally or partially remove pain through a number of techniques (check out Chapter 11 for more on these). However, if even a remote possibility exists that your pain may be a result of an undiagnosed physical problem, most hypnotherapists use hypnosis in a way that leaves a trace element of the pain, as a reminder of a potentially unresolved problem. A distinction exists between this sort of condition and pain that's a stress reaction, where total pain removal's more appropriate.

Problem Drinking

Excessive drinking – especially alcoholism – is a medical condition requiring medical attention first. Only a medical professional can diagnose alcoholism, so even if your angry partner calls you an alcoholic, this may or may not be relevant. You need to get the problem checked out medically first.

However, if like many people you aren't an alcoholic but struggle to keep your drinking within acceptable amounts, hypnotherapy can be an invaluable tool. (Turn to Chapter 15 for more information.)

Sexual Problems

Sexual problems can have root causes with medical and/or emotional origins. If you have the least doubt about any physiological issues, you should consult a doctor first.

But also keep in mind that hypnotherapy's a useful therapeutic tool for strengthening your ego, as well as addressing a range of sexual problems that individuals or couples may face. *Hypnotherapy For Dummies* incorporates specific work that you can do in this area.

Smoking

Smoking is a habit that is often associated with a wide variety of activities and emotions. You may find that you use smoking as a 'crutch' to help get you through rough patches in your life. Hypnotherapy is a great way to help you quit the habit (see Chapter 14), however if you feel that you won't be able to cope emotionally without cigarettes then you should seek help from a hypnotherapist or counsellor to help you cope with your emotions before quitting. The self-hypnosis exercises found in Chapter 10 will also help strengthen your ability to cope.

You may find that quitting on your own is too daunting and that you want outside help in the form of a hypnotherapist or smoking cessation counsellor. Though designed to help you quit on your own, the exercises found in Chapter 14 will provide you with an invaluable resource that complements the good work you are doing with these professionals.

Appendix A

Self-Hypnosis and Hypnotherapy Resources

• •

This Appendix is a useful guide to information and resources that can help you find out more about hypnotherapy in general as well as enhancing your experience of self-hypnosis.

Hypnotherapy Organisations

If you want to learn self-hypnosis from a professional or visit a therapist for 1-to-1 therapy then check these out. These resources are grouped by country in no particular order.

United Kingdom

British Association of Medical Hypnosis, Suite 296, 28 Old Brompton Road, London, SW7 3SS. Tel: 020 8998 4436. Web site: www.bamh.org.uk

The British Society of Clinical Hypnosis has the largest number of highly qualified hypnotherapists in the United Kingdom. 125 Queensgate, Bridlington, North Humberside, YO16 7JQ Tel: 01262 403 103. Web site: www.bsch.org.uk

National Association of Counsellors Hypnotherapists and Psychotherapists, PO Box 719, Burwell, Cambridge, CB5 0NX. Tel: 0870 850 5383. Web site: www.nachp.org

United States

American Society of Clinical Hypnosis. An interdisciplinary organisation that includes psychologists, psychiatrists, clinical social workers, marriage and family therapists, mental health counsellors, medical doctors, masters-level nurses, and dentists. 140 N. Bloomingdale Road, Bloomingdale, IL 60108-1017. Fax: 630/351-8490. Web site: `www.asch.net`

American Psychotherapy and Medical Hypnosis Association, 1100 Kittitas Street, Wenatchee, WA 98801. Tel: (509)662-5131. Website: `http://apmha.com`

International Medical and Dental Hypnotherapy Association, 4110 Edgeland, Suite 800, Royal Oak, MI 48073-2285. Tel: (248) 549-5594 / (800) 257-5467. Website: `www.imdha.com`

National Guild of Hypnotists, PO Box 308, Merrimack, NH, 03054. Tel: (603) 429-9438. Fax: (603) 424-8066. Website: `www.ngh.net`

Canada

Canadian Federation of Clinical Hypnosis. Website: `www.clinical hypnosis.ca`. Tel: Contact via website.

Professional Board of Hypnotherapy. Website: `www.hypnosiscanada.com`. Tel: 1 (888) 686-6163. Email: info@hypnosiscanada.com

Australia

Australian Society of Clinical Hypnotherapists, PO Box 471, Eastwood, NSW, 2122. Tel: 612 988 4997. Website: `www.asch.com.au`

Useful Script Books

The books here are some of the most relevant with regard to being a source of ideas for developing your own self-hypnosis scripts. They are all written for the professional hypnotherapist, however the ideas they contain are readily accessible to all.

The Handbook of Hypnotic Metaphors and Suggestions

Author: D. Corydon Hammond (W W Norton & Co Ltd, 1990).

If hypnotherapy were to have a script Bible, this would be it. Frequently referred to simply as 'Hammonds', it is probably the most complete reference book available. However, that does come at a price, as this worthy tome is quite expensive.

Scripts and Strategies in Hypnotherapy: The Complete Works

Author: Roger P. Allen (Crown House Publishing, 2004).

This is a tried and trusted source of scripts that is very accessible and comes in at a reasonable price.

More Scripts and Strategies in Hypnotherapy

Author: Lynda Hudson (Crown House Publishing, 2010).

The companion volume to *Scripts and Strategies*, this is an excellent source of script ideas with the added advantage of analysing exactly what is going on in each for those interested in the technical ins-and-outs.

Appendix B
About the CD

• •

*T*he CD which accompanies this book contains seven tracks to help you with your adventures in self-hypnosis.

What You'll Find on the CD

Table A-1 shows you the various tracks to be found on the CD. It also shows you whose voice you are hearing, and how long the track continues for.

Table A-1		CD track listing	
Track No	**Title**	**Recorded by**	**Time (minutes:seconds)**
1	Introduction and safety message	Peter	3:10
2	Progressive relaxation induction and 10 to 1 deepener	Peter	6:34
3	General ego boosting	Mike	9:10
4	Weight control	Peter	8:02
5	Smoking	Mike	6:52
6	Anxiety	Mike	8:53
7	Insomnia	Mike	7:29
8	Unconscious self-hypnosis	Mike	4:51
9	Awakening	Peter	1:15

Tracks can be played individually. However, for those with programmable CD players or those who rip the CD to an MP3 player the tracks can be programmed to run in a specific order. For example, for someone working on anxiety they will play tracks 2 + 3 + 6 + 8.

The playing of tracks 2 + 3 + 8 will benefit everyone who reads the book irrespective of what they are working on.

Customer Care

If you have trouble with the CD-ROM, please call Wiley Product Technical Support at 800-762-2974. Outside the United States, call 317-572-3993. You can also contact Wiley Product Technical Support at `http://support.wiley.com`. Wiley Publishing will provide technical support only for installation and other general quality control items. For technical support on the applications themselves, consult the program's vendor or author.

To place additional orders or to request information about other Wiley products, please call 877-762-2974.

Index

• E •

FOR DUMMIES®

Do Anything. Just Add Dummies

UK editions

BUSINESS

978-0-470-51806-9

978-0-470-99245-6

978-0-470-75626-3

FINANCE

978-0-470-99280-7

978-0-470-99811-3

978-0-470-69515-9

PROPERTY

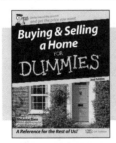

978-0-470-99448-1

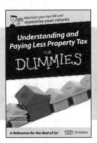

978-0-470-75872-4

978-0-7645-7054-4

Backgammon For Dummies
978-0-470-77085-6

Body Language For Dummies
978-0-470-51291-3

British Sign Language
For Dummies
978-0-470-69477-0

Business NLP For Dummies
978-0-470-69757-3

Children's Health For Dummies
978-0-470-02735-6

Cognitive Behavioural Coaching
For Dummies
978-0-470-71379-2

Counselling Skills For Dummies
978-0-470-51190-9

Digital Marketing For Dummies
978-0-470-05793-3

eBay.co.uk For Dummies,
2nd Edition
978-0-470-51807-6

English Grammar For Dummies
978-0-470-05752-0

Fertility & Infertility For Dummies
978-0-470-05750-6

Genealogy Online For Dummies
978-0-7645-7061-2

Golf For Dummies
978-0-470-01811-8

Green Living For Dummies
978-0-470-06038-4

Hypnotherapy For Dummies
978-0-470-01930-6

Available wherever books are sold. For more information or to order direct go to www.wiley.com or call +44 (0) 1243 843291

13902_p1

FOR DUMMIES®

A world of resources to help you grow

UK editions

SELF-HELP

Cognitive Behavioural Therapy FOR DUMMIES
978-0-470-01838-5

Neuro-linguistic Programming FOR DUMMIES
978-0-7645-7028-5

Emotional Freedom Technique FOR DUMMIES
978-0-470-75876-2

HEALTH

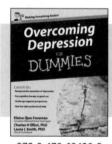
Overcoming Depression FOR DUMMIES
978-0-470-69430-5

IBS FOR DUMMIES
978-0-470-51737-6

Low-Cholesterol Cookbook FOR DUMMIES
978-0-470-71401-0

HISTORY

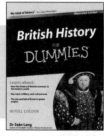
British History FOR DUMMIES
978-0-470-99468-9

Twentieth Century History FOR DUMMIES
978-0-470-51015-5

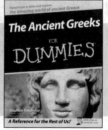
The Ancient Greeks FOR DUMMIES
978-0-470-98787-2

Inventing For Dummies
978-0-470-51996-7

Job Hunting and Career Change All-In-One For Dummies
978-0-470-51611-9

Motivation For Dummies
978-0-470-76035-2

Origami Kit For Dummies
978-0-470-75857-1

Personal Development All-In-One For Dummies
978-0-470-51501-3

PRINCE2 For Dummies
978-0-470-51919-6

Psychometric Tests For Dummies
978-0-470-75366-8

Raising Happy Children For Dummies
978-0-470-05978-4

Starting and Running a Business All-in-One For Dummies
978-0-470-51648-5

Sudoku For Dummies
978-0-470-01892-7

The British Citizenship Test For Dummies, 2nd Edition
978-0-470-72339-5

Time Management For Dummies
978-0-470-77765-7

Wills, Probate, & Inheritance Tax For Dummies, 2nd Edition
978-0-470-75629-4

Winning on Betfair For Dummies, 2nd Edition
978-0-470-72336-4

Available wherever books are sold. For more information or to order direct go to www.wiley.com or call +44 (0) 1243 843291

13902_p2

FOR DUMMIES®

The easy way to get more done and have more fun

LANGUAGES

978-0-7645-5194-9

978-0-7645-5193-2

978-0-471-77270-5

MUSIC

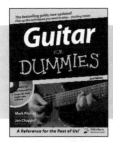

978-0-7645-9904-0

978-0-470-03275-6
UK Edition

978-0-7645-5105-5

SCIENCE & MATHS

978-0-7645-5326-4

978-0-7645-5430-8

978-0-7645-5325-7

Art For Dummies
978-0-7645-5104-8

Baby & Toddler Sleep Solutions For
Dummies
978-0-470-11794-1

Bass Guitar For Dummies
978-0-7645-2487-5

Brain Games For Dummies
978-0-470-37378-1

Christianity For Dummies
978-0-7645-4482-8

Filmmaking For Dummies, 2nd
Edition
978-0-470-38694-1

Forensics For Dummies
978-0-7645-5580-0

German For Dummies
978-0-7645-5195-6

Hobby Farming For Dummies
978-0-470-28172-7

Jewelry Making & Beading For
Dummies
978-0-7645-2571-1

Knitting for Dummies, 2nd Edition
978-0-470-28747-7

Music Composition For Dummies
978-0-470-22421-2

Physics For Dummies
978-0-7645-5433-9

Sex For Dummies, 3rd Edition
978-0-470-04523-7

Solar Power Your Home For Dummies
978-0-470-17569-9

Tennis For Dummies
978-0-7645-5087-4

The Koran For Dummies
978-0-7645-5581-7

U.S. History For Dummies
978-0-7645-5249-6

Wine For Dummies, 4th Edition
978-0-470-04579-4

**Available wherever books are sold. For more information or to order direct go to
www.wiley.com or call +44 (0) 1243 843291**

13902_p3

FOR DUMMIES®

Helping you expand your horizons and achieve your potential

COMPUTER BASICS

978-0-470-27759-1

978-0-470-13728-4

978-0-471-75421-3

DIGITAL LIFESTYLE

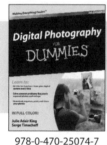

978-0-470-25074-7

978-0-470-39062-7

978-0-470-17469-2

WEB & DESIGN

978-0-470-19238-2

978-0-470-32725-8

978-0-470-34502-3

Access 2007 For Dummies
978-0-470-04612-8

Adobe Creative Suite 3 Design Premium
All-in-One Desk Reference For Dummies
978-0-470-11724-8

AutoCAD 2009 For Dummies
978-0-470-22977-4

C++ For Dummies, 5th Edition
978-0-7645-6852-7

Computers For Seniors For Dummies
978-0-470-24055-7

Excel 2007 All-In-One Desk Reference
For Dummies
978-0-470-03738-6

Flash CS3 For Dummies
978-0-470-12100-9

Mac OS X Leopard For Dummies
978-0-470-05433-8

Macs For Dummies, 10th Edition
978-0-470-27817-8

Networking All-in-One Desk Reference
For Dummies, 3rd Edition
978-0-470-17915-4

Office 2007 All-in-One Desk Reference
For Dummies
978-0-471-78279-7

Search Engine Optimization For
Dummies, 2nd Edition
978-0-471-97998-2

Second Life For Dummies
978-0-470-18025-9

The Internet For Dummies, 11th Edition
978-0-470-12174-0

Visual Studio 2008 All-In-One Desk
Reference For Dummies
978-0-470-19108-8

Web Analytics For Dummies
978-0-470-09824-0

Windows XP For Dummies, 2nd Edition
978-0-7645-7326-2

**Available wherever books are sold. For more information or to order direct go to
www.wiley.com or call +44 (0) 1243 843291**

13902_p4

Clinch-Powell Regional Library
130 N. Main St. Suite 2
Clinton, TN 37716-3691